Y0-BIZ-333

Social Attitudes in Contemporary China

Unlike many studies of social attitudes, which are based on large scale quantitative surveys, or which focus on the attitude of elites, this book considers the views of ordinary people, and is based on in-depth, qualitative interviews. This approach results in rich, nuanced data, and is especially helpful for highlighting ambivalent attitudes, where respondents may hold positive and negative views on a particular topic, views which are liable to change. The book examines attitudes on a range of subjects of current importance, including views on nationalism and internationalism, housing preferences, and educational ambitions. Throughout, the book explores how far attitudes are influenced by traditional Chinese values or by the neoliberal outlook fostered by recent reforms, and concludes that materialism and individualism have increased.

Yu Chen is a researcher at Shaan'xi Provincial Institution of Educational and Scientific Research, China.

Wei Fang is a researcher at Tsinghua University, Beijing, China.

Liqing Li is a freelance researcher and writer, formerly of the University of Bristol, UK.

Paul Morrissey is a freelance researcher and writer, formerly of the University of Bristol, UK.

Chen Nie is a lecturer and researcher at Beihang University, Beijing, China.

Routledge contemporary China series

1. **Nationalism, Democracy and National Integration in China**
   Leong Liew and Wang Shaoguang

2. **Hong Kong's Tortuous Democratization**
   A comparative analysis
   Ming Sing

3. **China's Business Reforms**
   Institutional challenges in a globalised economy
   Edited by Russell Smyth, On Kit Tam, Malcolm Warner and Cherrie Zhu

4. **Challenges for China's Development**
   An enterprise perspective
   Edited by David H. Brown and Alasdair MacBean

5. **New Crime in China**
   Public order and human rights
   Ron Keith and Zhiqiu Lin

6. **Non-Governmental Organizations in Contemporary China**
   Paving the way to civil society?
   Qiusha Ma

7. **Globalization and the Chinese City**
   Fulong Wu

8. **The Politics of China's Accession to the World Trade Organization**
   The dragon goes global
   Hui Feng

9. **Narrating China**
   Jia Pingwa and his fictional world
   Yiyan Wang

10. **Sex, Science and Morality in China**
    Joanne McMillan

11. **Politics in China Since 1949**
    Legitimizing authoritarian rule
    Robert Weatherley

12. **International Human Resource Management in Chinese Multinationals**
    Jie Shen and Vincent Edwards

13. **Unemployment in China**
    Economy, human resources and labour markets
    Edited by Grace Lee and Malcolm Warner

14 **China and Africa**
Engagement and compromise
Ian Taylor

15 **Gender and Education in China**
Gender discourses and women's schooling in the early twentieth century
Paul J. Bailey

16 **SARS**
Reception and interpretation in three Chinese cities
Edited by Deborah Davis and Helen Siu

17 **Human Security and the Chinese State**
Historical transformations and the modern quest for sovereignty
Robert E. Bedeski

18 **Gender and Work in Urban China**
Women workers of the unlucky generation
Liu Jieyu

19 **China's State Enterprise Reform**
From Marx to the market
John Hassard, Jackie Sheehan, Meixiang Zhou, Jane Terpstra-Tong and Jonathan Morris

20 **Cultural Heritage Management in China**
Preserving the cities of the Pearl River Delta
Edited by Hilary du Cros and Yok-shiu F. Lee

21 **Paying for Progress**
Public finance, human welfare and inequality in China
Edited by Vivienne Shue and Christine Wong

22 **China's Foreign Trade Policy**
The new constituencies
Edited by Ka Zeng

23 **Hong Kong, China**
Learning to belong to a nation
Gordon Mathews, Tai-lok Lui, and Eric Kit-wai Ma

24 **China Turns to Multilateralism**
Foreign policy and regional security
Edited by Guoguang Wu and Helen Lansdowne

25 **Tourism and Tibetan Culture in Transition**
A place called Shangrila
Åshild Kolås

26 **China's Emerging Cities**
The making of new urbanism
Edited by Fulong Wu

27 **China–US Relations Transformed**
Perceptions and strategic interactions
Edited by Suisheng Zhao

28 **The Chinese Party-State in the 21st Century**
Adaptation and the reinvention of legitimacy
Edited by André Laliberté and Marc Lanteigne

29 **Political Change in Macao**
Sonny Shiu-Hing Lo

30 **China's Energy Geopolitics**
The Shanghai Cooperation Organization and Central Asia
Thrassy N. Marketos

31 **Regime Legitimacy in Contemporary China**
Institutional change and stability
Edited by Thomas Heberer and Gunter Schubert

32 **U.S.–China Relations**
China policy on Capitol Hill
Tao Xie

33 **Chinese Kinship**
Contemporary anthropological perspectives
Edited by Susanne Brandtstädter and Gonçalo D. Santos

34 **Politics and Government in Hong Kong**
Crisis under Chinese sovereignty
Edited by Ming Sing

35 **Rethinking Chinese Popular Culture**
Cannibalizations of the canon
Edited by Carlos Rojas and Eileen Cheng-yin Chow

36 **Institutional Balancing in the Asia Pacific**
Economic interdependence and China's rise
Kai He

37 **Rent Seeking in China**
Edited by Tak-Wing Ngo and Yongping Wu

38 **China, Xinjiang and Central Asia**
History, transition and crossborder interaction into the 21st century
Edited by Colin Mackerras and Michael Clarke

39 **Intellectual Property Rights in China**
Politics of piracy, trade and protection
Gordon Cheung

40 **Developing China**
Land, politics and social conditions
George C.S. Lin

41 **State and Society Responses to Social Welfare Needs in China**
Serving the people
Edited by Jonathan Schwartz and Shawn Shieh

42 **Gay and Lesbian Subculture in Urban China**
Loretta Wing Wah Ho

43 **The Politics of Heritage Tourism in China**
A view from Lijiang
Xiaobo Su and Peggy Teo

44 **Suicide and Justice**
A Chinese perspective
Wu Fei

45 **Management Training and Development in China**
Educating managers in a globalized economy
Edited by Malcolm Warner and Keith Goodall

46 **Patron-Client Politics and Elections in Hong Kong**
Bruce Kam-kwan Kwong

47 **Chinese Family Business and the Equal Inheritance System**
Unravelling the myth
Victor Zheng

48 Reconciling State, Market and Civil Society in China
The long march towards prosperity
Paolo Urio

49 Innovation in China
The Chinese software industry
Shang-Ling Jui

50 Mobility, Migration and the Chinese Scientific Research System
Koen Jonkers

51 Chinese Film Stars
Edited by Mary Farquhar and Yingjin Zhang

52 Chinese Male Homosexualities
Memba, *Tongzhi* and Golden Boy
Travis S.K. Kong

53 Industrialisation and Rural Livelihoods in China
Agricultural processing in Sichuan
Susanne Lingohr-Wolf

54 Law, Policy and Practice on China's Periphery
Selective adaptation and institutional capacity
Pitman B. Potter

55 China–Africa Development Relations
Edited by Christopher M. Dent

56 Neoliberalism and Culture in China and Hong Kong
The countdown of time
Hai Ren

57 China's Higher Education Reform and Internationalisation
Edited by Janette Ryan

58 Law, Wealth and Power in China
Commercial law reforms in context
Edited by John Garrick

59 Religion in Contemporary China
Revitalization and innovation
Edited by Adam Yuet Chau

60 Consumer-Citizens of China
The role of foreign brands in the imagined future china
Kelly Tian and Lily Dong

61 The Chinese Communist Party and China's Capitalist Revolution
The political impact of the market
Lance L.P. Gore

62 China's Homeless Generation
Voices from the veterans of the Chinese civil war, 1940s–1990s
Joshua Fan

63 In Search of China's Development Model
Beyond the Beijing consensus
Edited by S. Philip Hsu, Suisheng Zhao and Yu-Shan Wu

64 Xinjiang and China's Rise in Central Asia, 1949–2009
A history
Michael E. Clarke

65 Trade Unions in China
The challenge of labour unrest
Tim Pringle

66 China's Changing Workplace
Dynamism, diversity and disparity
Edited by Peter Sheldon, Sunghoon Kim, Yiqiong Li and Malcolm Warner

67 **Leisure and Power in Urban China**
Everyday life in a medium-sized Chinese city
Unn Målfrid H. Rolandsen

68 **China, Oil and Global Politics**
Philip Andrews-Speed and Roland Dannreuther

69 **Education Reform in China**
Edited by Janette Ryan

70 **Social Policy and Migration in China**
Lida Fan

71 **China's One Child Policy and Multiple Caregiving**
Raising little Suns in Xiamen
Esther C.L. Goh

72 **Politics and Markets in Rural China**
Edited by Björn Alpermann

73 **China's New Underclass**
Paid domestic labour
Xinying Hu

74 **Poverty and Development in China**
Alternative approaches to poverty assessment
Lu Caizhen

75 **International Governance and Regimes**
A Chinese perspective
Peter Kien-Hong Yu

76 **HIV/AIDS in China – The Economic and Social Determinants**
Dylan Sutherland and Jennifer Y. J. Hsu

77 **Looking for Work in Post-Socialist China**
Governance, active job seekers and the new Chinese labor market
Feng Xu

78 **Sino-Latin American Relations**
Edited by K.C. Fung and Alicia Garcia-Herrero

79 **Mao's China and the Sino-Soviet Split**
Ideological dilemma
Mingjiang Li

80 **Law and Policy for China's Market Socialism**
Edited by John Garrick

81 **China-Taiwan Relations in a Global Context**
Taiwan's foreign policy and relations
Edited by C. X. George Wei

82 **The Chinese Transformation of Corporate Culture**
Colin S.C. Hawes

83 **Mapping Media in China**
Region, province, locality
Edited by Wanning Sun and Jenny Chio

84 **China, the West and the Myth of New Public Management**
Neoliberalism and its discontents
Paolo Urio

85 **The Lahu Minority in Southwest China**
A response to ethnic marginalization on the frontier
Jianxiong Ma

86 **Social Capital and Institutional Constraints**
A comparative analysis of China, Taiwan and the US
Joonmo Son

87 **Southern China**
Industry, development and industrial policy
Marco R. Di Tommaso, Lauretta Rubini and Elisa Barbieri

88 **State-Market Interactions in China's Reform Era**
Local state competition and global market building in the tobacco industry
Junmin Wang

89 **The Reception and Rendition of Freud in China**
China's Freudian slip
Edited by Tao Jiang and Philip J. Ivanhoe

90 **Sinologism**
An alternative to Orientalism and Postcolonialism
Ming Dong Gu

91 **The Middle Class in Neoliberal China**
Governing risk, life-building, and themed spaces
Hai Ren

92 **The Chinese Corporatist State**
Adaption, survival and resistance
Edited by Jennifer Y.J. Hsu and Reza Hasmath

93 **Law and Fair Work in China**
Sean Cooney, Sarah Biddulph and Ying Zhu

94 **Guangdong and Chinese Diaspora**
The changing landscape of Qiaoxiang
Yow Cheun Hoe

95 **The Shanghai Alleyway House**
A vanishing urban vernacular
Gregory Bracken

96 **Chinese Globalization**
A profile of people-based global connections in China
Jiaming Sun and Scott Lancaster

97 **Disruptive Innovation in Chinese and Indian Businesses**
The strategic implications for local entrepreneurs and global incumbents
Peter Ping Li

98 **Corporate Governance and Banking in China**
Michael Tan

99 **Gender, Modernity and Male Migrant Workers in China**
Becoming a 'modern' man
Xiaodong Lin

100 **Emissions, Pollutants and Environmental Policy in China**
Designing a national emissions trading system
Bo Miao

101 **Sustainable Development in China**
Edited by Curtis Andressen, Mubarak A.R. and Xiaoyi Wang

102 **Islam and China's Hong Kong**
Ethnic identity, Muslim networks and the new Silk Road
Wai-Yip Ho

103 **International Regimes in China**
Domestic implementation of the international fisheries agreements
Gianluca Ferraro

104 **Rural Migrants in Urban China**
Enclaves and transient urbanism
Fulong Wu, Fangzhu Zhang and Chris Webster

105 **State-Led Privatization in China**
The politics of economic reform
Jin Zeng

106 **China's Supreme Court**
Ronald C. Keith, Zhiqiu Lin and Shumei Hou

107 **Queer Sinophone Cultures**
Howard Chiang and Ari Larissa Heinrich

108 **New Confucianism in Twenty-First Century China**
The construction of a discourse
Jesús Solé-Farràs

109 **Christian Values in Communist China**
Gerda Wielander

110 **China and Global Trade Governance**
China's first decade in the World Trade Organization
Edited by Ka Zeng and Wei Liang

111 **The China Model and Global Political Economy**
Comparison, impact, and interaction
Ming Wan

112 **Chinese Middle Classes**
China, Taiwan, Macao and Hong Kong
Edited by Hsin-Huang Michael Hsiao

113 **Economy Hotels in China**
A glocalized innovative hospitality sector
Songshan Sam Huang and Xuhua Michael Sun

114 **The Uyghur Lobby**
Global networks, coalitions and strategies of the World Uyghur Congress
Yu-Wen Chen

115 **Housing Inequality in Chinese Cities**
Edited by Youqin Huang and Si-ming Li

116 **Transforming Chinese Cities**
Edited by Mark Y. Wang, Pookong Kee and Jia Gao

117 **Popular Media, Social Emotion and Public Discourse in Contemporary China**
Shuyu Kong

118 **Globalization and Public Sector Reform in China**
Kjeld Erik Brødsgaard

119 **Religion and Ecological Sustainability in China**
Edited by James Miller, Dan Smyer Yu and Peter van der Veer

120 **Comparatizing Taiwan**
Edited by Shu-mei Shih and Ping-hui Liao

121 **Entertaining the Nation**
Chinese television in the twenty-first century
Edited by Ruoyun Bai and Geng Song

122 **Local Governance Innovation in China**
Experimentation, diffusion, and defiance
Edited by Jessica C. Teets and William Hurst

123 **Footbinding and Women's Labor in Sichuan**
Hill Gates

124 **Incentives for Innovation in China**
Building an innovative economy
Xuedong Ding and Jun Li

125 **Conflict and Cooperation in Sino-US Relations**
Change and continuity, causes and cures
Edited by Jean-Marc F. Blanchard and Simon Shen

126 **Chinese Environmental Aesthetics**
Wangheng Chen, translated by Feng Su, edited by Gerald Cipriani

127 **China's Military Procurement in the Reform Era**
The setting of new directions
Yoram Evron

128 **Forecasting China's Future**
Dominance or collapse?
Roger Irvine

129 **Chinese Migration and Economic Relations with Europe**
Edited by Marco Sanfilippo and Agnieszka Weinar

130 **Party Hegemony and Entrepreneurial Power in China**
Institutional change in the film and music industries
Elena Meyer-Clement

131 **Explaining Railway Reform in China**
A train of property rights re-arrangements
Linda Tjia Yin-nor

132 **Irony, Cynicism and the Chinese State**
Edited by Hans Steinmüller and Susanne Brandtstädter

133 **Animation in China**
History, aesthetics, media
Sean Macdonald

134 **Parenting, Education and Social Mobility in Rural China**
Cultivating dragons and phoenixes
Peggy A. Kong

135 **Disability Policy in China**
Child and family experiences
Xiaoyuan Shang and Karen R. Fisher

136 **The Politics of Controlling Organized Crime in Greater China**
Sonny Shiu-Hing Lo

137 **Inside Xinjiang**
Space, place and power in
China's Muslim far Northwest
*Edited by Anna Hayes and
Michael Clarke*

138 **China's Strategic Priorities**
*Edited by Jonathan H. Ping and
Brett McCormick*

139 **China's Unruly Journalists**
How committed professionals are
changing the People's Republic
Jonathan Hassid

140 **The Geopolitics of Red Oil**
Constructing the China threat
through energy security
Andrew Stephen Campion

141 **China's Socialist Rule of Law Reforms Under Xi Jinping**
*Edited by John Garrick and
Yan Chang Bennett*

142 **Economy, Emotion, and Ethics in Chinese Cinema**
Globalization on speed
David Leiwei Li

143 **Social Attitudes in Contemporary China**
*Yu Chen, Wei Fang, Liqing Li,
Paul Morrissey and Chen Nie*

144 **Media Power in Hong Kong**
Hyper-marketized media and
cultural resistance
Charles Chi-wai Cheung

Social Attitudes in Contemporary China

Yu Chen, Wei Fang, Liqing Li,
Paul Morrissey and Chen Nie

Routledge
Taylor & Francis Group
LONDON AND NEW YORK

First published 2016
by Routledge
2 Park Square, Milton Park, Abingdon, Oxon OX14 4RN

and by Routledge
711 Third Avenue, New York, NY 10017

Routledge is an imprint of the Taylor & Francis Group, an informa business

© 2016 Yu Chen, Wei Fang, Liqing Li, Paul Morrissey and Chen Nie

The right of Yu Chen, Wei Fang, Liqing Li, Paul Morrissey and Chen Nie to be identified as the authors of this work has been asserted by them in accordance with sections 77 and 78 of the Copyright, Designs and Patents Act 1988.

All rights reserved. No part of this book may be reprinted or reproduced or utilised in any form or by any electronic, mechanical, or other means, now known or hereafter invented, including photocopying and recording, or in any information storage or retrieval system, without permission in writing from the publishers.

Trademark notice: Product or corporate names may be trademarks or registered trademarks, and are used only for identification and explanation without intent to infringe.

British Library Cataloguing in Publication Data
A catalogue record for this book is available from the British Library

Library of Congress Cataloging in Publication Data
Names: Chen, Yu, 1979 April 19-
Title: Social attitudes in contemporary China / Yu Chen, Wei Fang, Liqing Li, Paul Morrissey, Chen Nie.
Description: 1 Edition. | New York, NY : Routledge, 2016. | Series: Routledge contemporary China series ; 143 | Includes bibliographical references and index.
Identifiers: LCCN 2015036558| ISBN 9781138910690 (hardback) | ISBN 9781315693286 (ebook)
Subjects: LCSH: Attitude (Psychology)–China. | Youth–Attitudes–China. | Culture.
Classification: LCC HM1181 .C44 2016 | DDC 303.3/80951–dc23
LC record available at http://lccn.loc.gov/2015036558

ISBN: 978-1-138-91069-0 (hbk)
ISBN: 978-1-315-69328-6 (ebk)

Typeset in Times New Roman
by Wearset Ltd, Boldon, Tyne and Wear

Printed and bound in Great Britain by
TJ International Ltd, Padstow, Cornwall

Contents

Preface		xiv
Acknowledgements		xv
1	**Introduction** PAUL MORRISSEY	1
2	**Exploring Chinese young people's attitudes towards online communication and relationship formation: liberation, autonomy and ambivalence** WEI FANG	21
3	**Probing into attitudes and perceptions towards nation and nationalism in contemporary China: uncertainty, scepticism and disdain** LIQING LI	64
4	**Attitudes to housing tenures among young people in transitional China** CHEN NIE	97
5	**Beliefs and behaviours: accessing higher education in contemporary China** YU CHEN	153
6	**Conclusions** PAUL MORRISSEY	186
	Index	195

Preface

The central idea behind this book is the desire to take the reader into the lives of young Chinese respondents and to listen to their voices. We hope that those voices will introduce the reader to some of the feelings, beliefs and behaviours of young Chinese citizens, and the complexity that surrounds them. We do not aspire to be the curators of attitudes in the PRC; nor do we intend that this book should be a distillation of such attitudes, but we do wish to contribute to the literature in this area.

It is important to point out that all the norms of rigorous social science research conventions of a British university have been strictly adhered to, and the voices are anonymous. Respondents names are fictitious names, where they are used. Where Chinese names legitimately appear in the text, including the names of the writers of Chapters 2, 3, 4 and 5, the family name appears first, followed by the given name, for example, Chen Nie.

We foresee that different readers will want to use this book in different ways. Some will be most interested in the interview data, as a transmitter of attitude and interest. Some may want to delve more deeply into a particular topic, such as beliefs about nationalism, or the theoretical development of attitudes to housing tenures. With this notion of selective reading in mind, we have endeavoured to point the reader to particular sections in each chapter.

Paul Morrissey

Acknowledgements

This book has benefitted from the expertise of staff of the Faculty of Social Science and Law at the University of Bristol, expertise which was available to all the writers during their studies from 2005 onwards. In particular, we would like to thank all the staff at the Centre for East Asian Studies, the Centre for Policy Studies, the Department of Sociology and the Graduate School of Education for their encouragement and assistance during our studies and research. Professor Ka Ho Mok, Professor Roger Dale, Professor Susan Robertson, Dr. Misa Izuhara, Dr. Patricia Kennett, Professor Ray Forrest, Professor Thomas Osborne, Dr. Lee Marshall, Ms. Paula Surridge, Professor Maurizio Marinelli and Dr. Yang Chen need a special mention for their contribution to our collective education, and thus to this volume. The University of Bristol sponsored the PhD studies of Wei Fang, Liqing Li and Paul Morrissey, and also provided travel funds to some of the writers for the purposes of data gathering in China. The University of Hong Kong also provided funds for Paul to travel to a conference at that great institution.

Wei and Chen both would like to thank their young daughter Nie Rui (Tuotuo) for all the joys she brought them during the writing of their chapters.

This book draws upon the extensive body of written material in the social sciences and on modern China. While it may be invidious to mention individual scholars from those mentioned in the bibliography, we have collectively been particularly influenced by Pierre Bourdieu, Roger Dale, Richard Ronald and Teun A. van Dijk.

Much of the data in the book has been gathered from young citizens of the People's Republic, and our heartfelt thanks goes out to all of those individuals who have so generously given of their time to allow us insights into their perspectives, and to analyse those perspectives. These young citizens are drawn from a variety of locations in China, from the large cities of the eastern seaboard, to the more traditional centres in the West, and to communities which are defined as rural. It is the perspectives of these anonymous contributors that we have sought to represent and we are greatly in their debt.

Our data was reviewed by participants at a number of conferences, and we would like to thank the many attendees for their patience and comments. Especially useful were the British Sociological Association Annual Conference in

Leeds, 2012, the Social Sciences Conference in Hong Kong, 2009, the East Asian Social Policy 10th International Conference (Social Policy Responses and Changing Governance in East Asia) at Beijing Normal University, July 2013, the International Sociological Association (Housing and the Credit Crunch – International Experiences and Responses) in Glasgow, September 2009.

Helen Morrissey deserves particular thanks for her proofreading of the manuscript, which took many hours and great skill.

We profited greatly from the editorial guidance of Peter Sowden and his staff at Routledge, and the anonymous review of the proposal.

1 Introduction

Paul Morrissey

It has always struck me as remarkable, almost improbable, that in the late 1970s, Deng Xiaoping redirected the course of China's economy at the same time as President Reagan and Prime Minister Thatcher set course for a radically conservative capitalism, as if all three were reading von Mises, Hayek and Friedman at the same time. The last 40 years has seen a tumult of political, economic, social and technological change which has affected China as much as any country on the globe, and an awareness of these changes, presented later, may permit some understanding of the attitudes and ideologies presented in this book. But the question which this book attempts to address is: have these tumultuous changes also brought about a revolution in the Chinese psychological landscape?

What does the Chinese citizen think, feel and believe about her economic, political, technical and social environment? Where would she like to go college? Where would she prefer to live? What does she think about the world beyond her national boundaries? Who does she communicate with when she goes online? How have these feelings and beliefs changed from those of previous generations? Our goal in this book is to contribute to what is recorded about the feelings, thoughts and beliefs of people in contemporary China, through a number of case studies and the analysis of the primary data that these have allowed. We do not aspire to provide a meta understanding of the field, but we do aspire to offer fresh insights and to stimulate the reader's thinking in ways that might lead to further fruitful investigation. We do not regard the feelings, thoughts and beliefs of the contemporary Chinese citizen to be starkly simple; indeed, we offer a complexity, a level of nuance and a catalogue of inconsistency regarding these which both contribute to and extend the existing work.

There is plenty of easily digestible information available to the Western reader should he be interested in the questions outlined previously. Let's take an example. On a beautifully presented website, with very accessible graphics, Eli Bildner tells us that 80 per cent of Chinese are satisfied with their country's economic direction, as they have been for many years, and that Chinese respondents once again topped the list in terms of their level of satisfaction over their nation's development (www.tealeafnation.com). Further, Bildner informs us that a similar percentage of Chinese respondents also agree that people can live better in a free market economy, a figure which surpasses that of the US and European nations and is at the forefront of satisfaction ratings worldwide. The site claims to use data from the Pew Global Attitudes Survey, a resource that I will return to later, and states that Pew conducted more than 3,100 surveys in China to collect the data. But comments on the site are encouraged and true to the style of many such internet spaces, typify the sorts of problems which this genre of data, and its methodology, faces. I found one such comment, relating to the 'do people live better in a free market economy' question, particularly pointed:

> To be honest I don't understand the questions. It is not true that China is a free market economy. China is a mixed economy in which economic development is a combination of market forces and state planning and intervention. Just like Singapore or South Korea, which have a market-driven economy with large state intervention. I find it astonishing that such polls put questions that assume that market economy is the same thing everywhere.
>
> (Ibid.)

This book is not a critique of the survey methodology; indeed, the authors all concur that surveys have their rightful place in rigorous research. We accept that because it is easy, cheap and convenient, the conventional method of measuring social attitudes is to ask questions, often in writing, regarding an imaginary, or symbolic, situation; and because of this ease, convenience, economy and mechanical nature, the survey questionnaire has rightfully become a major tool in sociological and socio-psychological methodology. Indeed, all of the authors of this book have used the survey methodology in their own work in one way or another: survey data does appear in some of the chapters to follow. But we also accept that there are spaces into which the survey cannot go. Richard LaPiere famously painted a verbal picture for his students 80 years ago regarding the disjuncture between the symbolic Armenian lady on the bus and the symbolic negative reaction of the Armenian male (as a respondent to a questionnaire, in the comfort of a coffee shop) to the question of whether he should stand up for her, with the experience of the same Armenian male being on the bus with all the emotional reality of 'stolidly avoiding the hurt eyes of the hypothetical woman and the derogatory stares of the other occupants of the bus' (LaPiere 1934). His point was that an attitude or belief does not always equate to behaviour.

Our contribution here emerges from material relating to social, economic, technological and international dimensions, using the words and recorded preferences of PRC residents, material which has been collected within the last five years. We emphasise that all the data for this piece has been collected in China from ordinary Chinese citizens; the words and views are not of any elite group, nor of individuals who have been granted special permission to speak to the researchers. While the reliability of some research into attitudes in the PRC has often been questioned by Western scholarship, due to a lack of methodological transparency, we argue that the data here has been collected with due rigour.

Following this introduction, there are four further sections in this chapter. First, there will be a review of other writing relating to attitudes, values and ideologies in contemporary China, after which this will be an examination of the attitude construct, and an exploration of the qualitative and pro-qualitative methodology, the methodology which was used to collect much of the data for this piece; the final section will attempt to outline the contexts which frame the case studies which form the landscape of this book.

A review of work on attitudes in China

This section will draw upon examples of published work on attitudes in the PRC by both Chinese and Western scholars, in order to demonstrate the scale of this literature and to demonstrate some of the issues surrounding the collection of data on attitudes (see, for example, Johnston, A. and Stockman, D. on anti-Americanism, Cao, S., Chen, L. and Liu, Z. 2009 on attitudes to the environment, Chen, X. *et al.*, on attitudes to child rearing, and Fairbrother, G. on attitudes to political education). It will point out and discuss the fact that some of these studies use elite interviews as a data collection method, while others collect the data from 'ordinary' citizens; some studies use data which has been collected from online or other surveys. Also discussed will be the work of the Pew Research Centre, in particular the Pew Global Attitudes Survey, which has presented a number of China-based topics using face-to-face interviews.

But before the review of this literature, one must acknowledge that in discussing attitudes, it is impossible to ignore other concepts such as values, beliefs, opinions and ideologies. Certainly, these concepts will be mentioned in the following chapters. It's important here to outline my position regarding the enormous amount of theoretical and empirical literature on the concepts of values, attitudes and beliefs. Some have described this literature as contradictory: 'Often, these concepts are used indiscriminately, even interchangeably, creating confusing and misleading theoretical propositions and empirical research results' (Bergman 1998: 81). I accept Bergman's summary that we should regard 'an attitude (as) the cognitive construction and affective evaluation of an attitude object by an agent', and 'a value ... as the cognitive and affective evaluation of an array of objects by a group of agents' (ibid.: 87). This makes it clear that 'value' has more to do with the collective and a more general outlook, while 'attitude' has more to do with the individual and a defined, specific object. What I see is an inverted pyramid of concepts rooted in the Chinese psyche; I concur with Faure when he asserts that in China, what can be observed and recorded are behaviours, feelings and beliefs, and that behind these behaviours, feelings and beliefs, deeper in human personality, are anchored values:

> Values elicit behaviours, explain them. Before surveying the set of values that makes the Chinese so specific to Westerners, we have to touch upon something even less visible: Chinese perception and thinking.
>
> (Faure, G.O. 2002)

Let us start our review of the literature here, with Faure's notion of 'Chinese perception and thinking'. De Menthe's *The Chinese Mind: Understanding Traditional Chinese Beliefs and Their Influence on Contemporary Culture* is typical of the genre of work that appears to be aimed at a wide readership. De Menthe's piece is an examination of contemporary Chinese culture, offering insights into the values, attitudes and behaviour patterns of modern China – and their roots in the history of the nation. He insists that certain historical concepts are vital for an understanding of contemporary China and contemporary Chinese attitudes and behaviour, including *yin* and *yang*, the search for balance in all things, *mianji*, the importance of face, *hong*, looking at things holistically, *de*, the power of virtue, *guo cui*, the national essence of the Chinese, *zhong fu*, the pursuit of insight, and, *bi*, unity the Chinese way. His approach is of course fundamentally different from that of all the others described here in that *The Chinese Mind* is based on secondary data, and is his own reinterpretation of erstwhile cultural elements; the other writings, including this book, are based on fresh, or at least fresher, primary sources.

There is a great variety of empirical survey work by Chinese scholars interested in specific attitude objects, and projects which are designed to investigate an array of attitude objects. The reasons for such work are myriad, but it is interesting to note Sun's comment that it is not only academics who concern themselves with how people feel and behave; he asserts that how the public feel and behave are becoming more important to the carrying out of domestic and foreign policies, and that therefore the Chinese government has extended a great deal of effort in seeking to understand what the public think (Sun 2013).

The Beijing Area Studies Survey of Beijing Residents (BAS) is one of the larger and longer term projects: surveys started in 1995, giving the project a unique longitudinal perspective. The BAS has been conducted annually since 1995 by the Research Centre on Contemporary China (RCCC) at Beijing University, and was apparently modelled on the University of Michigan's Detroit Area Study (Johnson and Stockman 2007). The survey claims that sampling is done according to probability proportional to size (PPS), a form of stratified random sampling, and involves lengthy face-to-face interviews with respondents conducted by trained graduate students. Among its limitations is the fact that BAS responses are only from residents of the Beijing area, and only from residents with a Beijing *hukou* (see Chapter 2 for a discussion of the *hukou* system), thus excluding both migrants resident in Beijing and all those Chinese citizens who live outside the capital.

We can see from the title of a research project under the auspices of the Chinese Academy of Social Sciences, 'China General Social Survey' (www.uchicago.cn), that academics are certainly very interested in observing changing perspectives. I choose an example here from data provided by the 'China General Social Survey' to provide an insight into the contextual complexity, hitherto unmentioned here, and the procedural problems inherent in studying social attitudes in a nation which is so structurally fractured. Peilin Li and Yi Zhang suggest that the unprecedented social transformation and the ensuing complexity of the social reality in China have brought great importance, and great difficulties, to the research on the middle class in China. It is this group, the middle class, who are considered the nation's actual and potential change-makers, those whose opinions ought to be taken into account (Peilin and Yi 2008). Peilin and Yi were interested in the definition and scale of the middle class in transitional China and whether those defined as middle class perceive themselves as middle class (op. cit.). Their research was based on data collected for the project 'China General Social Survey' (op. cit.) for 2006 using 7,063 questionnaires covering the whole country.

Drawing on various definitions and measurements of the middle class by scholars from different countries and in different social realities, the authors employ three variables – income, occupation and educational capital – to identify the Chinese middle class. And interestingly, the authors report the social and cultural factors which caused complications. Average income, for example, is taken as the average income of urban *hukou* holders, rather than a national average income. Further, there is the cultural tradition of being reticent regarding one's wealth; to overcome this reticence, the authors readjusted income reported by respondents to improve the reliability of the data. How this readjustment was calculated and what effect it had on the results is not known, but the results are nevertheless very interesting. Those who met all three criteria variables – income, occupation and educational capital – are seen as 'core middle class', those who meet two are 'half-core middle class', and those who meet one are referred to as 'the marginal middle class'. Research data showed that nationwide, the middle class constituted 12.1 per cent of the population, with 3.2 per cent 'core middle class' and 8.9 per cent 'half-core middle class'; a further 13.7 per cent were defined as 'marginal middle class'. However, 25.4 per cent of the urban population (7.0 per cent 'core middle class' and 18.4 per cent 'half-core middle class') were identified, with a further 24.3 per cent seen as 'the marginal middle class'.

This work, and the thinking behind it, is significant. Within the literature relating to the study of contemporary Chinese attitudes, the problem of 'who one should ask' frequently emerges. Lu and Alon's study (2004) into changing perspectives notes a new socio-type, and it is this socio-type – the young and educated – with which they engage in their empirical work. Lu and Alon aim to define the group within the current social strata of China and to differentiate it from other social groups, and they argue that not only do the young and educated form a significant consumer base, but they are a barometer of changing attitudes. This arises partly because of their role as a specialized labour force for multinational companies, and their consequent contact with external ideas. In the chapters which follow, the authors engage with the same socio-group, the young and educated, whose responses are recorded and analysed.

I now turn to some pieces from Western literature which focus on social attitudes. Johnson and Stockman's 2007 article is an example of that category which investigates a particular attitude or sub-set of attitudes. They use language analysis, interviews, quantitative content analysis and survey data to examine

Chinese attitudes towards the United States from multiple angles. One of the reasons for my choice of this article is that the topic under review has a certain resonance with Liqing Li's contribution in Chapter 3, and there are other reasons. Johnson and Stockman provide useful comments on methodological issues which face this area of study:

> ...the problem is that conventional wisdom has come from sources which are methodologically problematic; anecdotal evidence based on US media reporting, selective attention to popular publications in China, and conversations with a relatively small group of group of Chinese scholars and officials.
>
> (Johnson and Stockman 2007)

Johnson and Stockman also list the problems with many Chinese surveys and claim that it is the methodology that is most often unclear. Many are either badly designed or they do not provide sufficient information about sampling techniques. For example, one of the most well-known polls is the China Youth Daily poll from the mid 1990s. These polls claimed the US was the most disliked country among Chinese youth. These results are often cited as evidence of growing anti-Americanism among Chinese youth, but further investigation revealed that the survey was in fact a readers' voluntary response survey, not a random sample. Other studies, they claim, have been based on street polling; they describe examples of polls where conduct was problematic, where sampling was entirely random. Further, they provide descriptions of sampling techniques which are so vague that it is difficult to determine how representative the survey samples really are. Two other problems reported by Johnson and Stockman relate to issues with wording of questions and perhaps more importantly, to the fact that they could find no surveys in their domain which were part of a times-series. All the information about Chinese attitudes about the US, whether these are anecdotal impressions of US politicians, or more systematic qualitative and quantitative data, comes from urban China, and most in fact comes from Beijing, or Beijing scholars, officials, analysts or interviewees. The authors are hesitant to generalise too much about how representative their conclusions are. I think this hesitancy is well advised, and concerns about the quality of methodology and/or representation may well apply to much of the literature on attitudes, including this piece.

Let us now take a closer look at the previously mentioned Pew Global Attitudes Survey. I should point out here that the information is from secondary sources, as Pew would not discuss with me the nature of their survey work. I take time to dwell on this survey for two reasons. First, it appears to have some impact, in that it is the source for regular, if not frequent, writing in the media (see for example, 'China finding superpower path no cake-walk', an article specially prepared by Pew for CNN, 8/6/2013 and 'Reached middle-class status? Start complaining about it', an article specially prepared by Pew for CNBC, 11/8/2011), and is thus part of the contemporary narrative about the PRC.

Second, the survey claims to collect data through face-to-face interviews, which is the method used in this research. We saw earlier how, according to Bildner, 80 per cent of Chinese are satisfied with their country's economic direction (www.tealeafnation.com), information gleaned through data from Pew Global Attitudes Survey. The official website for the Survey informs us that it conducts public opinion surveys, under the direction of Princeton Survey Research Associates International, on a broad array of subjects and in a wide variety of countries, ranging from people's perspectives of their own lives and their assessment of their own nation's progress, to their views about the current state of the world and important issues of the day; we are told that 400,000 interviews in 63 countries have been conducted as part of the project's work (www.pewglobal.org). The Survey forms part of the output from the Pew Research Centre, which claims to be a nonpartisan fact tank that informs the public about the issues, attitudes and trends shaping America and the world, without taking policy positions. Pew tells us, for example, that most Chinese feel that they enjoy a higher standard of living than their parents (Growing Concerns in China about Inequality and Corruption, September 2012), but the Chinese public is increasingly concerned about the quality of the country's air (Environmental Concerns on the Rise in China, September 2013).

We are informed that Pew's China surveys are based on a multi-stage cluster sample stratified by China's three regional-economic zones, which include all provinces except Tibet, Xinjiang, Hong Kong and Macao, with a disproportional sampling of the urban population. Twelve cities, 12 towns and 12 villages were sampled covering central, east and west China; the details of the towns and cities sampled are given, though not the villages. The mode of data collection for these surveys is face-to-face interviews, carried out in Mandarin and local dialect, with adults at least 18 years old. The data cited by Pew are from the Horizon Consultancy Group. Pew provides the caveat that in addition to sampling error, readers of these surveys should bear in mind that question wording and practical difficulties in conducting surveys can introduce error or bias into the findings of opinion polls.

The Centre also provides details of the survey instruments, and what is interesting in the context of this book is that although there is a claimed to be a face-to-face element, the principal instrument used appears to be a five-stage Likert scale; this instrument is discussed in a later section of this chapter (see 'Ambivalence'). For example, respondents are asked to respond to the issue of air pollution:

> Now I am going to read you a list of things that may be problems in our country. Tell me if you think (air pollution) is a very big problem, a moderately big problem, a small problem or not a problem at all.
> (Environmental Concerns on the Rise in China, September 2013)

As the question implies, the respondents have five choices in response to the question. They can choose between 'very big problem', 'moderately big problem', 'small problem', 'not a problem at all' and 'don't know/refused'. Of course, this instrument allows for the possibility of scale, though it does not provide an opportunity for respondents to add comments or qualify their responses. This is an important point for the approach herein, which centres on the contribution which qualified responses can add to this field of attitudinal study in contemporary China; I will return to the idea in the following section, which looks at the theoretical bases surrounding the attitude construct.

The attitude construct

From a Western scholarly viewpoint, the attitude construct has been of central importance to the understanding of our psychological lives. Without attitudes, 'one would go about daily life without the ability to think in terms of 'good' and 'bad', 'desirable' and 'undesirable', or 'approach' and 'avoid' ... existence would be truly chaotic and probably quite short' (Fazio and Olson 2003). For decades attitudes have played a central role in the field of social psychology (Allport 1935, McGuire 1985); indeed, the study of attitudes was at one time considered synonymous with this field (Thomas and Znaniecki 1918, Bergman 1998). A brief review of the literature on the attitude construct reveals the common assertion that evaluation is a pervasive part of everyday experience.

The traditional view of the attitude is of an unobservable psychological construct manifested in feelings, beliefs and behaviours, the so-called three component or tripartite model (Eagly and Chaiken 1993). The researcher cannot look into the mind of the Chinese citizen when he enquires about his attitude to roast duck, but the researcher can seek a response to the citizen's feeling about roast duck, as in 'Do you enjoy the prospect of eating duck?'; the researcher can seek knowledge about the citizen's beliefs, for example, 'Do you think that eating duck is good for your health?'; and he can ask about the citizen's behaviour patterns, as in 'How often do you eat roast duck?'

Fazio and Olson suggest that the tripartite view has been useful in cataloguing various attitudinal responses in providing a framework for their study, in providing a road-map for research on attitude formation and change, and in matching the intuitive distinction between the three components (Fazio and Olson 2003). However, research suggests that the strength of an attitude can be determined by which component is at the root of said attitude, and that an attitude can form as a result of just one of the components. Further, an individual may not experience a harmony or consistency between all three components, though the tripartite model implies this. For example, a Chinese citizen may believe that the 'one-child policy' is essentially necessary, but at the same time she may have reservations about the circumstances of an abortion. Further, she may have beliefs about the rights of a woman to have authority over her body, from a humanist or feminist perspective, but she may have a negative, visceral reaction to the mechanisms of the procedure.

We should also be aware in this study of the work on attitude formation, and the conceptualisations of the attitude construct, as being formed by means of cognitive, affective and behavioural processes. Regarding the cognitive, attitudes are thought to form when the attitude object is thought to possess desirable or undesirable elements, or when the attitude object is considered to bring about desirable or undesirable outcomes. Attitudes formed from affect stem from emotional reactions to attitude objects, when positive or negative feelings result from contact with the attitude object in question. When a subject has neither feelings nor beliefs regarding an attitude object, there may still be past experience of it, sufficient to induce an attitude towards it. But more significant to this project is the work on attitudes which is rooted in the conflicting relationships between the elements, and we now look at one of the features of the structural qualities of attitudes, namely ambivalence.

Ambivalence

Within the attitude construct literature is the situation where an individual may possess both positive and negative feelings, beliefs or thoughts about an attitude object; the individual's attitude can then be regarded as 'ambivalent' (Kaplan 1972).

Commonly-used measures of attitudes assume that attitudes exist somewhere between negative and positive, and often require respondents to place their attitude toward a given object somewhere on a Likert or bipolar single scale, usually defined at one end with 'dislike' or 'disagree' and at the other end with 'like' or 'agree' (Likert 1932). It is here that we come across the challenges which the survey methodology throws up, challenges which are recognised and addressed as far as they can be by workers in this field. As Fazio and Olson inform us, 'such scales deny the possibility that someone might feel *both* positively and negatively toward a given object (that is, ambivalent), or *neither* positively or negatively toward a given object (that is, indifferent)' (Fazio and Olson 2003). If the respondent to a questionnaire were to feel both positivity and negativity about an attitude object, then the meaning of the zero or neutral point on the scale becomes questionable, because respondents might respond somewhere near the zero or neutral point (Kaplan 1972). Some researchers who acknowledge ambivalence have attempted to reduce the problem by requesting that respondents make two judgements regarding a given object – one relating to their positive feelings toward the object, and another relating to their negative feelings toward the object.

Ambivalence is also recognised as an unstable and subjectively uncomfortable state (e.g. Newby-Clark *et al.* 2002); also recognised is the notion that there are consequences of ambivalence. As a result of this instability, ambivalent attitudes are prone to change, are relatively less predictive of behaviour, and are also more context dependent, meaning that whether the positive or the negative component is activated depends on the particular situation (Fazio and Olson); a further consequence is 'ambivalence amplification', the notion that behaviour towards an attitude object is amplified, either positively or negatively, in a subjective effort to reduce ambivalence (e.g. Hass *et al.* 1991). These notions are very useful in the context of this book and their significance will be examined in the later data chapters.

In conclusion, it is clear that there are well-documented difficulties regarding the use of survey methodology in attitudinal research, and much thought has been given to how these difficulties might be overcome. Of course, the survey method has the advantage of scale. However, where the collection of nuance is considered more important than the gathering of numbers, then there is a strong argument for a different methodology. It is this position that the authors in this book take. It is precisely because interviews are perhaps most often used to elicit opinions or attitudes, and to form hypotheses about the motivations behind such attitudes and consequent behaviours, that the authors used this method of data collection. In the next section, I consider the opportunities and benefits of using qualitative, semi-structured interviews in attitudinal research.

A qualitative approach

As has been pointed out earlier, a major feature of this book is that it presents an analysis of four sets of primary data collected through a series of intensive interviews. Thus, the nature of the investigation is qualitative: it is broad, deep and subjective; the responses to the questions posed involve description and explanation. Since the qualitative approach sees the world as socially constructed, and recognises the subjective viewpoints of interviewer and interviewee, it is able to offer the promise of a deep understanding of social reality (Warren 2004: 524). What makes the approach for this research fit for purpose are the recurrent characteristics in qualitative research, reproduced here from Miles and Huberman (1994: 10), each phrase of which echoes the intentions here:

- 'Qualitative research is conducted through an intense and/or prolonged contact with a ... life situation. These situations are typically ... normal, reflective of the everyday life of individuals, groups...
- The researcher's role is to gain a "holistic" overview of the context under study...
- The researcher attempts to capture data on the perceptions of local actors "from the inside", through a process of deep attentiveness, [and] empathetic understanding...'

In choosing a qualitative approach, we make certain philosophical assumptions. Regarding ontology, we embrace the position that there are multiple realities which may arise out of differences of culture, power and values; we accept that different researchers may interpret things differently, 'as do also the individuals being studied and the readers of ... the study' (Creswell 2007: 18). In a study of this nature, which crosses cultural boundaries, it was always highly probable that we would encounter different viewpoints. Our epistemological position is anti-essentialist; rather than a real world where one can find objective facts, we take the stance that no observer can be objective because he is bound up by social constructions (Marsh and Furlong 2002: 17) By implication, we chose to conduct the research in the 'field', as close as possible to the participants/respondents and their sites of working and living, in order to have a better understanding of the contexts of their opinions. We also embrace the rhetorical assumption that the writing needs to be personal, using the 'first person', and focusing on the meanings and understandings which the respondents bring to the study. Likewise, the methodology of this research has emerged from our experience in collecting the data, rather than being *only* informed by theory.

In this research, we adopt a 'magpie approach' with regard to the stances we take in order to interpret the data. Thus, we have been influenced by a number of theoretical positions, which have led to a personalised approach. We attempt to make sense of, or interpret, the meanings which our respondents have about their attitudes to choosing colleges of higher education or choosing their housing tenure; their attitudes to how they conduct their digital lives, and in their views about China's relationship with the outside world. Here, we claim to take a social constructivist stance. Interpretivist theory is relevant for its microsociological focus. It is based on a belief that social actors construct a world of lived reality by attaching specific meanings to local situations. 'It looks for culturally derived, and historically situated, interpretations of the social lifeworld' (Crotty 1998: 67). Interpretivists believe that knowledge is always local and embedded in organisational sites. We assume that beliefs, feelings, thoughts and behaviours can only be created or understood from the point of view of the individual. Since a researcher's interpretations are based on his own experiences, there may be different understandings and interpretations of reality. Objectivity is not a claim of this school of thought since we assume that our understanding of others can only be filtered through our own experiences. This position allows the double hermeneutic: the world is interpreted by actors (one hermeneutic level) and their interpretation is interpreted by the observer or researcher (the second hermeneutic level) (Marsh and Furlong 2002: 29). Hatch insists that this interpretive stance cannot allow the researcher to claim full understanding of another's meaning but has the advantage that it 'will open you to deep listening' (Hatch 2006: 15).

A consideration of interviews

> Whatever the aims of the social scientist, none can be reached without an understanding of the lives of the people who live in the society and the world. Qualitative interviewing is a tool for such an understanding.
> (Warren 2004: 524)

The above gives a clue as to the importance given in this study to what informants revealed to the authors. Interviewing was such a significant element in this research that it seems appropriate to devote some detailed attention to this instrument. From the literature regarding interviewing emerges a consensus 'that different types of interviewing are suited to different situations' (Fontana and Frey 1994: 373). The standardised or structured interview uses an order and wording of questions which is repeated from one interview to the next. The responses are recorded on a schedule, perhaps conveying the formality of the event. The semi-standard or unstructured interview allows a little more flexibility, and is particularly applicable to situations where 'you are on new ground' (ibid.: 125).

> (The) object (of the non-standard interview) is to find out what kinds of things are happening rather than to determine the frequency of predetermined kinds of things that the researcher already believes can happen.
>
> (Loftland 1971: 76)

In the semi-standard interview, the major questions are common to each interview but sequence may vary and the interviewer is free to probe more deeply for additional information. This may allow for differences in, for example, the level of comprehension of the interviewee, and for the fact that in answering one question, an interviewee may well be responding to another (ibid.: 124).

The literature points to the myriad pitfalls which may trap the unwary interviewer. O'Connel Davidson and Layder also argue that social researchers should continually reflect on the ways in which their values, mores and identity affect the information they seek to gather (O'Connel Davidson and Layder 1994: 53) and on the interpretation of those findings (ibid.: 28). It was particularly important in this study, where information gathering took place across cultures, to be reflective in this regard. I often reflected on Said's warnings, which seemed pertinent to my situation:

> ... the reality is ... (that) ... no-one has ever devised a method for detaching the scholar from the circumstances of life, from the fact of his involvement with a class, a set of beliefs, a social position, or from the mere activity of being a member of society (Said 1978: 10) ... with a European or an American studying the Orient there can be no disclaiming his actuality: that he comes up against the Orient as a European or an American first, as an individual second.
>
> (Ibid.: 11)

Of course, this was not so for my fellow authors here, as they were gathering responses to attitude objects in their own culture. Nevertheless, as with any scholarly work involving interviews, it is equally important for them, as for me, to guard against self-delusion on the part of the analyst with respect to the conclusions which they might make (Miles 1979: 591); illumination of issues may be possible, rather than generalisations (ibid.: 591).

Studies which have the interview as the central methodology should always carry the health warning that data gathered in this way is often less than neutral (Holstein and Gubrium 1995: 72; Hammersley 2003). In particular, the notion that 'open' interviews capture the genuine voices of interviewees is often questioned; rather, such voices can be 'a methodically constructed social product that emerges

Introduction 13

from its reflexive communicative practices' (Holstein and Gubrium op. cit.: 11). Thus, as Holliday points out, '...take what they say as evidence of what they wish to point out, rather than as information about where they come from' (Holliday *et al.* 2004: 48).

There is much questioning in the literature regarding the interview process about the 'capacity of interviews to provide accurate representations, either of the self or of the world' (Hammersley op. cit.: 1). Such doubts emerge from the view that interviews are more constructed social interactions than opportunities to collect objective data about beliefs or ideas of behaviour. Thus the interview is seen as a contextual social situation where the respondent may well be driven by the need to self-represent, possibly at the persuasion of the interviewer. Ozga and Gewirtz's phrase 'the disturbing and contaminating presence of the researcher' captures the extreme perception of this social situation (Ozga and Gewirtz 1994: 133). Others take a more realist view; writing about the tradition of reflexive disclosure on the part of researchers, Troyna is unconvinced that 'baring their souls' necessarily enhances the rigour of the research (Troyna 1994). However one positions oneself in this debate, we feel an obligation here to involve ourselves in 'intelligent self awareness or self examination' (the OED's definition of reflexivity).

> To be reflexive we need to be *aware* of our personal responses and to be able to make choices about how to use them. We also need to be aware of the personal, social and cultural contexts in which we live and work and to understand how these impact on the ways we interpret the world.
>
> (Etherington 2004: 18)

The following section leaves behind these important considerations of methodology and focuses on the contexts against which the case studies are written.

A consideration of context

> We live in a world of overlapping communities of fate, where the trajectories of countries are deeply enmeshed with one another.
>
> (Held 2004: 4)

As I have stated before, the last 40 years has seen a tumult of political, economic, social and technological change which have affected China as much as any country on the globe, and the reader will need an awareness of these changes to allow an understanding of the some of the attitudes and ideologies presented in this book. Regarding the political and the economic, the twin concepts of globalisation and neoliberalism frame much of the content of the case studies which follow; care needs to be taken in the use of these terms as they are used loosely in the wider literature.

First, then, the case studies are grounded in the concept of *globalisation*; from the many definitions written by scholars, I choose to reproduce Yang's here, for reasons which will be explained in a later section:

> Globalisation is the result of the compression of time and space that has occurred since advanced technology allowed the instantaneous sharing of information around the world, leading to a cross-border flow of ideas, ideologies, people and goods, images and messages, capital and financial services, knowledge and technologies, creating a borderless world economy. It has a material base in capitalism and an ideological genesis in neo-liberalism.
>
> (Yang 2003: 28)

Over the last decade, scholars and writers have increasingly discussed the nature and import of globalisation at political, economic, social and cultural levels (see, for example, Held and McGrew 2000, Schirato and Webb 2003); one scholar has demonstrated that the references to globalisation in social science journals have increased exponentially during the 1990s (Smith 2006: 5). Some of these references go beyond the political, economic, social and cultural to include technical or legal aspects and others issues relating to social justice and human rights (Held 2004).

Academics and researchers do not agree on many aspects of the form or direction of globalisation; for example, Vaira points out that some describe globalisation as a 'meta-myth' (Vaira 2004). There have been debates about its significance, and how it is to be defined; Held and McGrew are amongst those scholars who have attempted to identify categories of 'sceptics', 'globalists' and 'transformationists' in the globalisation debate (Held and McGrew 2000: 3). Mattelart, for example, takes the sceptical view: he considers that today's world situation is merely a continuation of trends which have developed over the last 400 or 800 years, and that the current situation is simply an intensification of the European (colonial) dominated global systems of the nineteenth century (Mattelart 2000: 75). Over 200 years ago the philosopher Kant wrote that 'we are unavoidably side by side', referring to the level of international integration that he perceived, (and wished to encourage further) at the end of the eighteenth century (Kant 1795). Held agrees with the sceptics: 'It needs to be pointed out that there is nothing new about globalisation per se' (Held, op. cit.: 2); he argues that there have been many phases of globalisation in the past, including the spread of empires and world religions, the Age of Discovery, and the development of trading blocs (ibid.: 2).

In contrast to sceptics, 'globalists' posit that 'globalisation is a real and significant global event' (Held and McGrew op. cit.: 3). Further, 'transformationists' consider that the effect of globalisation will be to create a new stratified global order of winners and losers in the world, requiring a revision of the existing nomenclatures of developed and developing nations (Mok 2006). Yang's definition of globalisation (as mentioned earlier) clearly reveals his position on the 'globalist' side of the debate and underlines his belief that the market is a cornerstone of the process, stressing the link to neoliberalism; markets are certainly to the fore in the case studies which follow relating to housing, higher education and social media. 'Hyperglobalists' argue that increasing interaction between different nation-states and the freer interchange of capital, goods, services, people, technologies, information, and ideas, suggest an inevitable convergence of human activities (Ohmae 1990; Fukuyama 1992); the notion of convergence may resonate with some readers, should they recognise some situations and attitudes which we describe in China.

There is little disagreement, however, about the forces which are driving the process: the electronic revolution, the development of global markets in goods and services, and of supranational bodies, and the rapid growth of migration and the movement of peoples. Of these factors, it is the rapid flow of capital that is seen by many as *the* determinant in the social, cultural and political issues of sovereign states (Mattelart 2000: 75). And in this context arises a further discussion among scholars. Where globalists see the disempowerment of the nation-state and the formation of a single consumer culture across societies (Fukuyama 1992; Waters 1995), others argue that there is heterogeneity of national responses to global processes (Schmidt 1999; Friedman 1999).

There are some important points which have great relevance to the case studies which follow. If globalists such as Yang (ibid.) are right, how are the processes of globalisation revealed in attitudes to the world beyond China's borders? Further, will the transformationist's argument, that globalisation creates a new stratified global order of winners and losers, be revealed in the preferences for particular HE institutions, or social media platforms, both of which may be competing for a particular niche within the internal market? Many scholars argue that this competition has been nurtured, and intensified, by neoliberal political and economic policies. Will Fukuyama's claim that there has been 'a shift in the balance between state and market strongly in favour of the latter' (Fukuyama 2006: 121) be evidenced in the case study relating to housing tenure? Highly relevant is the question regarding the disempowerment of the nation-state and the formation of a single consumer culture across societies (Fukuyama 1992; Waters 1995); a convergence of practice might counter the claims of heterogeneity of national responses to global processes (Schmidt 1999; Friedman 1999).

That market forces are integral to globalisation is essential to an understanding of the phenomenon; while some see globalisation as an inexorable process of global economic integration (Fukuyama 1992), others see it as a deliberate policy project which celebrates the market as economic saviour (Yang op. cit.: 28). Beyond dispute is the fact that both the Anglo-Saxon world and greater China are bound up in this process, as evidenced by Harvey and others (Harvey 2005), thus providing some legitimacy for the case studies used in this study.

Liberalisation or *neoliberalism* is a term used to describe the political-economic philosophy that focuses on free market methods, 'a shift in the balance between state and market strongly in favour of the latter' (Fukuyama 2006: 121). The neoliberal philosophy, with its roots in an intellectual movement promoted by scholars such as von Mises (1949) and Hayek (1960, 1976), advocates the reduction of the role of government, the opening of national markets, free trade, flexible exchange rates, deregulation, the transfer of assets from the public to the private sector, the transfer of the disciplines of the private sector into the routines of the public, and an international division of labour. Some scholars argue that we can trace the first manifestation of the philosophy back to the 1975 fiscal crisis in New York, and the subsequent financial remodelling (Harvey 2005: 44–48). This political-economic agenda is often referred to as the Washington Consensus (Bayliss and Smith 2001: 189, Stiglitz 2002: 20); though it might be argued that it is more of an ideology than a consensus.

A major theme emerging from the political-economic aspect of globalisation is the increased significance of competition. 'National competitiveness has increasingly become a central preoccupation of governance strategies across the world' (Watson and Hey 2003: 299). Scholars such as Jessop (for example, 2002, 2004), Cerny (1990) and Ball (2007) argue that during that last quarter century, many nations have evolved their political and economic structures to become 'competition states', which aims to 'secure economic growth within its borders and/or to secure competitive advantages for capitals based in its borders' (Jessop 2002: 96). This has been achieved by a complex structural coupling, 'an accommodation between accumulation and regulation' (Ball 2007: 3), which has resulted from the failure of previous 'command economies'. These systems had produced a shared condition known as 'the overloaded state' (Cerny 1990: 221), where capital was unable to play its full role in the economic system because of a series of crises in the social, financial and political fields (crises such as demographic change, unemployment, un-governability, etc.) (Ball 2007: 4). The competition state has emerged not as a unified project but as a piecemeal dismantling of previous arrangements, always limited by the 'political reach of regulation' (Ball op. cit.: 5). Importantly for this study, Ball points out that such arrangements emerge from and within existing state structures, and that therefore the response varies greatly from one nation to the next.

Returning to the Washington consensus, this powerful agenda has its critics: Stiglitz, for example, suggests that the implementation of this agenda in many nations around the world has led to a situation where there is 'global governance without global government' (Stiglitz 2002: 21). One might exemplify this with reference to the financial service industry: this has been criticised as being globally active (and perhaps globally irresponsible) but only nationally regulated. The Washington consensus has achieved this (partial) implementation by favouring treaty devices such as the World Bank and the World Trade Organization (WTO) (Fukuyama 2006: 121).

How have these meta-contexts of globalisation and the neoliberal agenda affected the attitudes of the Chinese citizen in the twenty-first century, if at all? For China, there has been a socio-economic transformation, which has included changes in both the distributive systems as well as the value systems. First, the distribution structure founded upon the principle of 'equal' income under Mao Zedong's regime has changed into one characterised by the variability of individual income; and second, there has been a move from a system of collectivism and selfless contribution to one based upon private property, individual achievement and the cult of self-interest (Lu and Alon). The chapters that follow explore both these contexts and consequent attitudinal reactions in greater detail.

Road map

Underlying Wei Fang's chapter (Chapter 2) are two profound transformations, with one taking place within a country and one spanning the globe, that indicate the forces which constitute our current era. In China, the phenomena of marketisation, urbanisation and globalisation have radically transformed social equity. At the same time, worldwide, the extensive diffusion of the internet and social media has brought in new modes of sociality, autonomy and agency. Based on materials from fieldwork in Hebei Provence, Wei's chapter will reveal young people's attitudes to particular social media sites, and to those who are in different social groups. How do young urban dwellers in China view their peers in rural areas? What are the social and geographical dimensions of this much discussed urban divide? Do the new digital technologies and their potential to cross social boundaries offer a hope for transforming the existing patterns of social inclusion-exclusion? Can the internet play a positive role in transforming rural–urban inequality? Is there a possibility that rural and urban youth may be able to increase their mutual social capital through communication online?

In the light of globalisation, a new world order and economic transformation in contemporary China, Liqing Li's Chapter 3 looks into university students' attitudes and perceptions towards the so-called 'rising nationalism' which is, allegedly, proving to be most evident among China's university students in urban areas, both through their participation in street demonstrations and their online activities (Xu 2008; Wang 2009). In turn, such attitudes and perceptions tellingly reflect the nationalism among university students themselves, which, as will be demonstrated in the chapter, contradicts the usual understanding of student nationalism based on larger scale survey studies.

What are young peoples' perceptions regarding various tenures and living arrangements in urban China? How have these perceptions changed during the reform era? How are the current trends in living arrangements underpinned by intergenerational lending, and how do such activities strengthen traditional family relations? Chen Nie's Chapter 4 is grounded in the economic reforms since the early 1980s and in the consequent housing policy for the New China. These reforms have transformed the nation and have overturned the structures which determined housing for most citizens in the Mao era, particularly for urban residents. Nie identifies the dominant assumptions, conceptions and processes in terms of a new home ownership ideology. The development of concepts of homeowners' groups and young people's views regarding home ownership are presented and analysed, as are its impact on society, the economy, the emerging housing market and importantly, individuals' perceptions and choices. Based on materials from fieldwork in Beijing, it examines young people's discourse about home ownership, private rental, and living in parents' homes.

In Yu Chen's chapter (Chapter 5), attitudes to accessing higher education are the focus. What are the perceived benefits of attending higher education in China? Is there an equality of opportunity for entering elite universities for students from different social, economic, cultural and educational backgrounds? Which students have the greatest chance to enter elite universities: does it depend on good academic results or are other factors involved? Yu Chen's chapter asks whether it is possible to measure the idea of social equity in HE access, against a wider enquiry as to the distribution of social, economic and cultural resources in contemporary Chinese society. She demonstrates a context of reform and restructuring in the field of higher education, and the change from an elite system to a mass system. Has this change allowed some individuals to improve their social status, or has it been manipulated by some to reproduce existing social structures? Students' socio-economic background is the main focus of her study. Yu's analysis is based on fieldwork in Xian and Shaanxi province.

References

Allport, G.W. 1935 'Attitudes', in *A Handbook of Social Psychology*. Murchison C.A. (Ed.) Worcester, MA: Clark University Press.

Ball, S. 2007 *Education plc: Understanding Private Sector Participation in Public Sector Education*. Abingdon: Routledge.

Bayliss, J. and Smith, S. 2001 *The Globalization of World Politics*. Oxford: Oxford University Press.

Bergman, M.M. 1998 'A Theoretical Note on the Differences between Attitudes, Opinions, and Values'. *Swiss Political Science Review* 4 (2) pp. 81–93.

Bildner, E. Accessed at www.tealeafnation.com on 6 September 2014.

Cao, S., Chen, L. and Liu, Z. 2009 'An investigation of Chinese attitudes toward the environment'. *Ambio: Journal of the Human Environment* 38 (1) pp. 55–64.

Cerny, G. 1990 *The Changing Architecture of Politics: Structure, Agency, and the Future of the State*. London: Sage.

Chen, X., Hastings, P.D., Rubin, K.H., Chen, H., Cen, G., Shannon, L. and Stewart, S.L. 1998 'Child rearing attitudes and behavioural inhibitions in Chinese and Canadian toddlers'. *Developmental Psychology* 34 (4) pp. 677–686.

China General Social Survey. Accessed at www.uchicago.cn on 13 September 2014.

Crotty, M. 1998 *The Foundations of Social Research*. Sydney: Allen and Unwin.

Creswell, J.W. 2007 *Qualitative Inquiry and Research Design*. London: Sage.

De Menthe, B. 2009 *The Chinese Mind: Understanding Traditional Chinese Beliefs and Their Influence on Contemporary Culture*. Vermont: Tuttle.

Eagly, A.H. and Chaiken, S. 1993 *The Psychology of Attitudes*. Orlando, Florida: Harcourt Brace Jovanovich College Publishers.

Etherington, K. 2004 *Becoming a Reflexive Researcher*. London: Jessica Kingsley.

Fairbrother, G. 2003 'The effects of political education and critical thinking on Hong Kong and Mainland Chinese university students' national attitudes.' *British Journal of Sociology of Education* 24 (5).

Faure, G.O. 2002 *China: New Values in a Changing Society*. Accessed at www.ceibs.edu on 6 September 2014.

Fazio, R.H. and Olson, M.A. 2003 'Attitudes: Foundations, Functions and Consequences', in Hogg, M.A. and Cooper, J. (Eds), *The Sage Handbook of Social Psychology*. London: Sage.

Fontana, A. and Frey, J.H. 2005 'Interviewing: the Art of Science', in Denzin, N.K. and Lincoln, Y.S. (Eds) *Handbook of Qualitative Research.* Thousand Oaks, California: Sage.
Fukuyama, F. 1992 *The End of History and the Last Man.* London: Hamilton.
Fukuyama, F. 2006 *After the Neocons.* London: Profile Books Ltd.
Hammersley, M. 2003. 'Recent Radical Criticism of Interview Studies', in *Qualitative Interviewing.* University of Essex 2004, Essex Summer School.
Harvey, D. 2005 *Neoliberalism.* New York: Oxford University Press.
Hass, R.G., Katz, I., Rizzo, N., Bailey, J. and Eisenstadt, D. 1991 'Cross-racial appraisal as related to attitude ambivalence and cognitive complexity.' *Personality and Social Psychology Bulletin* 17 (1).
Hatch, M.J., with Cunliffe, A. 2006 *Organisational Theory.* Oxford: Oxford University Press.
Hayek, F. 1994 *The Road to Serfdom.* Chicago: University of Chicago Press.
Held, D. 2004 *Global Covenant: The Social Democratic Alternative to the Washington Consensus.* Oxford: Polity.
Held, D. and McGraw, A. (Eds) 2000 *The Global Transformations Reader: An Introduction to the Globalization Debate.* Malden MA: Polity Press.
Holliday, A., Hyde, M. and Kullman, J. 2004 *Intercultural Communication: An Advanced Resource Book.* London: Routledge.
Holstein, J.A. and Gubrium, G.F. 1995 *The Active Interview.* Thousand Oaks, California: Sage.
Jessop, B. 2002 *The Future of the Capitalist State.* Oxford: Polity Press.
Johnston, A.I. and Stockmann, D. 2007 'Chinese attitudes toward the United States and Americans', in *Anti-Americanisms in World Politics.* Katzenstein P.J. and Keohane R.O. (Eds) Ithaca: Cornell University Press.
Kant, I. 1795 *Critique of Pure Reason.* Translated 1986 by J.M.D. Meiklejohn. London: Dent.
Kaplan, K.J. 1972 'On the ambivalence-indifference problem in attitude theory and measurement'. *Psychological Bulletin* 77 (5).
LaPiere, R.T. 1934 *Social Forces* 13 (2) pp. 230–237. Oxford: OUP.
Likert, R. 1932 'A Technique for the Measurement of Attitudes'. *Archives of Psychology* 140: 1–55.
Loftland, J. 1971 *Analysing Social Settings.* Belmont California: Wadsworth.
Lu, L. and Alon, I. 2004 'Analysis of the Changing Trends in Attitudes and Values of the Chinese: The Case of Shanghai's Young & Educated'. *Journal of International and Area Studies* 11 (2) pp. 67–88.
Marsh, D. and Furlong, P. 2002 *Ontology and Epistemology in Political Science* in Marsh, D. and Stoker G. (Eds) *Theory and Methods in Political Science.* Hampshire: Palgrave Macmillan.
Mattelart, A. 2000 *Networking the World, 1794–2000,* trans. Liz Carey-Libbrecht and James A. Cohen. Minneapolis MN: University of Minnesota Press.
McGuire, W. 1985 'Attitudes and Attitude Change', in Gardner Lindzey and Elliot Aronson (Eds) *The Handbook of Social Psychology* 2. New York: Random House.
Miles, M.B. 1979 'Qualitative Data as an Attractive Nuisance: The Problem of Analysis'. *Administrative Science Quarterly* 24 (4) pp. 590–601.
Miles, M.B. and Huberman, A.M. 1994 *Qualitative Data Analysis.* California: Sage.
Mok, K.H. 2006 *Education Reform and Education Policy in East Asia.* London: Routledge.
Newby-Clark, I.R., McGregor, I. and Zanna, P. 2002 'Thinking and caring about cognitive inconsistency: When and for whom does attitudinal ambivalence feel uncomfortable?' *Journal of Personality and Social Psychology* 82 (2), 157–166.

Ohmae, K. 1990 *The Borderless World: Power and Strategy in the Interlinked Economy*. New York: Harper Business.

Ozga and Gewirtz. 1994 'Sex, Lies and Videotape: interviewing the Educational Policy Elite' in Halpin, D. and Troyna, B. (Eds) *Researching Education Policy: Ethical and Methodological issues*. London: The Falmer Press.

O'Connel Davidson, J. and Layder, D. 1994 *Methods, Sex and Madness*. London: Routledge.

Peilin, L. and Yi, Z. 2008 'The Scope, Identity, and Social Attitudes of the Middle Class in China'. *Chinese Journal of Sociology* 28 (2).

Rosenberg, M.J. and Hovland, C.I. 1960 'Cognitive, Affective and Behavioural Components of Attitudes' in Hovland, C.I. and Rosenberg, M.J. (Eds) *Attitude Organisation and Change: An Analysis of Consistency Among Attitude Components*. New Haven, CT: Yale University Press.

Said, E.W. 1978 *Orientalism*. London: Routledge & Kegan Paul.

Schirato, T. and Webb, J. 2003 'Bourdieu's concept reflexivity of as metaliteracy.' *Cultural Studies* 17 (3–4).

Schmidt, V.A. 1999 *States and Sovereignty in the Global Economy*. California: Psychology Press.

Stiglitz, J. 2002 *Globalisation and its discontents*. London: Penguin.

Sun, L. 2013 'Different perceptions of the EU in urban China', in Lisheng Dong, Zhengxu Wang and Henk Dekker (Eds) *China and the European Union*. Oxford: Routledge.

Thomas, W.I. and Znaniecki, F. 1918 *The Polish Peasant in Europe and America*. 5 Vols. Boston MA: Badger; Chicago IL: University of Chicago Press.

Troyna, B. 1994 'Critical social research and education policy.' *British Journal of Educational Studies* 42 (1).

Vaira, M. 2004 'Globalisation and higher education organisational change: a framework for Analysis.' *Higher Education* 48 (4) pp. 193–206.

von Mises, L. 1949 *Human Action: A Treatise on Economics*. New Haven: Yale University Press.

Warren, C. 2004 'Interviewing in Qualitative Research', in Lewis-Beck, M., Bryman, A. and Liao, T. *Statistical Research Methods*. California: Sage.

Waters, M. 1995 *Globalization*. London: Routledge.

Watson, M. and Hay, C. 2003 'The discourse of globalisation and the logic of no alternative: rendering the contingent necessary in the political economy of New Labour'. *Policy & Politics* 31 (3) pp. 289–305.

Xie, Chang Da. 2004 'Viewing the New Generation – Globalization and Changes in the Values of the Youth'. Accessed at www.ccyl.org.cn/dcyjwz/ on 10 July 2014.

Yang, R. 2003 'Globalisation and Higher Education Development: a Critical Analysis'. *International Review of Education* 49.

Zhang Lihua. 2013 Accessed at http://carnegietsinghua.org on 6 September 2014.

2 Exploring Chinese young people's attitudes towards online communication and relationship formation

Liberation, autonomy and ambivalence

Wei Fang

Underlying this chapter are two profound transformations, with one taking place within a country and one spanning the globe, that indicate the forces that constitute our current era. In China, the phenomena of marketisation, urbanisation and globalisation have radically transformed social equity. At the same time, the extensive worldwide diffusion of the internet and social media has brought in new modes of sociality, autonomy and agency.

The internet has been increasingly adopted by young people in China. It has been configured for self-presentation, communication and expanding relationships and networks. It is crucial to understand Chinese young people's attitudes towards online communication and relationship formation, which are defined as attitude objects in this chapter, such as their feelings towards special features of online communication, their beliefs in the extent of liberation and autonomy facilitated by the internet in communication and relationship formation, and their behaviours of building relationships online. Furthermore, it is significant to scrutinise whether there are differences in these attitudes between rural and urban young people so as to examine whether the internet facilitates the transformation of social inequality as assumed by some utopian writers.

The emergence and diffusion of the internet worldwide has stimulated expectations surrounding its role in transforming social inequality. Special modes of communication enabled by the internet, such as greater anonymity and the ability to transcend time and space, are conceived as having this transformational potential. Online communication is seen as having the potential of easing the pressure of self-disclosure with strangers and thus increasing the possibility of establishing new relationships (Bargh *et al.* 2002; Kang 2000; McKenna *et al.* 2002). Furthermore, these newly developed relationships can now cross both geographical and social boundaries due to the aforementioned special qualities of online communication (Chesebro and Bonsall 1989; Ebo 1998; Hert 1997; Lea and Spears 1992; Rice and Love 1987; Siegel *et al.* 1986; Sproull and Kiesler 1986). As such, this relationship formation among people from different social backgrounds seems to provide potential for transforming social inequality if these connections are able to transform the unequal distribution of resources.

This chapter consists of four major parts with eight sections. The first part which includes the first to third sections presents the theoretical framework of this chapter. It centres on discussions regarding utopian writers' attitudes towards the potential of the internet in transforming communication and relationship formation, empirical studies that examine these assumptions, and the Chinese context of rural–urban inequality and internet development. The second part (section four) introduces the procedure of data collection. The third part which consists of the fifth to seven sections presents research findings, including social media utilised for communication and rural and urban young people's attitudes towards the attitude object. The fourth part (section eight) discusses the conclusions of this study.

The utopian perceptions surrounding relationship formation on the internet

The utopian perspective sees the internet as facilitating interactions and relationship formation across geographical and social boundaries (e.g. Adams 1996; Kelly 1996; Lea and Spears 1992; Stewart 1996; Rheingold 1993; Sproull and Kiesler 1986). The utopian writers hold optimistic attitudes surrounding the role of the internet in interaction and relationship formation. They propose that special features of the internet and online communication would facilitate relationship formation among people from different social divisions and which may result in a creation of a more equal society.

The utopian assumptions of the social consequences of the internet are based on the technological capabilities of online communication, specifically greater anonymity and its capabilities in transcending time and space, compared to face to face communication. Face-to-face communication has rich cues of physical context:

> Body-to-body, people have a full range of communicative resources available to them. They share a physical context, which they can refer to nonverbally as well as verbally (for instance, by pointing to a chair). They are subject to the same environmental influences, such as distractions. They can see one another's body movements, including the facial expression through which so much meaning is conveyed. They can use each other's eye gaze to gauge attention.... They can also hear the sound of one another's voice. All of these cues – contextual, visual, and auditory – are important to interpreting messages and creating a social context within which messages are meaningful.
>
> (Baym 2010: 9)

In addition to physically contextual cues, face-to-face communication also provides social cues in terms of age, gender, class, race, authority, etc. When communicating in a face-to-face context, one can tell each others' social contexts from the way they speak, the tone and accent they use, their style of dress, their gestures and so on. Besides rich physical and social cues, communication in real life is restricted by time and space as it requires people to be together at the same space and same time. All these features of face-to-face communication make people more likely to meet people in similar situations.

In contrast, online communication is argued to have a greater level of anonymity and the ability to transcend time and space. Due to its greater anonymity, when communicating with people met online, one has less knowledge of whom one is interacting with in terms of physical and social contexts. The famous *New Yorker* cartoon of two dogs explaining 'On the Internet, nobody knows you're a dog', depicted vividly the anonymity of online communication. In addition, through the internet, one can connect with distant others and make asynchronous interaction; hence online communication enables interactions transcend space and time.

Hence, utopian writers assume that people have positive attitudes towards developing relationships with strangers due to the special qualities of online communication. They argue that these technological capabilities of online communication would make relationship formation online much more attractive, as well as easier. The greater anonymity of online communication encourages relationship formation with people who they have never met face to face. Online communication is seen as resembling the 'strangers on the train' phenomenon described by Rubin (1975; also Derlega and Chaikin 1977, quoted in Bargh and McKenna 2004). Its relative anonymity would ease the pressure of self-disclosure with strangers and thereby increase the possibility of developing close and intimate relationships with them (McKenna *et al.* 2002). As noted by Kang:

> Cyberspace makes talking with strangers easier. The fundamental point of many cyber-realms, such as chat rooms, is to make new acquaintances. By contrast, in most urban settings, few environments encourage us to walk up to strangers and start chatting. In many cities, doing so would amount to a physical threat.
>
> (Kang 2000: 1161)

One early empirical study regarding relationship formation online suggests that people tended to like those first met online more than those first met face to face (McKenna *et al.* 2002). Another study found that people were more likely to be able to express their true self to people they interact with over the internet than face to face and once they liked each other, they tended to project qualities of their ideal friends onto each other (Bargh *et al.* 2002).

As people are motivated to develop relationships with people first met online, it is possible that they can connect with people without geographical restrictions with the help of the internet. The increased penetration rate of the internet has allowed users to build and maintain relationships with distant others (Chesebro and Bonsall 1989; Rice and Love 1987; Siegel *et al.* 1986). Before the internet era, people were more bound to the traditional communities (e.g. neighbourhood, school and workplace). Due to the segregation of society based on social status, people from similar status are more likely to interact with and form relationships with similar others. But in the internet era, people have more opportunities to reach out of their traditional communities and build connections with people from geographically different communities. This may increase the diversity of one's networks and contribute to social ties built between members of a different social status.

Besides transcending geographical boundaries, the internet is also conceived by the utopians as enabling communication and relationships formation across social boundaries. First of all, online communities provide a more equal environment for developing relationships due to its lean cues and special structure. When online, anonymous communication would make one's physical and social contexts less salient and thus less meaningful (Hert 1997; Lea and Spears 1992; McKenna *et al.* 2002; Sproull and Kiesler 1986). Racial or other identities which constitute a stigma in many societies (Crocker and Major 1989) could more easily be concealed over the internet than face to face and this would facilitate the disruption of racial or social stereotypes (Kang 2000). In addition, the internet 'deemphasizes hierarchical political associations, degrading gender roles and ethnic designations, and rigid categories of class relationships found in traditional, visually based and geographically bound communities' (Ebo 1998: 3). Hence, people are supposedly able to interact equally online and relationships formed in this environment tend to transcend social boundaries.

Second, the development of relationships online relies on the content of message rather than the social categories one belongs to. When people first meet face to face, how they conceive and interact with one another is largely shaped by their social status, which can easily be told from the physical context. But when first met online, the content they communicate, more than what they look like and which group they belong to in real life, determines the quality of communication and their relationship formation. In other words, the founding of relationships is based on more substantive bases, such as shared interests (McKenna *et al.* 2002). Thus, online communication offers more opportunities for facilitating egalitarian communication and relationships formation as people would emphasise the content of messages instead of the social status of the source (Hert 1997; Lea and Spears 1992; Rice and Love 1987; Siegel *et al.* 1986). As noted by Baym:

> On a societal level, anonymity opens the possibility of liberation from the divisions that come about from seeing one another's race, age, gender, disabilities, and so on … early rhetoric about the Internet often speculated that the reduction of social cues would lead to people valuing one another's contributions for their intrinsic worth rather than the speaker's status. The internet would lead to the world Martin Luther King Jr. dreamed of, in which people would be judged by the content of their character rather than the color of their skin. A now-legendary MCI advertisement that ran during the 1997 Superbowl described it like this: 'There is no race, there are no genders, there is no age, there are no infirmities, there are only minds. Utopia? No, the Internet'.
> (Baym 2010: 34)

Hence, many utopian writers 'praised the internet's ability to bring together disparate people from around the world into what Marshall McLuhan called the "global village": the internet would allow relationships to flourish in an environment of equality and respect' (Boase and Wellman 2006: 3). Thus, social relationships move from traditional close-knit family groups, physical communal neighbourhoods, and schools and professional environments, to virtual communities and online relationships (Negroponte 1995; Rheingold 1993; Schuler 1996, quoted from Ebo 1998).

From the utopian perspective, this universal connection on the internet would lead to a more equal society. If people from different social categories are universally connected in the 'global village', social inequality would be transformed, as this universal connection suggests more opportunities for disadvantaged individuals to access institutional resources. In this way, unequal distribution of resources among the dominant and dominated groups would be transformed. Then the social inequality caused by differential distribution of resources would itself be transformed. The internet, therefore, through bringing people of different statuses together, acts as a social equaliser.

Many of these utopian accounts described above were written by a small number of academics and high-tech corporate commentators who were early internet users, as it was only open to such people at that time (Boase and Wellman 2006). They showed optimistic attitudes towards the role of the internet in social relationships and the social consequences. With the increased access to the internet and proliferation of online communication, a great number of empirical studies have been conducted to examine the attitudes of young social media users towards the attitude object.

Empirical studies in online communication and relationship formation

According to the utopians who hold positive attitudes towards the attitude object, the internet would encourage positive relationship development across geographical and social boundaries. The internet provides an anonymous environment which would encourage self-disclosure and ease the pressure of communication and thereby encourage people to be more interested in meeting new people online. Due to the greater anonymity, development of relationships would rely on the content of the message rather than the status of the source; hence people from different groups would be connected with one another. In other words, people would be interested in utilising the internet to create new relationships with others, in particular those from different groups. But empirical studies surrounding internet use and relationships seemed to provide mixed outcomes, which will be presented in the following parts of this section.

Relationships online: mostly pre-existing ties, only a few new ties

Despite the opportunities provided by the internet for acquiring social resources by expanding relationships online, the internet tends to be employed by young people predominantly for maintaining relationships with their offline friends. These pre-existing relationships can be strong ties such as close friends and family members or weak ties such as those who study at the same school but are not close friends. Teenagers were found to be more interested in maintaining offline relationships using different communicational platforms online. Based on studies among young people from the EU, especially the UK, Sonia Livingstone, a UK based leading scholar on young people's online practices, noted that:

> The question of making new friends is the subject of debate among young people themselves. Most are little interested in talking to people they do not know on the internet, preferring to communicate with friends. Indeed, children who have chatted to strangers online described it as 'weird' or 'dodgy', they don't see the point. Older teenagers tend to prefer instant messaging to chat rooms because 'you know who you're talking to' – a phrase used over and over in the UK Children Go Online focus groups.
>
> (Livingstone 2009: 95)

Results from the Pew Internet project and the American Life Project showed that most teenagers are using the Social Networking Sites (SNSs) to keep in touch with pre-existing social ties: either friends they see a lot (91 per cent), or friends they rarely see in person (80 per cent) (Lenhart and Madden 2007). Among these users, more than two-thirds (69 per cent) reported that they did not have unmet friends in their network. Several other empirical studies regarding teens and young people's Instant Messaging (IM) use have also demonstrated that IM was predominantly used to maintain relationships with pre-existing relationships (e.g. Quan-Haase 2007; Grinter and Palen 2002; Valkenburg and Peter 2009). Similarly, college students were also found to utilise the internet overwhelmingly to keep in touch with old friends as well as connecting with college friends made offline (Ellison and Steinfield 2007; Lampe *et al.* 2006; Steinfield *et al.* 2008).

Despite the fact that the internet does not cause a widespread flourishing of new relationships, there are still cases of relationship formation online. In 1995 and 2000, two large-scale national surveys in the US demonstrated that around 10 per cent of internet users have met unknown people online (Katz and Aspden 1997; Katz and Rice 2002). Two studies regarding newsgroups and relationships also demonstrated that people had made new friends online and some of them had moved these relationships to offline life (McKenna *et al.* 2002; Parks and Floyd 1996). Despite the fact that young people's main purpose for using IM was to keep in contact with existing friends, some reported using IM to make new friends (Grinter and Palen 2002; Lenhart *et al.* 2001).

With regard to SNSs, although people mainly use them to maintain existing relationships, there are opportunities for forming new relationships. The public display of connections on the social networking sites provide potential to activate latent ties which refer to 'ones that exist technically but have not yet been activated' (Haythornthwaite 2002) by developing friendships with friends' friends. For example, a survey in the US showed that 70 per cent of social networking teens with unmet friends reported that some of these people had a connection to their offline friends, such as the older sister of a classmate, or the cousin of a good friend (Lenhart and Madden 2007).

Besides forming relationships with friends' friends, many practices on the social networking sites such as affiliating with celebrities, musicians and political candidates provide opportunities to meet new people. Data from a Pew Internet and American project regarding teens' online relationships showed that among 9 per cent of online teens who reported meeting unmet friends, more than half (53 per cent) of them had unmet friends with no connection to their online or offline friends (Lenhart and Madden 2007).

Based on these discussions, we know that teens and young people have created new relationships through many platforms for online communication. Technologically, online communication provides opportunities to connect with people without restrictions of time and space (geographical and social). In order to see whether this utopian assumption has any validity, in the following part we will examine what kinds of new friends youths from different social groups made online.

Composition of new ties formed online: more similar than disparate others

The fact is that, despite the technological potential of online communication to connect people from different backgrounds, the principle of homophily, which refers to people being more likely to connect with similar others, still plays an important role in developing online friends. In other words, internet users tend to befriend similar others in terms of age, gender, education, class, race, ethnicity, etc. Many empirical studies regarding young people's practices of developing online relationships have demonstrated that online relationships are more likely to reproduce than transform offline relationships.

Given the popularity of internet use among adolescents, research focusing on their online friendship formation has started to emerge. Many of these studies mainly focus on the comparison of online and offline friendship formation. Actually, evidence has shown that, in a longer time frame, online and offline relationships may have similar qualities. For example, in a study of friendships in the real world and in online newsgroups, which was conducted among Hong Kong young internet users, Chan and Cheng (2004) found that offline and online friendships seemed to grow in different ways. At first, offline friendships were found with higher degrees of breadth, depth, code change, understanding, interdependence, commitment and network convergence compared to offline friendships. However, as the duration of the relationship increased (about six months to one year), the difference in quality between online and offline friendships diminished. This suggests that, as noted by Walther:

> Given sufficient time and message exchanges for interpersonal impression formation and relational development to accrue, and all other things being

equal, relational (communication) in later periods of CMC [computer-mediated-communication] and face to face communication will be the same.
(Walther 1992: 69)

Some scholars focus on comparing factors such as age, gender and geographic proximity among friends made online and offline. Mesch and Talmud (2007) conducted a study comparing similarities between friends made offline and online among Israeli adolescents. They found that though there was higher rate of similarity in terms of age, gender and place of residence in friends made offline than that made online, social similarity mattered even for friends met online. Moreover, they also found that the more similar friends made online were, in terms of residence and gender, the stronger was the social tie. This suggests that geographic proximity and homophily may play a less important role in making friends online, but they are still strong predictors of online friendship formation.

Besides examining the similarity of demographic characteristics such as age, gender and place of residence, some scholars started to pay attention to the similarity in social position in terms of race/ethnicity and class. Considering the prominent role of SNSs in online communication for teens and young people, many of these studies focused on how different choices of SNSs, in particular MySpace and Facebook, reflected social divisions (e.g. race, ethnicity and class).

Evidence from several empirical studies suggests that those from similar social backgrounds are more likely to make a similar choice for choosing SNSs which provide them with opportunities to form relationships with people unmet offline. Through observation of teens' online practices and face-to-face interviews, Boyd noticed that:

> While plenty of teens chose to participate on both sites (Facebook and MySpace), I began noticing that those teens who chose one or the other appeared to come from different backgrounds. Sub-culturally identified teens appeared more frequently drawn to MySpace while more mainstream teens tended towards Facebook. Teens from less-privileged backgrounds seemed likely to be drawn to MySpace while those headed towards elite universities appeared to be headed towards Facebook. Racial and ethnic divisions looked messier, tied strongly to socio-economic factors, but I observed that black and Latino teens appeared to preference MySpace while white and Asian teens seemed to privilege Facebook.
>
> (Boyd 2011: 9)

While Boyd was uncertain whether her observations can be generalised, results from several other studies conducted among different age groups have shown strong support towards her findings. With regard to the teens' group, data from a national survey conducted among teens aged 12 to 17 years old in the US have demonstrated demographic variation in terms of choice of social networking sites (Lenhart *et al.* 2011). Facebook users were over-represented among whites, older teens (14–17), and those whose parents had at least some college experiences, while MySpace users were more likely to be Latino teens and those whose parents did not go to college. One study among US teens (12–18) also supported the finding that offline social divisions predict young people's online communities (Ahn 2012). Another study focusing on the relations between high school students' social networking sites habits and school rank showed that students from lower ranked schools tended to be more active on MySpace while students from higher ranked schools seemed to be more active on Facebook (Lam 2007a, 2007b). Similar patterns can also be found among college students (Hargittai 2007; Watkins 2009).

These studies suggest that young people and utopian writers seem to differ greatly in their attitudes towards online communication and relationship formation. Utopian writers tend to have optimistic feelings and believe that the internet can bring different people together. However, young people are more likely to communicate and maintain relationships with pre-existing relationships online than develop new relationships. Moreover, despite a few new relationships developed online, they were more likely to be with similar, rather than different, others.

Rural–urban inequality and internet development in China

As most of the studies discussed in this section were conducted among young people in the Western countries, little was known about young people's attitudes towards this attitude object in the context of China. Before examining this issue, we need to understand the social reality in which young people situate, such as rural–urban inequality, and the development of the internet in China.

Rural–urban inequality: a historical perspective

Faced with the huge rural–urban gap in contemporary China, many may find it hard to imagine that the countryside and farmers were not seen as inferior to city dwellers and urbanities in China's modern history. Prior to the mid nineteenth century, there was a relatively small disparity between cities and the countryside. In traditional China, mainly characterised as an agricultural society, farmers were at a relatively higher rank of the social hierarchy (gentry, farmers, craftsmen and merchants) (Liang 1989). Despite urban residents 'despising peasants for their simplicity and ignorance, and ridiculing country rustics' and peasants' distaste for urban people,

> the discrimination that came from both sides was part of a greater multifaceted, and dynamic culture, and neither side was so strong in its prejudices that they constituted a deep cleavage between the rural and urban sectors of traditional Chinese life.
>
> (Lu 2010: 29)

Later, the industrialisation which started from the late nineteenth century reshaped traditional rural–urban relations. The industrialisation of the city and the deterioration of the rural economy made cities a better place with more opportunities; thus the rural–urban continuum was gradually replaced by a rural–urban gulf (Lu 2002).

In the early twentieth century, the construction of discourse around peasants and rural society by Chinese intellectuals and political elites reinforced the superiority of the city and urban residents:

> For the elite, China's rural population was now 'backward' and a major obstacle to national development and salvation. For them, rural China was still a 'feudal society' of 'peasants' who were intellectually and culturally crippled by 'superstition'.
>
> (Cohen 1993: 154)

Peasants, therefore, have become a purely cultural category for many Chinese and Westerners alike (Cohen 1993). Yet the status barriers between rural and urban residents were not large, considering the rate of upward and downward mobility, as well as the relative freedom of movement of the population (Whyte 2010).

The unprecedentedly sharp rural–urban gap was created after the Chinese Communist Party (CCP) established power over China in 1949. The main reason for this huge rural–urban gap is the *hukou* system, established by Chinese Communist Government (CCG) in the 1950s, which prohibited, and still prohibits, rural residents from migrating to urban areas and discriminates in favour of the urban population with regards to resources. The next part of this section will first introduce this *hukou* system briefly and then address its impact on rural–urban inequality.

A brief introduction to the hukou system

The *hukou* system was established for the purpose of consolidating administrative control by the CCG. When the CCP took power in 1949 there was no restriction regarding rural to urban migration. A huge number of rural residents migrated to cities, consisting of members of the revolutionary army of who were largely rural recruits (who then took over management of cities) and other rural residents who were recruited, or migrated by themselves, to offices and factories in cities (Whyte 2010). The control of migration of rural residents to cities was conceived by revolutionary leaders who were concerned about the control and management of cities after taking power, as 'free migration' was bringing more difficulties in their control of cities. Under this circumstance the *hukou* system was introduced in the 1950s to strengthen administrative control.

There are two classifications in this system: the first is the place of registration (*hukou suo zai di*) based on one's residential location, and the second is the type of registration (*hukou lei bie*) which is generally referred to as 'agricultural' and 'non-agricultural' *hukou* or 'rural' and 'urban' *hukou* (Chan and Zhang 1999). The registered people are treated differently in almost every aspect of their lives according to the different categories and locations, and they are restricted in their migration between regions. Although the *place* of registration has some impact on life chances for Chinese citizens to some extent, it is the *type* of registration that has created a pronounced distinction in socio-economic entitlements among Chinese citizens and has significantly shaped the order of social stratification in the country (Wu and Treiman 2004). The division of people into either agricultural or non-agricultural population has acted as an invisible 'wall' separating rural from urban areas, as well as prohibiting migration from countryside to cities, since unauthorised migrants cannot access many resources allocated to urban residents (Chan 1994; Cheng and Selden 1994). With only a few reform attempts and limited alterations, the *hukou* system still enjoys a strong institutional legitimacy in China and continues to be the backbone of Chinese institutional structure in the 2000s (Wang 2005).

The *hukou* system, in addition to differentiated distribution of resources, also shapes social and cultural aspects of rural–urban relations. As 'the central institutional mechanism defining the city-countryside relationship and shaping important elements of state-society relations in the People's Republic', the *hukou* system 'not only provided the principal basis for establishing identity, citizenship and proof of official status, it was essential for every aspect of daily life' (Cheng and Selden 1994: 644). As Peng concluded, the *hukou* system has been 'affixing people's social career, role, personal identity, production and living space; restricting the free migration of people and labor; maintaining and strengthening the dual economic and social structure between the urban and the rural areas' (Peng 1994, quoted in Wang 2005: 23). Hence, rural residents, who account for the majority of the Chinese population, have been disadvantaged in terms of access to economic, social and political opportunities, activities and benefits, compared to the much smaller urban population (who constitute between 14 and 26 per cent of the whole population) (Wang 2005).

The classification of each member of the population as having rural or urban status, entitled to differentiated resources and opportunities, has reinforced and accelerated the rural–urban gap in Communist China. The *hukou* system fundamentally touches and determines the life of every Chinese citizen through comprehensively collecting data on everyone, identifying and stratifying people and regions, controlling population movement, and allocating resources and opportunities (Yu 2002). As such, it has played a crucial role in shaping rural and urban residents' positions in the social stratification as well as in distinguishing them socially and culturally.

Internet development in China

Over the last two decades, the government of the People's Republic of China (PRC) has been encouraging the development of information and communication technologies (ICTs). This process is guided by the strategy of 'informatisation' which is defined by the government as 'the transformation of an economy and society driven by information and communication technology' (Hanna and Qiang 2010: 128). Underlying the discourse of informatisation is the role of ICTs as a means of boosting economic growth, as well as enhancing a 'socialist harmonious society'. Meanwhile, the government has invested heavily in telecommunications infrastructure, which has provided foundations for the nationwide penetration of ICTs, in particular the internet.

The number of internet users in China has increased dramatically from 22.5 million in 2000 to 538 million in June 2012, making up nearly a quarter (22.4 per cent) of the world's internet population.[1] According to a report released by the UN Broadband Commission, by 2015 the number of users accessing the internet in Chinese will overtake English language users.[2] Despite the vast number of internet users and relative high rate of adoption, however, the internet has not spread equally among rural and urban populations.

There are insufficient studies regarding how people from different social groups use the internet. In explaining why insufficient empirical attention is paid to who uses the internet and how they use it, Jens Damm noted:

> One reason is that Western research on the Internet in China is often influenced by Chinese dissidents, now working in various departments of U.S. universities. And these dissidents are well aware of the high priority given to questions of censorship by the U.S. mainstream media. Another reason is that anyone seeking to carry out a content analysis of the Chinese Internet faces the problem of how to deal with the sheer mass of available content. Finally, the Chinese Internet providers are reluctant to provide researchers, whether Westerners or Chinese, with data on Internet usage, such as information about the exact numbers of accesses.... Much of the research on the Internet in China is now being carried out by commercial institutes (such as CCID Saidi-consultant), which have strong interests in promoting e-business and e-commerce. Although these institutes are concerned with lifestyle and consumerist attitudes, they generally do not focus attention on aspects of identity-politics and societal changes, concentrating instead on matters of brand-name building and how to increase the efficiency of the Internet in selling products.
> (Damm 2007: 281)

Although some official organisations like China Internet Network Information Center (CNNIC) have published reports regarding internet use in China, the information mainly includes user demographics, access locations, and average online behaviour. With regard to online communication, these reports are capable of answering questions as to 'what' rural and urban youth do online but fail to answer their attitudes towards the internet and online communication.

This chapter aims to fill the gap by examining rural and urban young people's attitudes towards the internet and its implications for rural–urban inequality in China. More specifically, it will centre on questions including their feelings, beliefs and behaviours surrounding online communication and relationship formation.

Research methods

In order to interpret rural and urban young people's attitudes towards online communication and relationship formation from their perspectives, qualitative research[3] was selected for guiding this project. I considered qualitative research most suitable since it 'claims to describe life-worlds 'from the inside out', from the point of view of the people who participate' and thereby 'seeks to contribute to a better understanding of social realities and to draw attention to process, meaning patterns and structural features' (Flick *et al.* 2004: 3).

This research was designed as a case study. A county-level city named Zunhua, located in the northern part of China, was chosen as the case study location of this study.[4] Zunhua was selected as the case study location for this study for several reasons. The initial reason lies in the previous quantitative study conducted in Zunhua which provided information including demographic factors, practices of internet use in terms of information, communication and education, and the consequences of internet use; second, despite the diffusion of the internet nationwide, little attention was paid to how people from county-level divisions utilise the internet and its impact on their lives; third, one of the most important reasons is because it can be seen as one representative or typical case which exemplifies a broader category of cases which refer to county-level divisions in China (e.g. counties, county-level cities).

Participants for this project were selected among students (senior secondary and college) and non-students of a similar age in Zunhua.[5] The rationale behind this choice is largely based on young people's high level of internet use nationwide. In most of the reports released by CNNIC, young people from this age group account for the most active internet users.

The procedure of selecting participants for this project was based on purposive sampling. Rather than selecting participants randomly, purposive sampling 'is to sample cases/participants in a strategic way, so that those sampled are relevant to the research questions that are being posed' (Bryman 2008: 415). The main criteria for selecting participants of this project included age, social background in terms of rural and urban status, and gender. As young people were the most active internet users (according to reports released by CNNIC), participants were selected from this age group. As the purpose of this project was to explore whether there are differentiated attitudes towards expanding social networks for rural and urban young people, the most important criterion for selection was social background in terms of rural and urban status. Another criterion was gender, since I also considered the role of gender in generating different attitudes. Overall, the participants of this project were expected to include male and female young people from rural and urban areas.

Based on these criteria, recruitment of participants was implemented through communication on QQ (an instant messaging software service developed by a Chinese company). The first step was creating a QQ account for accessing and contacting potential participants for this project. A QQ profile was created with my real personal information (e.g. name, age, gender, occupation) so as to gain trust. A brief introduction to my personal background, academic background, previous survey, and purpose of this project was written in the form of a blog on Qzone (QQ's social networking website). In addition to these, a number of photos depicting my life abroad were uploaded to Qzone with the purpose of verifying the authenticity of my identity provided in QQ as well as to attract attention from those potential participants. After the completion of the QQ account, I sent requests to be QQ friends to all QQ IDs (more than 80) which were left on the questionnaire from the previous quantitative study,[6] and received responses from more than half of them.

There are altogether 36 young people participating in this project. Of these 36, 15 are female and 21 are male. Female youth were more cautious than male youth in online communication and they were less likely to accept the invitation of a face-to-face interview, so there were fewer female participants. But the number of female participants (15) is sufficient for in-depth interviews which have more emphasis on quality rather than quantity. As place of origin (rural vs. urban) is another criterion for sampling, participants were selected based on whether they were from rural or urban areas. Hence, among the 36 interviewees, 14 were from urban areas, 12 were from rural areas, and 10 were rural youth with urban experiences.[7] Though the number of 36 participants may appear small compared to that of the quantitative study, the nature of qualitative research, as addressed earlier in this chapter, enables the acquisition of in-depth data.

The qualitative interview and observation were employed as methods for data collection. But different types of qualitative interviews, in terms of whether they were online or face-to-face interviews, and whether they were unstructured or semi-structured interviews, were conducted under different conditions in different stages of this project. The face-to-face semi-structured interview was designed as the main method for collecting data for this project. Another method, the online unstructured interview, was employed to collect complementary data by means of casual chatting before as well as after the face-to-face interview. Besides these two types of interview method, observation of online data was employed as another complementary method for data collection.

Social media utilised for communicational engagement online

Young people in China have been found to utilise diverse online services for self presentation and communication such as BBSs (Bulletin Board Systems) (Damm 2007; Giese 2004; Mackinnon 2008b; Yang 2009), Blogs (CNNIC 2010; Mackinnon 2008a; Nie and Li 2006), SNSs (Ho 2007), IM (e.g. CNNIC 2010) and online games (e.g. McLaren 2007). Respondents in this study mainly reported three platforms or means for making new friends through online communication: QQ, Renren (a real-name social networking internet platform in China) and online games. Previously, in the studies regarding online relationship formation, scholars examined how people perform in specific channels, such as chat rooms, newsgroups, IM, SNSs and online games.

Exploring Chinese young people's attitudes 35

However, in the context of China, it is better to address the name rather than the category of the platform as some have been integrating different forms of popular services in one platform to keep existing users or even to attract new users. For example, in China, QQ, which was initially developed to be an IM, has become a platform integrating IM, online games, SNS, etc. Each function provides opportunities to interact with strangers and form relationships with them through different mechanisms, but all of them are referred to as QQ. That is why when asked through which channel they form relationships online, respondents normally answered QQ first, rather than specifying QQ's IM function, SNS function, or games. Besides the popular QQ, Renren, which is popular among college students, and online games, were two other main means reported by young people interviewed for forming relationships online.[8]

This section provides a brief introduction to these three means of making online friends mentioned by young people interviewed. The introduction includes the basic information regarding design, functions, and their roles in developing relationships online. The focus will be QQ which was reported as the most popular platform for developing new relationships online. This introduction will provide a foundation for understanding the mechanism and dynamics of young people's online relationship formation.

QQ

As mentioned earlier, QQ was initially developed as an IM, like MSN, ICQ, Yahoo Messenger and others, by Tencent in 1999. It is the most popular IM in China now. As an IM, it provides services including text messaging, video and voice chat, and online documents transmission.

Though QQ functions primarily as a tool of IM, Tencent has also built up several other services which have been seamlessly integrated with QQ IM and can be accessed through users' QQ accounts. Among all these new services, Qzone, which is QQ's SNS service, as well as QQ Game, also provide opportunities for young people in China to develop relationships with people not known in offline life.[9] Qzone was created by Tencent as a social networking website in 2005. Users can write blogs, upload photos and music, update status and check their friends' updates. Qzone is customised to individuals' tastes because users can set their Qzone background and decorate their Qzones according to their preferences. However, as most Qzone services are not free, users need to spend money on obtaining 'diamond' level membership to access these services.

Another service, QQ Xiaoyou, which was created as another SNS targeting students from universities and secondary schools, was officially launched in 2009. Though not as popular as Qzone now, it has the potential to occupy this group in the future, considering the influence of QQ among young people.

Besides Qzone and QQ Xiaoyou, an online games platform provided by Tencent also creates opportunities for young people's online relationship formation. QQ users can access several types of online games provided by Tencent directly. They can play games with friends on their buddy lists or strangers they have never interacted with before. When people feel they can trust each other and want to keep in touch, they may give each other their QQ ID and continue their interactions outside the game.

Other services such as the 'drift bottle' also provide opportunities for users to establish relationships with strangers. Through this service, a user can write whatever he/she wants to say and let his/her words drift anonymously among all QQ users, and only one user would receive his/her 'bottle' and be able to reply. There are news reports on how young people developed new relationships with people they have never met and received instrumental support from one another. For instance, a female journalist named Xiaoli once received a QQ 'drift bottle' from a fourth-year male undergraduate describing his painful experiences and feelings in finding a job. This reminded Xiaoli of her own similar experiences and feelings when finding a job. So she sent back the 'drift bottle' describing her own experiences in finding jobs as well as giving him some advice for job hunting. After several letters sent in the 'drift bottle' between them, they finally became friends.[10] Some respondents, for example Jin (female, senior secondary student, rural), also reported developing new relationships through sending and receiving 'bottles'. Through this service, she has made new friends with students at the same grade. She shared school experiences and discussed issues of study with her newly developed friends through sending and receiving 'bottles'.

The Renren network

Just like Facebook, Renren is a popular SNS among college students in China. Here users can search for people based in colleges they currently attend, schools from which they graduated, and hometowns. A user can add existing friends or newly-acquainted friends to the friend list. Users can be also affiliated with groups, such as an existent class, school or organisation. They can upload photos, write blogs, update status, share photos, others' blogs and external links, and leave a message or comment on a photo, blog, status and so on. The interactive features of Renren facilitate maintaining relationships with existing friends as well as developing friendships with strangers.

The differences, particularly in the authenticity of the users' personal information, between Renren and QQ have caused different attitudes towards using them for making friends online. Renren's users are mainly college students and they feel safer making friends on this platform than on QQ. Some college students prefer Renren for making friends with strangers due to the authenticity of information on this platform. For example, as noted by Han (male, college student, urban):

> I feel Renren is more real (compared to QQ), because the personal profile is based on schools you have attended. For example, I can search for a person according to which school he graduated from and this is more real. But for QQ, I can write 'female' in my personal information while I am a male. Then I will chat with you as a girl online. So QQ seems to be too virtual.

Han created his profile on Renren after receiving an offer from his college as he wanted to know students from the college. He made several friends who were students at the college before he commenced his study, and thus gained some useful information regarding the college from his new friends. After entering the college he still kept in touch with these friends. Sometimes, he comments on their updated status and they normally would reply to his comments. He said that he trusted these friends more than those from QQ.

However, some of the respondents, especially girls, seemed to show a more cautious attitude towards making friends with unknown people on Renren. Their concerns also lie in the issue of safety. They normally provide real information, as they want to be connected with existing friends or friends' friends in offline life rather than with complete strangers. They do not feel safe with strangers in their friend lists on Renren. This suggests that facing the same platform and technological features, different people have different attitudes and behaviours toward making friends online.

Online games

Online games also play an important role for young people in China in making friends. These games include those which are provided by platforms like QQ and Renren as well as some professional game websites. The requirement of cooperation and communication among players during games facilitates the development of friendships. One respondent Xin (male, senior secondary student on suspension, urban) mentioned that after many times of playing games together, he preferred to befriend those with whom he had established trust. Sometimes, when he felt lonely, he would intentionally interact with strangers to make friends on the games' website.

Sometimes, when trust has been developed during playing games together, some respondents would continue their friendships outside the games. For example, Gang (male, college student, urban) reported that he trusted those with whom he usually played games together and they also communicated by other means or platforms. He has exchanged mobile phone numbers with them as well as added them into his QQ buddy list. Communication through different platforms helps increase both trust and intimacy among them. They then became 'old friends' and preferred to play games with each other and even invited each other to play some new games together.

Overall, different platforms facilitate the formation of online friendships for young people. But this does not mean the technological features of these platforms determine the development of friendships. Many young people have made friends online because they already held positive attitudes towards making new friends before using the internet. In other words, it is their choice to make new friends and their choices are influenced and facilitated by the platforms mentioned earlier. In addition to communication platforms on the internet, young people's attitudes towards developing new friendships online are shaped by the realities of the Chinese field in which they are situated. The next section will present why young people hold positive attitudes in building new friendships on the internet.

Liberation and autonomy: youth's perception of online communication and relationship formation

Compared to youth from other countries, Chinese youth tend to be more interested in forming relationships online. A study in the UK found 11 per cent of teens making acquaintances online (Livingstone and Bovill 2001). Another study in the US regarding teens reported 14 per cent of US teens making close online relationships (Wolak *et al.* 2003). A similar study conducted in Israel found that 12 per cent reported having at least one close friend made online (Mesch and Talmud 2006); while in China, a national survey regarding youth's internet use showed that 71.7 per cent of internet users under 25 reported having made many new ties online (CNNIC 2009). Hence, we can tell how positive Chinese youth's attitudes are towards making new friends online. This section will discuss why Chinese youth are so enthusiastic in meeting and developing relationships with people they have never met in real life.

Anonymous communication and liberation

There have been studies showing that the special qualities of online communication, especially its anonymity, facilitate the formation of online relationships (e.g. Kang 2000; McKenna *et al.* 2002; Peter *et al.* 2005). For example, Katelyn Y.A. McKenna and colleagues have articulated how the special qualities of internet communication attract people to disclose information about themselves, and this in turn facilitates the development of relationships with strangers (McKenna *et al.* 2002). They propose that the relative anonymity of online communication greatly reduces the risks of self-disclosure, which is similar to the 'strangers on the train' phenomenon, in which some quite intimate information tends to be shared among anonymous seatmates. Besides, they also assumed the lack of the usual 'gating features' such as physical appearance, apparent stigma, or visible shyness or social anxiety in online communication would also enable greater self-disclosure. These suggest that people may have positive attitudes towards making friends with strangers, as they can disclose information about themselves with relatively low risk compared to face-to-face communication with friends from real life.

The anonymity of online communication which reduces the risk of self-disclosure plays an important role in promoting positive attitudes for young people in Zunhua when making online friends. When asked why they make friends with unknown people online, their answers reflect the attraction of the anonymity of online communication. Sometimes, bad things happen and they do not want to share those with friends or family members. So they turn to the internet and make friends with people who are not involved with their offline life. It appears much safer to reveal their unhappy experiences to friends made online.

Mei (female, senior secondary student, rural), mentioned that she preferred to chat with friends made online because she could talk about whatever she wanted without worrying about gossip among friends in offline life. Another example from Han (male, college student, urban) also shows how the low risk of online communication due to anonymity, stimulates online relationship development. When asked what kind of things he preferred to talk about with strangers, he mentioned:

> Something bad in offline life, such as unhappy experiences with school friends or family members. There's probably more bad than good things (to talk about with online friends). It does not matter if you talk with real-life friends about happy things. But if I told one friend the unhappy experiences between me and another friend, maybe these two people know each other, and there would be some bad influence.

Moreover, the lack of 'gating features' of anonymous communication also helps to stimulate positive attitudes for young people to make new friends online. In particular, those who see themselves as less physically attractive or socially skilled tend to turn to the anonymous online communication for friendships. For example, Yu (female, senior secondary student, rural), who considered herself as having an ugly appearance due to vitiligo, reported that she had made a lot of friends online. She revealed that she preferred talking with online friends compared to friends from real life. Another example from Gu (male, senior secondary student, rural) indicates that anonymity helps to ease shy people's anxiety in communication. He has been always active and enthusiastic when chatting with me online. But when I asked him for a face-to-face interview, he seemed to be stressed and said that he preferred an online interview as he is too shy to interact with people face-to-face. He also reported having made many friends online with people he has never met before. Examples from these two interviewees show that for those who consider themselves less attractive and less sociable, the internet enables them to communicate with people with more confidence.

Young people also claimed to be attracted by the internet's ability to enable relationship formation transcending time and space. Almost all young people interviewed claimed curiosity and excitement at how the internet can connect them with people they have never seen before. Most started surfing on the internet when they were primary school students. At this early stage of internet adoption, they mainly utilised QQ for online communication. Special features of QQ, for example the public display of all users, facilitate the interaction between strangers. As teenagers, they claimed that it felt 'incredible' to meet unknown people online and were eager to make friends with some of them. For example, Zhen (male, senior secondary student, urban) felt very excited when he started using QQ and was eager to befriend and to talk with strangers, particularly not from local areas. He felt 'really fantastic' to have friends from other areas. As he described it:

When I first got my QQ account, I felt it was so interesting. I was especially eager to add strangers from different places in my QQ buddy list. I felt very good having friends from other places and talking with them online.

For Ann (female, senior secondary student, rural), a lack of access to the internet at home did not inhibit her eagerness to talk with unknown people online. She went to the internet cafe to chat with her new friends almost every day.

As they were attracted by online communication, they started accumulating online friends to compete for status and popularity, revealing the consistency of their feelings, beliefs and behaviours towards the attitude object. As reported by the respondents, with the wide spread of the internet, making friends by QQ with unknown people became a fashion among young people. Some competed with each other for the number of friends made online. For instance, Pan (male, senior secondary student, urban) said that 'they all had QQ friends, and I did not want to fall behind, so I also made some online'. In a similar way, many youths reported making a large number of friends online. Han (male, college student, urban) reported proudly that he used to have several hundred friends on his QQ buddy list. This is similar to Western teens who use IM to 'maintain as many ties as possible rather than striving for fewer, more meaningful relationships' (Boneva *et al.* 2006: 623).

However, despite special technological features as mentioned earlier for making new friends online, not all chose to connect with strangers online. For those who reported less enthusiasm in making online friends, safety was the main concern. Interacting and connecting with strangers online was seen as not safe. Though they were curious, they preferred to utilise QQ for maintaining relationships with existing friends. But for others, who also felt unsafe making friends with unknown people, their curiosity outweighed the safety concerns. This suggests that facing the same technological features of online communication as well as the issue of safety, attitudes seem to differ between different people with different concerns.

Online communication and autonomy

The internet is perceived by many rural and urban young people as a technology that offers them freedom in making friends. Their attitudes were shaped by social and cultural factors surrounding youth's relationship formation in the context of China as well as characteristics of young people's developmental stage.

In the context of China, adults and especially parents' emphasis on education makes them more likely to want to control children's relationships. There is a long tradition of valuing education in China. This tradition endures across time and space. In other words, the emphasis on education, dating back more than 2,000 years, has influenced not only contemporary youth in China but also Chinese immigrants in other countries. This tradition, together with the limited opportunities to receive a higher education, mean that children are constantly pressured by both teachers and parents to gain academic achievement (e.g. Chen *et al.* 2003). Under these circumstances, Chinese parents manage to do whatever they can to promote their children's academic achievement. Besides providing all kinds of material and emotional support for education, parents also try to prevent children from doing things that they think may be harmful to their study.

With regard to children's friendships, parents prefer their children to connect with those who have a positive influence on their children's academic performance rather than those who may have a negative impact. According to data from the interviews, cross-gender relationships, in particular romantic relationships, are disapproved of by parents, as they think this type of relationship will distract children's attention from their study. Hence, parents seem to have negative attitudes to children's interactions with cross-gender peers, as they are afraid that this may lead to a romantic relationship. Such attitudes are demonstrated by Peng's (male, senior secondary student, rural) example:

> My mother is always very strict (in romantic relationships). She does not allow me to interact with girls too much. To be honest, I have never had a girlfriend till now. I do not dare to do that because my parents are really strict. I even do not dare to tell my female school friends my telephone number when they ask me.

Peng is very cautious in telling female friends his telephone number not because he does not want to keep in touch with them after school, but because he is afraid that his mother may think he has made a girlfriend if a female friend gives him a call. Another participant, Chan (male, senior secondary student, rural) reported similar experiences:

> Parents and teachers are always very strict. I am particularly scared of receiving mobile phone calls (when at home). When I answer, my mother will follow me to my room (to listen). Then she would ask who has called and I have to explain carefully who this person is.... When my friends ask for my contact number, I always give them the number of my mobile phone rather than the landline, as there may be trouble if my mother answers.

Besides parents, schools which share the same negative attitudes towards cross-gender relationships also engage in monitoring youth's cross-gender relationships, especially romantic relationships. According to the respondents, the schools at which they study, no matter if they are located in rural or urban areas, all have regulations regarding romantic relationships. As noted by the respondents, teachers consider that engaging in a relationship is no less serious than other types of misbehaviour, such as fighting with other students or teachers. If one is found to have a girlfriend or boyfriend by teachers or other school staff, one may be forced to leave school. Being forced to leave school due to engaging in romantic relationships would be seen as humiliating to both students and families. Hence, the possibility of being forced to leave school and the consequence of losing face make youth cautious in interacting with cross-gender peers at school.[11]

Underlying the power of parents and teachers is the relatively high degree of filial piety in China. In Chinese society, the Confucian teaching of filial piety, which is seen as the first of all virtues, requires young people to be respectful, caring and obedient to elders, families or otherwise (Ho 1994; Sung 1995). The filial piety, as noted by Yue and Ng (1999: 215), 'has served as a guiding principle for patterns of Chinese socialization and intergenerational communication for thousands of years'. This principle of filial piety, which requires young people's respect for parents, as well as obedience to them, facilitates parents' intervention in their children's development of cross-gender relationships.

Though some scholars claim that some aspects of filial piety, for instance absolute obedience, have been eroded in recent decades in China (e.g. Ho 1996), Chinese youth still seem to be obedient under the influence of the one-child policy.[12] The one-child policy, formally promulgated in 1979, has produced new generations often called 'little emperors' (*xiao huangdi*), as only children are often spoiled by the older generations. Empirical research confirms that parents in China are more involved in their children's care than in the past (Zhang *et al.* 2001). But as noted by Qiu (2009: 131), 'more care also means more control and less autonomy' as the parents 'devote their undivided attention and resources to the upbringing of their youngsters'. Considering the Chinese tradition of valuing education and the role of education in social mobility in China, many parents have devoted huge efforts to promote their children's educational achievement. For example, though Peng (male, senior secondary school, urban) is from a rural family, he was studying at the best senior secondary school in Zunhua. In order to provide him with a comfortable and quiet place to focus on study and to achieve a better academic performance, his parents rented a flat in the city and hired a maid to look after him. This is actually a big cost for a rural family whose income is mainly from the land and stock raising.

Parents' devotion, which is highly appreciated by their children, helps to maintain their obedience to them. In other words, Chinese youth tend to obey their parents not because they think they need to be absolutely obedient as children, but because they see obedience as a means of expressing their gratitude for their parents' devotion. Chinese children appreciate what parents have done for them and tend to believe that all parents want to do is for their own good. For example, though he disagreed with the notion that cross-gender relationships are harmful for study, Chan (male, senior secondary student, rural) showed understanding towards his parents' intervention in his personal relationships. Hence parents' devotion facilitates parents' control over youth's interaction with cross-gender peers, which is seen as having a negative impact on academic achievement.

Young people's attitudes surrounding the development of online relationships are therefore shaped by these key features of the Chinese society discussed earlier. The emphasis on education makes parents pay more attention to with whom their children socialise and to the impact of these peer relationships, in particular cross-gender relationships, on their children's educational performance. Meanwhile, Chinese parents tend to have a higher level of control over their children, due to the long tradition of filial piety and the one-child policy, facilitating their intervention in young people's peer relationships. This means that in China, young people, whether they are from rural or urban areas, tend to have less freedom in developing relationships with those of the opposite sex.

Youth obey their parents' restrictions regarding developing cross-gender relationships not because they show similar negative attitudes towards the attitude object, but because they do not want to disappoint their parents. Actually, young people, especially those at puberty are attracted by the opposite sex, and this sexual attraction starts to complement same-sex friend groups (Pascoe 2007). However, Chinese youth at puberty are not provided with sufficient sex education. In Chinese culture, discussion about sex-related issues is traditionally taboo, and hence most Chinese people feel uncomfortable in providing sex education to adolescents (Zhang *et al.* 2007). Very few Chinese parents talk about sexual issues with their children. At school, despite sex education which is in the form of 'puberty education' and has been recommended as part of the education curriculum, youth still cannot get appropriate information, due to teachers' lack of enthusiasm and the limited content of the curriculum (Cui *et al.* 2001). This inadequate sex education, together with parents' restrictions in interactions with cross-gender peers, may stimulate rather than suppress children's curiosity and desire in heterosexual relationships.

Thus the dilemma occurs. On the one hand, Chinese youth want to meet their parents' expectations by keeping a distance from their cross-gender peers. On the other hand, the sexual attraction resulting from biological processes of the body cannot be ignored. Hence a means of communication which provides not only freedom but also opportunities to meet cross-gender peers would be welcome among youth. Among all the disposable choices, young people often decide to choose the internet. The internet not only provides satisfactory platforms for them to form relationships with people of a different gender, but also offers them more freedom by avoiding the monitoring by parents and teachers.[13]

New communication technology is perceived as providing them with some degree of freedom. As claimed by interviewees, they can go to places outside the home and school to use the internet, for example internet cafes, which are cheap and popular, and friends' homes. In a study exploring urban youth's practices of going to internet cafes, Fengshu Liu wrote:

> There seems to be a close relationship between many urban Chinese youth and the Internet café *(wangba)* although home access is common today and despite the problematisation of the site as a den of iniquity by both the authorities and lay people ... young people came to the *wangba* for something that is lacking in those other sites, from which they need to escape from time to time. In particular, they are there for a sense of being equal, something that is hard to come by in today's China, which is characterised by sharp social stratification, fierce competition, lack of security, consumerism, corruption, and unfairness in the distribution of resources. The pressure entailed by these interrelated factors has been manifested especially clearly

in the case of the only-child family, where parents typically have very high expectations of the one and only child, and this is reinforced by the above-mentioned factors.

(Liu 2009: 182)

More importantly, with the development of mobile internet, they can access the internet and communicate with online friends on their mobile phones. Even during the interviews, some participants did not stop chatting with their friends online. When they communicate online without the presence of parents and teachers, they are free to interact with people as they like. Hence the new technology enables them to maintain and develop relationships without parents' and teachers' intervention.

Data regarding their preference in online relationships in terms of gender, and the composition of friendships developed online in terms of gender, have shown that youth preferred to develop cross-gender relationships, and their friends made online were more likely to be those from the opposite sex. The fact that they chose to use the internet to realise their communication and relationship formation with cross-gender peers suggests the freedom provided by online communication is an important characteristic.

It is interesting that when asked why they employed the internet to develop online relationships, interviewees rarely mentioned their motivation for obtaining freedom in engaging with cross-sex relationships. In other words, all they mentioned seemed to be related to how online communication enabled them to be connected with others online conveniently, rather than how this new form of communication helped them to be free from parents' control in developing cross-gender relationships. From my point of view, this may because they see me as one of those adults who will judge them for their desire and practices in cross-sex relationships. When talking about topics regarding romantic relationships, participants, in particular secondary school students, seemed to be shy and embarrassed.

To summarise, technology, youth and the social space they inhabit together shape youth's attitudes towards the attitude object. Technological features of online communication provide opportunities for people to maintain existing relationships as well as developing new relationships. But realities in different societies shape one's choices regarding communicational use of the internet. In Western countries which have a higher rate of internet adoption and a low level of adults' intervention in peer relationships, in particular cross-gender relationships, they seem more likely to emphasise the internet's capability of connectivity than liberation in terms of relationship management, as described by Livingstone:

> Intriguingly, this spontaneous and enthusiastic adoption by children and young people of online opportunities for self-presentation and relationships construction is not technology driven – the successive adoption of email, chatrooms, text messaging and social networking was hardly anticipated by

their producers, though each was keenly co-opted by them in developing new markets. Rather, what drives online and mobile communication is young people's strong desire to connect with peers anywhere, anytime.

(Livingstone 2009: 95)

In small cities in the context of China like Zunhua, young people's cross-gender relationships, which are considered as being harmful to their academic performance, are suppressed by adults in order to secure their educational opportunities. The internet, which facilitates anonymous and liberating communication, is perceived as being able to provide them with opportunities to develop new, especially cross-gender, relationships. They are more likely than their Western counterparts to adopt the internet to satisfy their curiosity and desire to interact with those of the opposite sex.

Young people's preferences in selecting online friends

Despite the technological potential for meeting various types of people, and their positive attitudes towards forming online relationships, young peoples' behaviours of online friendship formation is not random, thoughtless and unpredictable, as assumed by many adults. On the contrary, their friendships developed online reveal highly predictable structures. The principle of homophily, which refers to the tendency of individuals to bond with similar others, together with their passion in developing cross-gender relationships, as presented in the last section, strongly shape young people's preferences regarding with whom to be friends online. As shown in the interview data, interaction and friendship formation online are more likely to occur among cross-gender youth who share certain demographic characteristics and academic orientation.

Most previous studies regarding the quality of youth's online relationships focus on the similarity of relationships developed offline and online using quantitative research methods (e.g. Chan and Cheng 2004; Mesch and Talmud 2007). These studies have provided evidence in how similar young people's online relationships are to their offline relationships, but they fail to answer why the similarities in offline and online relationships happen. This section will fill this gap by providing analysis of how and why offline personal, social and cultural factors help to generate positive attitudes towards socialising and connecting with similar others online.

Preference in meeting cross-sex youth

With the help of online communication, many young people's desires in developing cross-gender relationships seemed to be satisfied. Both girls and boys stressed their positive attitudes for making cross-sex friends online. Many examples have shown the males' enthusiasm and obsession in meeting girls online. For instance, Zhang (male, senior secondary student, urban) reported that almost all of his friends made online were female, as he intentionally selected girls to talk with. He has met some males who send a request to be friends, but he never approved their requests. Interestingly, Zhang showed embarrassment when explaining his intention to eventually make a girlfriend online, because for secondary school students like him, it is considered as inappropriate to develop romantic relationships. This suggests how strong the normative factors imposed on young students at this age are.

Similar examples can also be found among girls interviewed. Nan (female, senior secondary student, rural) revealed that she only chose to interact with boys when dealing with strangers online. She reported that among all 'friends' from her QQ buddy list, all the girls are school friends. In other words, she has never developed relationships with female strangers online. Deng (female, senior secondary student, rural) claimed: 'I don't want to befriend girls.' When asked her reason, she said: 'It is just a kind of habit, anyway, I don't see the point of girls chatting with girls'.

Age: most prefer peers, only a few interested in non-peers

Their positive attitudes in developing relationships with the opposite sex guide their preferences regarding similarities in demographic characteristics, including age and place of origin. Despite the technological potential for connecting with people of any age online, the youth interviewed seemed to be more interested in interacting online with people of a similar age. Generally, young people prefer to interact with and build friendships with peers. Some even have an exact age range of people they want to befriend. For example, Wan (male, college student, rural) preferred those from 16 to 22 years old while Yun (female, senior secondary student, rural) chose to interact with those who are no more than two years older or younger than her. This is consistent with some studies on adolescents' friendship formation online in other countries. In a survey conducted among Israeli adolescents by Mesch and Talmud (2007), data showed that when the friend was met online, age similarity held for 42.4 per cent of the respondents. Though there are fewer age similarities in relationships formed online than formed in a face-to-face setting (80.4 per cent), we can still tell that age is a strong predictor of online friendship formation.

They preferred to interact with those of a similar age because they thought age mattered a lot in communication. When asked why they preferred to befriend peers, most explained that they had shared experiences that make communication easy and comfortable. Older adults were not welcome among most young people interviewed, as they considered them as having an 'outdated' thinking style which made communication difficult. The importance of age similarity in online communication lies in several structural factors. Many factors, as mentioned by Boyd (2008), such as the age-segregated institutions of school, after-school activities and sports, and youth-oriented consumer culture, are strong structuring influences for the similarity in the age of online friends. Besides, as mentioned earlier, the underlying force for many young people's online interaction is to develop romantic relationships. Hence they want to be with cross-gender peers as they have more to chat about online than with people from other age groups.

However, besides expressive ties built with cross-gender peers, a few instrumental ties were also reported by the youth interviewed. Several participants reported making a small number of older-adult friends online, though this type of friend accounts for only a few among all their online friends. In other words, even for those who have showed interest and made several older-adult friends, peers still account for most of their online friends. Their reasons for making friends with non-peers are practical and instrumental. They choose to befriend them because they think it is safer to deal with older people. For youth like Peng (male, senior secondary student, urban), dealing with older adults online gives him a sense of security in the virtual world. From his perspective, those adults are much older than him and he does not think they would have the motivation to deceive young people such as him. He reported that he had made almost 10 older-adult friends online. Peng's explanation may confuse people from a different cultural context. In Chinese society, a cultural tradition which can be depicted as 'respect for the old, love for the young' (*zun lao ai you*) has a significant role in relationships between young people and older people. In daily life, when meeting older people, it seems natural for young people like Peng to show respect and presume they are nice people. Normally, many older people would show their love for the young people and react in a respectful way. These offline relationships between young people and older people seem to extend to the online world. That is why Peng regarded older-adults as worthy of trust. Apart from the feeling of safety, another reason for making friends with older people seems more instrumental. They want to develop relationships with some older adults because they see them as potential support providers due to their experience in life. They are eager to benefit from the relationships built with those who have experience and resources.

However, though some youth have an interest in connecting with older-adults for support, it is not easy for them to build relationships with them. Just as not all young people are interested in making older-adult friends, not all adults are interested in connecting with young people either. From Peng's (male, senior secondary student, rural) experience, many of them had no interest in talking with him online. He also revealed he is used to being rejected by many adults for online friendship. But he claimed that he understood why he was rejected: 'I myself do not like to talk with those who are much younger than me, as I think they are too naïve'. He thought that this may be because secondary school students like him were seen as naïve by those older-adults. Hence, even for some youth who do not care much about the age of people they meet online, there are few opportunities for them to build instrumental ties with them.

Place of residence: local peers are more welcome

Besides gender and age, young people also reported preference in place of origin when selecting online friends. With regard to the place of residence, the youth interviewed reported a preference in communicating with local peers. When facing the technology that transcends the limitations of space, it may seem surprising to hear young people's preferences in utilising this technology to meet people who are local. Technologically, the internet provides potential for users to connect with any other users through many platforms. But young people from small cities like Zunhua have their own preferences in choosing online friends, based on their places of residence. They claimed that they preferred to meet and make friends with those from the local area. But it seems that the definition of 'local' varies among young people. Some defined 'local' as those from the same province, some preferred those from the same big city (which is administratively in charge of their hometown), while some only showed interest in those from their hometown. Only a few claimed that they did not care where people were from when making friends online.

Youths preferred meeting peers from the local area as they thought it was easy to talk with local people and develop intimate relationships. They thought it was easy to find common topics to talk about with local people due to their shared experiences in this area. It seems that the more they talk with each other, the more likely the development of intimate relationships between them. As noted by Nan (female, secondary school student, rural):

> I prefer to meet people from the local area. When talking with strangers online, we always talk about the places we are from. If they live very near, we may talk a lot and may become intimate friends. But if they live very far away, I only talk about something irrelevant. It will be just a casual but not intimate talk.

Moreover, relationships developed with local peers have the potential to extend to offline life. In other words, they wanted to make friends with peers from the local area because this would facilitate their face-to-face meetings. For those who desired to make boyfriends or girlfriends online, only developing intimate or even romantic online relationships through chatting with each other online is not enough. They wanted to check out what each other looks like or whether they can get on well in real life. As in offline life, one's appearance plays an important part in the formation of intimate relationships between strangers. As noted by Nan (female, secondary school student, rural):

> I like to befriend local (peers). It is not only because it is common to meet friends made online face-to-face, but also because we expect to meet each other. Despite some people's preferences in talking online rather than meeting offline, young people like me usually expect to meet online friends. This is because, after the meeting, I would have more talk with those good looking guys and may stop talking with those who are not good looking.

Thus for youth dedicated to developing romantic relationships online, it is not realistic to make friends with those who live far away due to its inconvenience for meeting offline.

Unlike secondary school students, those who have left their hometown to attend colleges have their own reasons for meeting people from their hometown. For example, Qi (male, college student, urban), who is currently a college student studying in the capital city, revealed that he always felt close to people from his hometown, because there are only two (including him) that are from the province that he comes from. He admitted that even online, there was some sense of belonging when communicating with people from his hometown. Actually, in many universities in China, it is common for students to join clubs which are organised around place of origin in order to obtain support. To some extent, the sense of intimacy and closeness when meeting people from their hometown online mirrors their feelings under the same circumstances offline.

The evidence above suggests that for Chinese youth, the pattern of selecting online friends based on demographic characteristics is guided by their orientation for developing cross-gender or even romantic relationships. Shared age and place of residence provide the basis for communication between cross-gender youth. But similarity in demographic features is not enough for developing relationships. Besides similarity in age and place of residence, they are also concerned that people they meet online have a similar academic orientation.

Similarity in academic orientation

Academic orientation, which plays an important role in youth offline friendship formation in the context of China, persists in online relationship development. In China, children confront constant pressure from teachers, parents and peers to perform optimally, and those who fail to obtain satisfactory academic achievement are seen as highly problematic (e.g. Wu and Tseng, 1985). Hence, it is more likely that in offline life, youth with a similar academic orientation tend to be friends with each other. When communicating with peers online, the youth interviewed also seem to care about their academic orientation and this stands as an important factor in youth's online relationship formation.

In the online space, academic orientation is displayed in the form of two categories: students vs. non-students. According to the youth interviewed, when meeting peers online, they would probably ask whether one is a student. If the answer was yes, then they would ask about their academic performance. They claimed that this is part of a process of knowing someone. In other words, one's academic orientation is part of one's identity for them. Social categories play an important role in structuring young people's social worlds in China. Labels like 'students and non-students' identify different social categories. Literally, it is not difficult to understand what 'students' refers to, but the implications for 'non-students', which refer to young people who have left school whilst still of school age, are more complicated.[14] In Zunhua young people normally leave school either because they have to, due to violations of school regulations, or because they themselves choose to leave due to their academic orientation.[15] As noted by Boyd (2008: 174): 'Each label is associated with stereotypes about tastes, practices, and attitudes'. The label of 'non-student' in China is no exception.

Non-students, particularly those who have no jobs but hang out in groups on the streets, are seen as bad youth with no future.

When selecting online friends, interviewees said they prefer to communicate with those of a similar academic orientation. That is, students want to befriend students, whereas non-students prefer to interact with non-students. This preference online is shaped by youth's experiences in offline life. In offline life, restraints from parents and a lack of shared experiences have resulted in difficulties in interacting and even developing friendships between students and non-students. Most students interviewed have reported restraints from parents regarding interacting with non-students, including those who are their former school friends. Chan (male, senior secondary student, rural) noted that when some of his former school friends who had quit school came to visit him, his mother always told him not to learn bad things from them. Besides parents' restraints, many students admitted that a lack of shared experiences caused by a differentiated social life also made the interactions between them and non-students difficult. For students in China, the main space for socialising is the school and the main task for them is to perform well in their studies and finally enter a good university, while non-students have different experiences in different social spaces. All these suggest the difficulties for students and non-students in China to interact and develop intimate relationships.

To summarise this section, despite the technological features of new communication technology which help to lower barriers of communication, it is difficult to completely abolish the effects of social constraints on attitudes towards social interaction. This is because the new technology does not completely change the structure of the social space in which youth are situated, and hence their dispositions, which generate preferences in selecting online friends, do not change completely in the online space. Thus, as in offline life, the odds of developing online relationships are higher among the demographically close (except for gender) and socially similar in terms of academic orientation. To some extent, these shared attitudes in selecting with whom to interact and establish relationships seems to open up opportunities for the internet to bring rural and urban young people together. Yet whether they can connect online is shaped by their perceptions of members of each group and orientations surrounding making friends online in terms of place of origin (rural vs. urban).

Ambivalence, inconsistency and conflicts: perceptions and orientations surrounding the development of online relationships

For both rural and urban youth, their perceptions of members of each group are shaped by their own life experiences in the villages and cities as well as by other experiences of villagers and city-dwellers. In the context of China, the rural–urban gap in almost every aspect of life, and the social and cultural construction of cities and urbanites, villages and peasants have together shaped rural and urban youth's perception of themselves and others. In other words, villages, rural people and rural lifestyles are constructed as inferior, whereas cities, city-dwellers and urban lifestyles are seen as superior. And these differentiated perceptions have enabled urban people's bias and discrimination towards their rural counterparts as well rural people's hatred of urban people's arrogance. When online, previous experiences together with new online experiences continue to shape rural and urban youth's perceptions of each group, and orientations of with whom to develop relationships online.

'Arrogant urbanite': rural youth's perception of urban youth and orientation in developing online relationships

It seems that offline perceptions extend to the online space and have significant impact on attitudes towards online relationship formation between rural and urban youth. Many rural youth interviewed complained about urban people's arrogance in offline life and claimed that they preferred not to be connected with urban people even online.

For example, Ao (male, worker, rural) and Ann (female, senior secondary student, rural) both have unhappy experiences involving city-dwellers during their short-time study in city schools. They talked about how urban people's arrogance made their adoption in city schools difficult. Hence they both chose to return to rural schools in which they felt like 'fish in the water'. Compared to other rural youth who have fewer opportunities to interact with urban people, they tended to have a higher level of dislike towards urbanites. They both said that they did not want to make friends with urban people online because they are so arrogant, and they felt isolated.

Examples from rural–urban migrants in China can help explain the impact of unhappy experiences in cities for rural youth. Like Ann and Ao mentioned earlier who have experienced living in city schools, these migrant workers manage to leave villages for cities. Despite their contribution to the development of cities, rural migrant workers are labelled by the media and by urban elites as poor, dirty, ignorant and prone to violence, which reflects and reinforces the notion of the inferiority of rural residents. Bias and discrimination against migrant workers, in particular in big cities, tend to be prevalent among urban residents. Consequently the stigma, together with other problems confronted by migrant workers, has contributed to their poorer mental health status compared to their non-migrant counterparts, urban residents, and the general population. This helps us understand why rural youth's personal experiences in the city increased their negative attitudes towards urban people. Hence, when they interact with people online, their offline experiences and orientation towards developing relationships are reflected online.

Some rural youth's perceptions of urban people's arrogance are shaped by their experiences of interactions with urban youth in their rural space. They seemed to put more weight on the inclination to avoid being hurt by arrogant urban people during online communication. Normally, this type of rural youth is more likely to have experiences of prejudice by urban people in offline life. They seem to be unable to get rid of these former experiences. So they intentionally choose to avoid being involved with those 'arrogant' urbanities online. For example, Gu (male, senior secondary student, rural) had the experience of being looked down upon by a city girl, and this has had great influence in his choice of selecting online friends. He said:

> When I was at the first grade of senior secondary school, I used to pursue a girl. I was very silly that time. She is from the city, while I did not know how to dress up and did not know how to talk properly. She told me that she did not have any intention of making a boyfriend with boys from our school. She used to attend the No. 1 senior secondary school before transferring to our school. At that time, I guessed that the reason for her not choosing a boyfriend from our school was that this is the countryside, which is rubbish. I firmly believed that this was the reason. But she told me that the real reason was that she was with a man who was several years older than her and had been waiting for her for seven years! I asked about the man's occupation; she said his job was fixing computers. Then I asked his parents' occupation; she said they were doing business in Guangdong province. But she finally became a girlfriend of my best friend from our village. His sister has a store selling clothes and his sister-in-law is the nephew of a very rich man in our town. His sister-in-law is also a manger of a very big supermarket. So you can say he is popular and rich. From this I have seen clearly many people. They are too hypocritical.

When Gu was refused by the girl the first time, he firmly believed that his failure was caused by his rural identity. Hence he was curious about the girl's boyfriend and his parents' occupation, so as to find out whether he was rejected due to his social background. We can tell how sensitive he is about his identity as a rural boy. Then when he found the girl was with a rich and popular rural boy, he realised that the reason for his failure in pursing this girl did not mainly lie in his rural background, but rather was in most part due to his family's socio-economic status. Moreover, the girl said many insulting words regarding his social background as a poor rural boy in order to reject him, which made him suffer a lot. His experiences dealing with this urban girl, which have structured his attitudes towards other urban girls, seem to generate his perceptions and preferences in online communications. He seemed very sensitive in what type of people (rural/urban) he met online. When he met someone (usually girls) behaving in an unfriendly manner, and they happened to be urban girls, he usually turned to their urban identity as an explanation of their bad attitude and behaviour.

One may think it is difficult to tell one's identity in terms of rural or urban origin during online communication. Actually, despite the anonymity of online communication, sometimes Gu could tell whether they were urban girls without asking them. For example, he told me that sometimes he could tell this from the photos uploaded in their QQ spaces. Many of the backgrounds in which the pictures are taken, for example tall buildings, reveal whether one is from a rural or urban area. After some unhappy experiences involving urban girls in the new online circumstance, his former perception of urban girls and preferences in developing relationships were reinforced. Then he gave up making online friends with urban girls and turned to rural girls whom he considered as nice and friendly. From his point of view, people's attitudes online are mainly determined by whether those concerned are from the countryside or the city.

'Inferior peasants': urban youth's perception of rural youth and orientation in developing online relationships

Unlike rural youth, urban youth seemed to be less conscious of their orientation towards developing online relationships in terms of place of origin (rural vs. urban). Many urban youth claimed that they cared less about identity differences in terms of rural and urban when interacting with people online. When told that rural youth did not like to befriend urban people because of their arrogance and prejudice towards rural residents, urban youth that were interviewed tended not to agree with this. Han (male, college student, urban) noted that not all urban people are arrogant. He saw arrogance as someone's personal attitude rather than a general feature of urban people. He thought only a few urban people are arrogant while most seem to be fine.

In fact, urban residents' negative attitudes (such as prejudice or arrogance) towards their rural counterparts seem to be persistent but in a more implicit way. Due to the government's efforts to reduce the negative attitudes towards migrant workers and to help them adapt to urban life, urban residents' prejudice has shifted from the explicit to implicit form. In other words, urban residents may not say directly that migrants are inferior but they may think they deserve a better life. Moreover, under the discourse of *suzhi* (quality), if urban residents express direct prejudice towards rural residents or migrant workers, they may be seen as having low *suzhi*. Hence, under this circumstance, urban youth also tend not to express their prejudice explicitly. For example, Gang (male, senior secondary student, urban) admitted that when he was young, he used to look down upon rural people, but he no longer had that kind of feeling because he had grown up.

However, from Gang and his friend's depiction of rural–urban differences, we can tell their sense of superiority. Gang (male, senior secondary student, urban) and Pan (male, senior secondary student, urban) are two urban students studying in a rural senior secondary school. When asked whether they had different feelings about studying in a school in which most students are from villages, Gang replied 'yes, I could not get on well with them (rural students), and I always feel that they are different from us in the style of talking and behaviour', while Pan said, 'they are not as bold as us'. The way they expressed their differences with rural students and the kind of language they used in the interview indicated their feeling of superiority over rural students.

Hence, when meeting online, it is not easy for rural and urban youth to overcome the obstacles caused by differences in attitudes towards each group in developing online relationships. Rural youth tend to prejudge urban youth as arrogant and consider themselves as inferior. Those who have experiences living in the countryside, including rural students attending urban schools and those who used to live in the countryside during their early life seem to understand how sensitive some rural people are, even online, due to their experiences with rural identity. For example, rural students who have attended urban schools like Shuang (female, college student, rural) and Wan (male, college student, rural) revealed that they are very careful when interacting with their rural friends because they know how sensitive their friends are. Even for Pan (male, senior secondary student, urban) who identified himself as an urban boy as his family moved to the city when he was very young, claimed that rural people's inherent feeling of inferiority when faced with urban people is a very important obstacle for these two groups to have a nice talk online.

But this is more difficult for urban young people to deal with rural people's sensitivity during online communication. They do not have experiences living in the countryside. Moreover, many of them even do not realise how sensitive rural people are because they are at a superior position. Though they did not claim explicitly their orientation in developing online relationships in urban youth, their implicit sense of superiority and perception of superiority seemed to imply their orientation in connecting with urban youth online. Hence, the differences in attitudes tend to generate different perceptions of each group and orientation in developing relationships between rural and urban youth.

Different social positions

Though rural and urban young people share similar preferences in their attitudes towards selecting online friends, their disparities in social position tend to play an important role in with whom they connect online.

The significant role of *guanxi* (personal relationships) in Chinese culture (see e.g. Bian 1997; Knight and Yueh 2008) tends to have a great impact on young people's preferences in selecting whom to befriend online in terms of their social status. That is, as members of Chinese society, both rural and urban youth tend to show positive attitudes in connecting with people with a high status. As mentioned in the previous section regarding youth's passions and standards for selecting online friends, they seemed to show practicality when making online friends, as they prefer to connect with resourceful others. As well as the motivation for developing cross-sex relationships, many showed the desire for connecting to people with higher status. Perhaps we can say that the purpose for developing cross-gender relationships and connecting with high-status people are not contradictory. In other words, if they have the choice, they would probably choose to connect online with someone who is both cross-gender and with high status.

This preference in connecting with high-status others seems to provide the potential for increasing social resources for both rural and urban youth. My own experiences of contacting them online and inviting them to participate in my interviews, together with evidence provided in the face-to-face interviews, have demonstrated their interest in connecting with people that they regard as high status and resourceful. As for rural young people, they were curious and excited at the prospect of being able to connect with me online. A rural boy (male and self-employed) who has left school was enthusiastic in chatting with me online. He talked about his plans for starting his own business and wondered if I could offer him some advice based on my experiences abroad. He also told me proudly that his mother had successfully built connections with someone working in the local government through online communication. Some even tried to show off to their friends about their connections with me. For example, after talks with me online, Le (male, worker, rural), who did not finish junior secondary school, invited me to his friend's birthday party to show them that he knew a person who had studied abroad. Wan (male, college student, rural) reported that his village friends also liked to show off their connections with some high-status people:

> In my village, students are seen as high-status. Sometimes my village friends told me friends they had made on Jinwu (one popular online dancing game) would probably say 'this is a college student' at first.

Among all the identities of friends developed online, Wan's village friends chose to introduce their college-student identity first as they considered that those college students were high-status people and they were proud that they had connections like that.

As for urban young people, most were also eager to develop relationships with those they considered to be high-status and resourceful. Data from the unstructured online interviews suggests that they saw people like me as being valuable to connect with, due to my academic experiences. Senior secondary school students, particularly those from the best school in Zunhua, like Zhen (male, senior secondary student, urban), were eager to seek tips for improving academic performance, so as to enter a better university. College student Han (male, college student, urban) wanted to obtain information on entering top graduate schools in China. Bei (male, college student, urban) was more interested in acquiring information about getting offers and scholarships from universities abroad. There are also college students like Qi (male, college student, urban) who was curious about what things are like in the UK regarding his future career.

However, despite rural and urban young people's shared positive attitudes in developing relationships with people they regard as high-status, they tend to differ in their definitions and choices for high-status people, due to their unequal positions in society. According to the interview data, perceptions of status vary between urban and rural youth. As rural and urban youth are embedded in quite different kinds of social networks, the same person who is seen as high-status by rural youth may be seen as low-status by urban youth; or one who is seen as having very high status by rural youth is less likely to be seen in the same way by urban youth. For example, the girls from some unknown college met online by Ju (male, worker, rural), and Wan's (male, college student, rural) village friends who did not go to university, are seen as high-status, but would be seen as low-status by urban youth who have more potential to go to better universities. Similarly, if some urban girls hear Deng (female, senior secondary student, rural) proudly telling me about one of her urban friends made online who did not finish secondary school, they would be surprised, as it is less likely for them to be involved with an unknown 'dropout' online, even if they are from urban areas, due to their low status. Even when dealing with me, rural youth were more likely to see me as higher status compared to urban youth, considering their reactions after knowing my real identity.

The rural–urban differences in the perceptions of high-status people play an important role in shaping their choices of who are worthy of connecting with. For many urban youth, their rural counterparts seem to belong to the low-status group with whom they have less interest in developing online relationships. They seemed to be more interested in developing relationships with those with similar or higher status than themselves, that is, young people who are more likely to come from urban areas. As stated by Shuang (female, college student, rural),

> all want to be connected to those with higher rather than lower status than themselves, those who are well educated want to be connected to others with a higher level of status, and they won't be involved with those drop outs.

But for rural youth, their range of high-status people is wider than that of urban youth. Besides urbanites, other rural people who have more capital than themselves are also seen as high-status people. But connecting with these high-status rural people is not perceived as increasing their social capital, as they appear to define urban people as those who are more likely to have access to various institutional resources.

Rural–urban differences in their choices of selecting online friends based on status are also revealed from analysing data collected from the unstructured online interviews, in particular their reactions after knowing my identity and the subsequent online communication. Rural youth were shown to be more curious, more excited and more interested in chatting with me online compared to urban youth. Urban youth were more likely to behave arrogantly and to ignore or even reject my request for an interview; this was less likely to happen among rural youth. When talking with Wan (male, college student, rural), who has been studying in city schools and then college since he was a primary school student, about observed rural–urban differences in online communication in terms of their reactions, his explanations confirm that these differences are mainly caused by the unequal distribution of social capital between rural and urban youth. Based on his knowledge of rural and urban people, he explained that it is rare for rural people to know someone who is studying abroad, and that they are eager to connect with people like me due to curiosity as well as for instrumental purposes.

But for urban people, they have seen people like me in their offline social relationships. One revealed that he would probably have ignored me had he not found out that he knew me, after I told him my identity online, as my background and experiences had not impressed him too much.[16] Another high-status urban girl rejected my request for interview and stopped chatting with me online after realising that I was less likely to provide her with guidance online and to be her personal tutor. She was a senior secondary student whose father worked in the state-owned electricity supply company whose employees are known for high income and authority, due to the high level of industrial development in Zunhua, where electricity supply plays an important economic role. Recently, it has become normal for employees from that company to send their children abroad. Thus for this high-status urban girl, if I could not give her the support that she demanded, I was not a valuable contact.

It seems that offline perceptions extend to the online space and are reinforced by online communication between rural and urban youth. Hence, both rural and urban youth have showed orientations in developing relationships with people from the same groups, even online. As members of the same society, they tend to have similar positive attitudes towards forming relationships, such as preference in developing relationships with high-status people, which is embedded in the Chinese *guanxi* culture. This does not challenge their orientations as they hold different positions and hence construct different standards with high-status people.

Conclusions

This research reveals that both rural and urban young people have shown positive attitudes towards online communication and relationship formation. Technological features of online communication, especially anonymity, which reduces the risk of self disclosure and eases the anxiety of social interaction, help to promote positive attitudes towards interacting with strangers and making friends with them. Moreover, adults' intervention in young people's relationship formation in offline life make young people more attracted to online communication and relationship formation. They believe that through online communication they can obtain more freedom and autonomy in with whom to interact and establish relationships. Their communication with strangers via various social media and establishing a number of relationships with them indicate the consistency of their feelings, beliefs and behaviours towards the attitude object. Yet this study also reveals inconsistency and ambivalence in attitudes towards with whom to communicate and form relationships online in terms of place of origin (rural vs. urban). Both rural and urban respondents tend to show negative attitudes towards developing relationships with members of the other group, as offline perceptions extend to the online space and have significant impact on attitudes towards online relationship formation between rural and urban youth. Besides negative attitudes towards interacting and connecting with each other, the disparity in social status between rural and urban young people also tends to make their behaviours in developing relationships with each other difficult.

Notes

1 Data retrieved from www.internetworldstats.com/top20.htm on 31 October 2012.
2 Data retrieved from www.telegraph.co.uk/technology/broadband/9567934/Chinese-internet-users-to-overtake-English-language-users-by-2015.html# on 1 November 2012.
3 The data from a survey conducted in the same area (Fang 2008) was used in this project as secondary data.
4 Though Zunhua is called a city, under China's system of administration, it covers both urban and rural areas. It includes sub districts named urban areas and residents who register there hold urban *hukou* status. Besides, it also includes towns and villages named rural areas and residents who register there are rural *hukou* holders.
5 Here college students refer to students who are from Zunhua but attending college outside their hometown.
6 In the questionnaire, there was an invitation saying 'you are welcome to leave your QQ ID if you do not mind'. And around 20 per cent of respondents chose to leave their QQ ID, which also suggests that they did not mind future contact with me. Actually, later on, as I also left my QQ ID in the introduction part of the questionnaire, a small number of participants added me on their QQ buddy lists and started chatting with me through QQ.
7 There was a group of youth who were born in villages and hold rural *hukou* status but also had experiences of attending city schools. They were not completely the same as either other village youth without experiences of studying and living in urban areas, or as urban youth who had their socialisation mostly in the city area, despite the similarities they share with youth of both groups. It is necessary to make them a different category.
8 Online games mentioned are provided by different platforms, including QQ, Renren and specific online game websites.
9 QQ's other new services may also provide opportunities for relationship formation online, but because they are not very popular and young people I interviewed did not mention them, the focus of new services for making friends online here refer to Qzone and QQ Game.
10 See news reported on http://news.cnwest.com/content/2011–02/26/content_4178154.htm.
11 Actually, things described here have not changed much from my experiences attending secondary school more than 10 years ago.
12 Many policies may contribute to the reinforcement of filial piety. But here the focus will be the one-child policy as it is the most relevant regarding parents' intervention in their children's cross-gender relationships.
13 Young people's preference in communicating and forming relationships with cross-gender peers on the internet will be presented in detail in the third section.
14 In this project, non-students refers to those who left school before finishing secondary school or college.
15 Because of the level of economic and educational development of Zunhua, it is less likely for young people from this area to drop out of school due to financial problems. Actually, among the interviewees who have dropped out of school, no one reported reasons related to financial problems.
16 Our families have been friends for years. When he was a senior secondary school student, he did the survey I conducted in 2008 and left his QQ account on the questionnaire. As his information on the questionnaire is anonymous, I did not know who he was when I first contacted him. After I revealed my real identity, he just realised who I was and told me who he was. Though his family live in a village, his father worked for a big state-owned steel company which distinguishes his family from most rural families in terms of economic, social, and cultural capital. He and his sister both attended the best city schools since they were primary school students. Hence, for him, it is not that rare to see a PhD student studying abroad compared to most other rural youth.

References

Adams, C.J. 1996 'This is not Our Fathers' Pornography: Sex, Lies, and Computers', in Ess, C. (Ed.) *Philosophical Perspectives on Computer-mediated Communication*. Albany: State University of New York Press.

Ahn, J. 2012 'Teenagers and social network sites: Do off-line inequalities predict their online social networks?' *First Monday* 17 (1–2).

Bargh, J.A., McKenna, K.Y. and Fitzsimons, G.M. 2002 'Can You Tell the Real Me? Activation and Expression of the 'True Self' on the Internet'. *Journal of Social Issues* 58 (1) pp. 33–48.

Bargh, J.A. and McKenna, K.Y.A. 2004 'The Internet and Social Life'. *Annual Review of Psychology* 55 pp. 573–90.

Baym, N. 2010 *Personal Connections in the Digital Age*. Cambridge, UK: Polity Press.

Bian, Y. 1997 'Bringing Strong Ties Back in: Indirect Ties, Network Bridges, and Job Searches in China'. *American Sociological Review* 62 pp. 366–385.

Boase, J. and Wellman, B. 2006 'Personal Relationships: On and Off the Internet', in Vangelisti, A. and Perlman, D. (Eds) *The Cambridge Handbook of Personal Relationships*. New York: Cambridge University Press.

Boneva, B.S., Quinn, A., Kraut, R., Kiesler, S. and Shklovski, I. 2006 'Teenage Communication in the Instant Messaging Era.' *Computers, Phones, and The Internet: Domesticating Information Technology*, pp. 201–218. Accessed at http://slo.sbcc.edu/wp-content/uploads/boneva04-teencommunicationinimera.pdf on 23 March 2015.

Boyd, D. 2008 *Taken Out of Context: American Teen Society in Networked Publics*. PhD Dissertation, University of California-Berkeley.

Boyd, D. 2011 'White Flight in Networked Publics? How Race and Class Shaped American Teen Engagement with MySpace and Facebook'. In Nakamura, L. and Chow-White, P.A. (Eds) *Race after the Internet*. New York: Routledge.

Bryman, A. 2008 *Social Research Methods* (3th ed.). New York: Oxford University Press.

Chan, K.W. 1994 *Cities with Invisible Walls*. Hong Kong: Oxford University Press.

Chan, D.K.S. and Cheng, G.H.L. 2004 'A Comparison of Offline and Online Friendship Qualities at Different Stages of Relationship Development'. *Journal of Social and Personal Relationships*. 21 (3) pp. 305–320.

Chan, K.W. and Zhang, L. 1999 'The Hukou System and Rural–urban Migration: Processes and Changes'. *The China Quarterly* 160 (1) pp. 818–855.

Chen, X., Chang, L. and He, Y. 2003 'The Peer Group as A Context: Mediating and Moderating Effects on Relations between Academic Achievement and Social Functioning in Chinese Children'. *Child Development* 74 (3) pp. 710–727.

Cheng, T.J. and Selden, M. 1994 'The Origins and Social Consequences of China's Hukou System'. *The China Quarterly* 139 pp. 644–668.

Chesebro, J. and Bonsall, D. 1989 *Computer-mediated Communication: Human Relationships in a Computerized World*. Tuscaloosa: the University of Alabama Press.

China Internet Network Information Center (CINIC) 2009. *China Youth Internet Report 2008–2009*. Beijing: China Internet Network Information Center.

China Internet Network Information Center (CNNIC) 2010 *Statistical Survey Report on Internet Use among Young People*. Beijing: China Internet Network Information Center.

Cohen, M.L. 1993 'Cultural and Political Inventions in Modern China: The Case of the Chinese "Peasant"'. *Daedalus* 122 (2) pp. 151–170.

Crocker, J. and Major, B. 1989 'Social Stigma and Self-esteem: The Self-Protective Properties of Stigma'. *Psychological Review* 96 (4) pp. 608–630.

Cui, N., Li, M. and Gao, E. 2001 'Views of Chinese Parents on the Provision of Contraception to Unmarried Youth'. *Reproductive Health Matters* 9 (17) pp. 137–145.

Damm, J. 2007 'The Internet and the Fragmentation of Chinese Society'. *Critical Asian Studies* 39 (2) pp. 273–294.

Ebo, B.L. 1998 'Internet or Outernet?', In Ebo. B.L. (Ed.) *Cybergetto or Cybertopia? Race, Class and Gender on the Internet*. Westport, CT: Praeger.

Ellison Nicole, B. and Charles, S. 2007 'The Benefits of Facebook "Friends": Exploring the Relationship between College Students' Use of Online Social Networks and Social Capital'. *Journal of Computer-mediated Communication* 12 pp. 1143–1168.

Fan, C.C. and Sun, M. 2008 'Regional Inequality in China, 1978–2006'. *Eurasian Geography and Economics* 49 (1) pp. 1–18.

Flick, U., von Kardoff, E. and Steinke, I. 2004 *A Companion to Qualitative Research*. London, Thousand Oaks, New Delhi: Sage.

Fleisher, B.M., Li, H. and Zhao, M.Q. 2010 'Human Capital, Economic Growth, and Regional Inequality in China'. *Journal of Development Economics* 92 (2) pp. 215–231.

Giese, K. 2004 'Speaker's Corner or Virtual Panopticon: Discursive Construction of Chinese Identities Online', in Mengin, F. (Ed.) New York: Palgrave.

Grinter, R.E. and Palen, L. 2002 'Instant Messaging in Teen Life'. *The ACM Conference on Computer-Supported Cooperative Work (CSCW '02)*. New Orleans, LA, November 16–20.

Hanna, N.K. and Qiang, Z.W. 2010 'China's Emerging Informatization Strategy'. *Journal of the Knowledge Economy* 1 pp. 128–164.

Hargittai. E. 2007 'Whose Space? Differences Among Users and Non-users of Social Network Sites'. *Journal of Computer-mediated Communication* 13 pp. 276–297.

Haythornthwaite, C. 2002 'Strong, Weak, and Latent Ties and the Impact of New Media'. *Information society* 18 pp. 385–401.

Hert, P. 1997 'Social Dynamics of An Online Scholarly Debate'. *The Information Society* 13 pp. 329–360.

Ho, D.Y. 1994 'Filial Piety, Authoritarian Moralism, and Cognitive Conservatism in Chinese Societies'. *Genetic, Social and General Psychological Monographs* 120 pp. 347–365.

Ho, D.Y. 1996 'Filial Piety and Its Psychological Consequences, in Bond, M.H. (Ed.) *The Handbook of Chinese Psychology*. New York, NY, US: Oxford University Press.

Ho, K.-C. 2007 'A Case study of Douban: Social Network Communities and Web2.0 in China'. *Masaryk: University Journal of Law and Technology* 2 pp. 43–56.

Kang, J. 2000 'Cyber-race'. *Harvard Law Review* 113 pp. 1130–1208.

Katz. J.E. and Aspden, P. 1997 'A Nation of Strangers?' *Communications of the ACM* 40 (12) pp. 81–86.

Katz, J.E. and Rice, R.E. 2002 *Social Consequences of Internet Use: Access, Involvement, and Interaction*. Cambridge: MIT Press.

Kelly, K. 1996 'The Electronic Hive—Embrace it'. In Kling, R. (Ed.) *Computerization and Controversy, 2nd edition*. San Diego: Academic Press.

Knight, J. and Yueh, L. 2008 'The Role of Social Capital in the Labour Market in China'. *Economics of Transition* 16 (3) pp. 389–414.

Lam, C. 2007a 'Analyzing Facebook Usage by High School Demographic'. *Data Strategy* 14 September.

Lam, C. 2007b 'Examining MySpace Usage by High School'. *Data Strategy* 19 September.

Lampe, C., Ellison, N. and Steinfield, C. 2006 'A Face(book) in the Crowd: Social Searching vs. Social Browsing'. *The 2006 20th Anniversary Conference on Computer Supported Cooperative Work.* New York.

Lea, M. and Spears, R. 1992 'Paralanguage and Social Perception in Computer-mediated Communication'. *Journal of Organizational Computing* 2 pp. 321–341.

Lenhart, A. and Madden, M. 2007 *Teens, Privacy, & Online Social Networks.* Washington, DC: Pew Internet & American Life Project.

Lenhart, A., Madden, M., Smith, A., Purcell, K., Zickuhr, K. and Rainie, L. 2011 *Teens, Kindness and Cruelty on Social Network Sites.* Washington, DC: Pew Internet and American Life Project.

Lenhart, A., Rainie, L. and Lewis, O. 2001 *Teenage Life Online: The Rise of the Instant-Message Generation and the Internet's Impact on Friendships and Family Relationships.* Washington, DC: Pew Internet and American Life Project.

Li, N. and Kirkup, G. 2007 'Gender and Cultural Differences in Internet Use: A study of China and the UK'. *Computers & Education* 48 (2) pp. 301–317.

Liang, S.M. 1989 *Zhongguo Wenhua Yaoyi (The Main Meanings of Chinese Culture).* Shanghai.

Liu, F.S. 2009 'It is not Merely about Life on the Screen: Urban Chinese Youth and the Internet Café'. *Journal of Youth Studies* 12 (2) pp. 167–184.

Liu, F.S. 2010 'The Internet in the Everyday Life – world: A Comparison between High – school Students in China and Norway'. *Comparative Education* 46 (4) pp. 527–550.

Livingstone, S. 2009. *Children and the Internet: Great Expectations and Challenging Realities.* Cambridge: Polity.

Livingstone, S. and Bovill, M. 2001 *Children and Their Changing Media Environment: A European Comparative Study.* Mahwah, NJ: Lawrence Erlbaum Associates.

Lu, H. 2002 'Urban Superiority, Modernity and Local Identity: a Think Piece on the Case of Shanghai'. In Faure, D. and Liu, T.T. (Eds) *Town and Country in China: Identity and Perception.* Hampshire: Palgrave.

Lu, H. 2010 'Small-Town China: A Historical Perspective on Rural–urban Relations'. In Whyte, M.K. (Ed.) *One Country, Two Societies: Rural–Urban Inequality in Contemporary China.* Harvard: Harvard University Press.

MacKinnon, R. 2008a 'Blogs and China Correspondence: Lessons about Global Information Flows'. *Chinese Journal of Communication* 1 (2) pp. 242–257.

MacKinnon, R. 2008b 'Flatter World and Thicker Walls? Blogs, Censorship and Civic Discourse in China'. *Public Choice* 134 (1) pp. 31–46.

McKenna, K.Y., Green, A.S. and Gleason, M.E. 2002 'Relationships Formation on the Internet: What's the Big Attraction?' *Journal of Social Issues* 58 (1) pp. 9–31.

McLaren, A.E. 2007 'Online Intimacy in a Chinese Setting'. *Asian Studies Review* 31 (4) pp. 409–422.

Mesch, G. and Talmud, I. 2006 'Online Friendship Formation, Communication Channels, and Social Closeness'. *International Journal of Internet Science* 1 (1) pp. 29–44.

Mesch, G.S. and Talmud, I. 2007 'Similarity and the Quality of Online and Offline Social Relationships among Adolescents in Israel'. *Journal of Research on Adolescence* 17 (2) pp. 455–466.

Negroponte, N. 1995 *Being Digital.* New York: Alfred A. Knopf.

Nie, M. and Li, J. 2006 'The Communication Characteristics of Celebrity Blogs (*Mingren boke de chuanbo tezheng fenxi*)'. *Social Science Journal of South Central University* 12 (6) pp. 746–751.

Parks, M.R. and Floyd, K. 1996 'Making Friends in Cyberspace'. *Journal of Communication* 46 (1) pp. 80–97.

Pascoe, C.J. 2007 *Dude, You're A Fag: Masculinity and Sexuality in High School.* Berkeley: University of California Press.

Peter, J., Valkenburg, P.M. and Schouten, A.P. 2005 'Developing a Model of Adolescent Friendship Formation on the Internet'. *CyberPsychology & Behavior* 8 pp. 423–430.

Qiu, L.C. 2009 *Working-Class Network Society: Communication Technology and the Information Have-Less in Urban China.* Cambridge: MIT Press.

Quan-Haase, A. 2007 'University Students' Local and Distant Social Ties: Using and Integrating Modes of Communication on Campus'. *Information, Communication & Society* 10 (5) pp. 671–693.

Rheingold, H. 1993 'A slice of Life in My Virtual Community', in *Global Networks.* Harasim, L.M. (Ed.). Cambridge: The MIT Press.

Rice, R. and Love, G. 1987 'Electronic Emotion; Socioemotional Content in A Computer-mediated Communication Network'. *Communication Research* 14 pp. 85–108.

Siegel, J., Dubrovsky, V., Kiesler, S. and McGuire, T.W. 1986 'Group Processes in Computer-mediated Communication'. *Organizational Behavior and Human Decision Processes* 37 pp. 157–187.

Sproull, L. and Kiesler, S. 1986 'Reducing Social Context Cues: Electronic Mail in Organization Communication'. *Management Science* 32 (11) pp. 1492–1512.

Steinfield, C., Ellison, N.B. and Lampe, C. 2008 'Social capital, Self-esteem, and Use of Online Social Network Sites: A Longitudinal Analysis'. *Journal of Applied Developmental Psychology* 29 pp. 434–445.

Stewart, T.A. 1996 'Boom Time on the New Frontier'. In Kling, R. (Ed.) *Computerization and Controversy (2nd ed.)* San Diego: Academic Press.

Sung, K.-T. 1995 'Measures and Dimensions of Filial Piety in Korea'. *The Gerontologist* 35 pp. 240–247.

Valkenburg, P.M. and Peter, J. 2009 'The Effects of Instant Messaging on the Quality of Adolescents' Existing Friendships: A Longitudinal Study'. *Journal of Communication* 59 pp. 79–97.

Walther, J.B. 1992 'Interpersonal Effects in Computer-mediated Interaction'. *Communication Research* 19 (1) pp. 52–90.

Wang, F.L. 2005 *Organizing through Division and Exclusion: China's Hukou System.* CA: Stanford University Press.

Watkins, S.C. 2009 *The Young & the Digital: What the Migration to SocialNetwork Sites, Games, and Anytime, Anywhere Media Means for Our Future.* Boston, MA: Beacon Press.

Whyte, M.K. 2010 'The Paradoxes of Rural–urban Inequality in Contemporary China'. In Whyte, M.K. (Ed.) *One Country, Two Societies: Rural–Urban Inequality in Contemporary China.* Harvard University Press.

Wolak, J., Mitchell, K.J. and Finkelhor, D. 2003 'Escaping or Connecting? Characteristics of Youth Who Form Close Online Relationships'. *Journal of Adolescence* 26 pp. 105–119.

Wu, X.G. and Treiman, D. 2004 'The Household Registration System and Social Stratification in China, 1955–1996'. *Demography* 41 pp. 363–384.

Wu, H. and Tseng, W.S. 1985 *Chinese Culture and Mental Health.* London: Academic Press.

Yang, G. 2009 *The Power of the Internet in China: Citizen Activism Online.* New York: Columbia University Press.

Yu, D.P. 2002 *Urban Rural Society: From Segmentation to Openness (Chengxiang Shehui: Cong Geli Zouxiang Kaifang)*. Jinan: Shandong renmin chubanshe.
Yue, X. and Ng, S.H. 1999 'Filial Obligations and Expectations in China: Current Views from Young and Old People in Beijing'. *Asian Journal of Social Psychology* 2 (2) pp. 215–226.
Zhang, Y., Kohnstamm, G.A., Cheung, P.C. and Lau, S. 2001 'A New Look at the Old Little Emperor: Developmental Changes in the Personality of Only Children in China'. *Social Behavior and Personality: an International Journal* 29 (7) pp. 725–731.

3 Probing into attitudes and perceptions towards nation and nationalism in contemporary China
Uncertainty, scepticism and disdain

Liqing Li

Decades ago, between 1930 and 1932, Richard LaPiere, along with his young Chinese student and the student's Chinese wife, travelled around the United States by car, during which, of 251 serving businesses, they were hosted at 66 hotels/auto-camps/'Tourist Homes' and were served in 184 restaurants/cafes throughout the country, and were only turned away once by those asked to serve them. Yet, at the end of their journey, when LaPiere posted a questionnaire survey to each of the serving businesses they had visited, with the question 'Will you accept members of the Chinese race as guests in your establishment?', of the 128 restaurants and 81 cafes and 47 hotels/auto-camps/'Tourist Homes' that responded, 92 per cent of the former and 91 per cent of the latter answered 'No'. While the survey results seemed to fit in with the then general (negative) attitude of Americans towards the Chinese as indicated by the 'social distance' studies (LaPiere 1934: 231), they also suggested, at least at face value, a sharp inconsistency between people's attitudes and behaviour. While LaPiere's finding has generated a wave of studies that give attention and concern to the correlation between attitude and behaviour, which are of course of importance, in this study, the research interest lies in the ways studies of attitudes are conducted. For its advantage of being easy, cheap and mechanical, the survey method, usually in the form of a questionnaire, seems to have become a customary and dominant research method into people's attitudes (LaPiere 1934: 230), yet, it is worth considering a more qualitative approach, or even a combination of both methods to examine people's attitudes and perception. In the case of LaPiere's study, one may wonder, what if LaPiere had designed his survey question to the serving businesses differently? What if he had further looked into the stories behind those high percentage 'No' responses by having in-depth interviews? Perhaps if LaPiere had probed deeper, the research results of the attitude being investigated would not have been so dramatically different from the reality behaviour, if not completely coherent. This is what the current chapter intends to do. It aims to demonstrate how attitudes and perceptions can be expressed differently when explored differently by researchers. More specifically, by looking into university students' attitudes and perceptions towards nation and nationalism in contemporary China, this chapter shows that attitudes and perceptions can be naturalised within a given social, cultural and political context. Hence, when examined in a more or less direct way, they can be produced, or reproduced, for the researcher without much reflection; yet, explored in a less direct way and probed in depth, more complex and even contradictory stories can be revealed.

Here the 'attitude object' is set as nation and nationalism in contemporary China, a field of growing interest to many in recent times due to the new wave of nationalism after the collapse of Soviet-type Communism in 1989 in general and the alleged rising nationalism in China in particular. As will briefly be presented further on, based on a series of eye-catching pro-China street demonstrations and nationalistic publications in recent times, the consensus has been that nationalism in China is rising, especially among China's university students, suggesting a fervent nationalistic outlook of the young Chinese; yet, apart from a few survey studies focused on university students' political attitudes, few have given attention to their attitudes towards and perceptions about nation and nationalism. Some might argue that such studies are not necessary because university students' actions (such as their participation in pro-China street demonstrations) are already speaking for themselves in this regard. While it is true that university students have been making up the majority of the participants in recent pro-China demonstrations, one has to remember that while many students took part in demonstrations, there are many more who did not, not to mention the non-nationalistic motivations behind those who did participate. Take the 1999 students' demonstration against the US bombing of the Chinese embassy in Belgrade as an example: while many, including public media reports as well as political science and international relations literature, have judged and portrayed it as the rise of anti-US nationalism, Yu and Zhao's (2006) empirical study found over three-quarters of the protest participants were 'uncommitted participants and opportunists' who had no serious commitment to the anti-US ideologies. So the causal link between students' seemingly nationalistic actions and their thoughts on nation and nationalism should not be taken for granted and easily assumed. Even if there is a coherent causal link, without knowing students' thoughts on nation and nationalism, it is still bewildering to try and understand their seemingly nationalistic actions at the scene. Therefore, by taking a reflexive approach, this study will take a step back at this point, and make the notion of nation and nationalism, especially the alleged rising nationalism among university students mentioned earlier, an independent attitude object, against which university students' attitudes and perceptions were investigated.

This chapter is organised in five key parts. The first two parts briefly outline the national background concerning the attitude object, as well as students' association with it, so that readers can gain a general background knowledge about the attitude object (nation and nationalism) and attitude subject (university students). After all, as Berger and Luckmann (1967: 68) argue: 'the self cannot be understood apart from the particular social context in which they were shaped'. Following this, the third part of this chapter outlines the research methods employed in the collecting of data used in this chapter. After that, the last two parts, utilising the idea of 'national habitus' as an analytical framework, demonstrate students' 'taken for granted' attitudes and perceptions shown in their initial responses, as well as more complex articulation about the attitude object when delved into deeper.

Nation and nationalism in China: a brief introduction

Although scholars may disagree with each other about the origins, content and ethics of nationalism, alongside the primordialists' interpretation of nationalism as being ancient and eternal, many share the view that nationalism is only a modern phenomenon that appeared with the emergence of the modern state. In the case of China, although Chinese official discourses and ardent nationalists alike have regarded China as a centralised multi-ethnic nation-state with 5,000 years of history, and insist that being an immense political driving force, nationalism long existed in China throughout its history (Zhao 2004), many scholars in the field of Chinese nationalism generally agree that modern nationalism arose in China as an ideological moment of anti-imperialism, anti-colonialism and anti-feudalism in the late Qing Dynasty (1841–1912). They argue, as the well-known culturalism-to-nationalism thesis demonstrates, that it was not until the mid-nineteenth century when China was defeated by modern Western forces that China was woken up from its old 'China centrality' (*huaxia zhongxin*) dream and started its transition from a cultural entity (the Confucian idea of state) to a political entity (the imported Western idea of nation-state). Motivated by the determination to 'blot out the humiliation and restore China to its rightful place' – not that 'of China at the centre of the world and Chinese culture as a universal set of values' but that of China standing on an equal footing with other major powers – the Chinese nationalists started their century-long national salvation and strengthening movement by modernising China (Zhao 2000). Since then, according to Zhao (1998: 290), 'the wave of nationalism steadily engulfed all that stood in its path'. He notes:

> While other movements and ideologies waxed and waned, nationalism permeated them all. Those who wanted to rule China had to propound and implement a program of national salvation.
>
> (Zhao 2000: 4)

Even the founding of the Chinese Communist Party (CCP) itself back in 1921, it has been argued, was the result of the emerging Chinese nationalism (Wu 2007), and the following Communist revolution was

> at core a movement of nationalistically inspired students, who subsequently reached out to other allies – first workers, then peasants – in an effort to topple a government that they charged was remiss in its responsibility to guard China's national sovereignty.
>
> (Perry 2001: 169)

So, the 'long-disguised quasi-Communist' CCP has never been a true Communist party from the beginning, but 'a purely nationalist party' (Wu 2007: 123). Unlike the classic Marxism that downplayed the significance of nationalism, the CCP's legitimacy to rule has rested on its nationalist credentials in fighting for China's independence and prosperity (Karl 2002). When President Mao Zedong (1949–1976) declared from the top of the Tiananmen Gate in Beijing that the 'Chinese people have stood up', on the founding day of the People's Republic of China (PRC) back in 1949, he was appealing to Chinese nationalism (Zhao 1998; Wu 2007). And subsequent Chinese presidents have done much the same, whether it was Deng Xiaoping (1978–1989), Jiang Zemin (1989–2002) or Hu Jintao (2002–2013), and 'no matter what kind of ideological line, practical policy or political institution they applied, the nationalism appeal has always been the driving force in their decision-making' (Wu 2007: 126). However, the salience of nationalism, it has been observed, had a brief 'holiday' from the late 1950s to the early 1970s because of the promotion of ideology centred on Marxism-Leninism and Mao Zedong Thought, by Mao's political campaigns (Zhao 1998). In the light of the '*san xin wei ji*' (the three belief crises – crisis of faith in socialism, crisis of belief in Marxism and crisis of trust in the Party (Chen 1995), which, it has been said, resulted in the Tiananmen demonstration in 1989 (Zhao 1998), and the rapid decline of official Communist ideology, nationalism was called back to work again, assured and bold with justice.

Together with the party-state's promotion of patriotic education – a state-led nationalism (Zhao 1998, 2004) – and a series of nationalistic publications featuring radical nationalist expressions in the 1990s such as the 'Say No' books[1] (written by five young writers led by Wang Xiaodong, who deployed a wide variety of means to arouse anti-Western sentiment), and other alleged anti-foreign demonstrations[2] carried out primarily by university students, it has been widely agreed both in popular media and academic studies that nationalism, or as some have claimed, anti-Western nationalism, in contemporary China is on the rise (Cf. Carlson 2009; also see for example, Chang 1998; Zhao 2002, 2004; Seckington 2005; Zhou 2005; Lee 2006). As Carlson (2009: 20) points out: 'It is logical to begin any discussion of Chinese nationalism with the now long standing conventional wisdom that such a sentiment has been on the rise in China over the last two decades'. The rising tide of nationalism, it has been observed, can be identified at least at three levels: in the state apparatus, in intellectual discourse, and within popular society (Zhao 2004; also see Wu 2007; Shen 2007). Zhao (2004: 8–11) notes, at the state level, that the CCP rediscovered the utility of nationalism, and launched a nationwide patriotic education campaign, positioning itself as the sole representative of the Chinese nation. At the intellectual level, due to China's changing position in the post-Cold War world, the dominant discourse of worshipping the West in the 1980s not only shifted but also turned into what Zhao describes as 'deep suspicion' of the West in the 1990s among Chinese intellectuals. At the populist level, Zhao maintains, the resurging of nationalism was evident in the publications of 'Say No' books and 'Mao fever' in the 1990s.[3]

All these phenomena embedded in the so-called rising nationalism, it has also been argued, have a broad external and internal background. Externally, following the collapse of Communist states in Eastern Europe and the former Soviet Union, and due to the philosophically contradictory natures of Communism and nationalism, a worldwide consensus has claimed that nationalism is on the rise in state socialist countries (Shen 2007). As the last major Communist country, China has also been incorporated into this broad backdrop. Internally, and in relation to the decline of Communist ideology worldwide, it has been argued that the CCP was facing a legitimacy crisis. Many analysts (for example, see Huang 1995; Chang 1998; Zhao 1998; Broudehoux 2004) believe that due to the decline of Communist ideology and the loss of attraction of Marxism-Maoism to the Chinese people, particularly after the 1989 Tiananmen demonstration and after the collapse of Communist states in Eastern Europe and the former Soviet Union, the CCP is desperate to embrace nationalism in order to maintain and strengthen its ruling legitimacy (Zheng 1999). At a time of rapid and unprecedented development of globalisation and China's growing integration with the outside world, some have also argued that although globalisation has increased interconnectedness and interdependence of countries, it also 'conveys visibility and awareness of the "other"' (Guibernau 2004: 138). In the light of these discussions, the rise or revival of nationalism in China becomes a fait accompli. Liu Xiaobo, a Chinese political dissident, states that 'since June 4, 1989, China has suddenly been engulfed in a wave of nationalism and patriotism, which reaches every corner of the land and involves every person' (Cf. Zhao 2004: 8).

Overnight, the perceived 'rise' or 'resurgence' of Chinese nationalism based on those eye-catching exemplars, almost like an alarm ringing, appears to have attracted great attention from both inside and outside China, both in media reports and in academic studies, adding more (probably negative) weight to the ongoing debate about the rise of China (being a friend or foe) in general. As Yuan notes:

> The past few years have seen growing Western interest in the study of Chinese nationalism. While the immediate academic attention has been triggered by recent events in China, in particular the strong outpouring of anti-foreign sentiments in the aftermath of the 1999 US/NATO bombing of the Chinese embassy in Belgrade, the 2001 mid-air collision of a US spy plane and a Chinese fighter aircraft, and the controversies over the Japanese history textbooks and the Yasukuni Shrine visits, the deeper concerns relate to the larger question of how China's rising nationalism, along with its growing economic power, political influence, and military capabilities will likely affect Beijing's foreign policy decisions.
>
> (Yuan 2008: 3)

According to Zhao,

> This development has fed the roiling sense of anxiety in many political capitals of Asian and Western countries about if a virulent nationalism has

emerged from China's 'century of shame and humiliation' to make China's rise less peaceful.

(Zhao 2005: 175)

Already, there are talks about the wider implications of this alleged rising Chinese nationalism. While Yu decodes the rising new Chinese nationalism as a desire to replace 'the dominant position of the West in the world and making the twenty-first century a Chinese century' (Cf. Zhao 2000: 2), Huntington (1996: 229) expresses his concern over China's intention to restore its historic position as 'the pre-eminent power in East Asia' and 'to bring to an end the overlong century of humiliation and subordination to the West and Japan'. While Lilley (1996) claims that 'there is a rallying cry for Chinese everywhere ... that after a century of humiliation and Mao's social and economic experiments China's time has come ... it [China] will rise in the world to the place it deserves' (Cf. Zhao 2000: 2), Bernstein and Munro (1997: 19) send out the warning message that 'driven by nationalist sentiment, a yearning to redeem the humiliations of the past, and the simple urge for international power, China is seeking to replace the United States as the dominant power in Asia'. While Friedman (1997: 5) asserts that 'an extraordinarily strong and sensitive nationalism infuses elite political circles in Beijing at the end of the 20th century' and that 'the new, post-Mao nationalism in China not only challenges Taiwan's autonomy, it also could endanger peace in the Pacific-Asia region', Ming Zhang (1997: 122) states that 'suspicion and hatred of the US have prevailed among the public interviewed, old and young, intellectual and less educated'. The list can go on but the 'gloomy concern with the worrisome nature' (Chen 2005: 35) of contemporary Chinese nationalism is clear. In extreme cases, some even equate it with fascism or Nazism.

It is in this context that university students are brought onto the scene as it has been suggested that the rising tide of nationalism appears to be most evident among China's university students. This will be further addressed later.

University students and nationalism

As has happened in many other Asian and African countries, when modern nationalism first arose in China, it was largely among the urban educated elite, amongst whom young students played a significant role. It has been suggested that student involvement in defending their motherland has been a traditional feature of both pre- and post-1949 China (Rosen 2009). Historically, influenced by the Confucian value that educated intellectuals should take responsibility for their nation, Chinese students, like their Korean counterparts, were always motivated by a sense of social responsibility, patriotic duty and quest for 'national salvation', and strongly believed they should be responsible for their country's future and ought to stand up on behalf of the Chinese people (Zhang 2002; Luo 2004). Indeed, in the light of the student movement in the 1960s worldwide, Lutz (1971) notes that the issue that could politicise student youth in

China was a threat to the Chinese nation. The student movement could, in Lutz's words, 'punctuate the definition of nationalism and provide exclamation points in its expression' (Lutz 1967: 627). Studies have suggested that the student protest in 1919 greatly helped the founding of the CCP itself (Rosen 2009; Guo 2004; Wasserstrom 2005); the student nationalistic movement demands of resistance towards imperialist countries and the bringing to an end to unpopular policies during 1927–1937, had profound effect at the time (Israel 1966); and the student movement in 1989 – with a patriotic intention to strengthen China through political reform (Zhao 2004, 2008) – posed a significant challenge to the government (Wasserstrom 2005) although it was eventually beaten down by the CCP.

The overriding appeal of nationalism, it has been claimed by some academic studies as well as popular mass media, is still strong amongst university students in post-1989 China (Wang 2009; Xi 2006). Yearly survey studies of university students' moral and political attitude organised by the Chinese Educational Bureau between the years of 1991 and 2009 consistently suggest that contemporary university students in China are a generation with great love for their country and people, and are a hopeful and trustworthy generation who can hold up the historical task of Chinese national rejuvenation (Wang and Cai 2009). Other survey studies also suggest university students' strong nationalistic attachment and commitment. For example, the national survey of university students conducted by China Youth and Children Research Centre (2004) reported that 91.9 per cent of university students were willing to make contributions against foreign aggression (Xi 2006). As a matter of fact, it has been put forward by some scholars, whether or not coincidentally with the alleged rising nationalism in China, that university students' nationalistic feelings have been riding high since the mid-1990s (Zheng 1998, cf. Ye and Zweig 2007; Chang 1998). In short, there are indications that university students in contemporary China are still strongly attracted to nation and nationalism (Wang 2009).

In the context of the increasing feelings of nationalism mentioned earlier, it has been suggested that the rising tide of nationalism is most evident among Chinese university students in urban areas (Xu 2008; Wang 2009). More precisely, it has been observed that in the first instance, university students made up the majority of the demonstrators (in recent pro-China demonstrations mentioned earlier) in terms of group number. This is clearly indicated in academic research as well as news reports at the time, although, without denial, other social segments also took part in the demonstrations. Second, they have been one of the key targets of the nationwide 'patriotic education', which, according to some, has proved to be working. For example, Chang writes:

> Since the 1989 Tiananmen incident, Beijing has mounted a patriotic nationalist campaign to regain popular support by shifting its basis of legitimacy from a bankrupt ideology to nationalism. That campaign appears to be effective, especially among youth and intellectuals.
>
> (Chang 1998: 83)

Similarly, Zhao (1998: 287–288) maintains as a state-led nationalist movement, the patriotic education campaign was 'directly responsible for the nationalistic sentiment of the Chinese people in the mid-1990s'. Huang (1995: 57) asserts that 'The strategy [patriotic education campaign] has worked, as evidenced by the recently rising anti-American sentiment'.

Third, while the nationalistic publication such as the series of 'Say No' books have been regarded by many both inside and outside China as evidence of the rising nationalism, it has also been suggested that the publication of such books are most popular among Chinese youth. With regard to the 'Say No' books, Chang notes:

> Not only did the authors claim to represent popular sentiment, the book received the recommendation of the Chinese government for its 'representative' reflection of the experiences and sentiments of Chinese youth and for its 'nationalist purpose'.
>
> (Chang 1998: 86)

With such evidence at hand, it seems natural to link university students with the now widely discussed and claimed 'anti-foreign' rising nationalism in contemporary China. University students in this picture have been portrayed as fervent nationalists, the most 'patriotic, establishment-supporting people' (Forney 2008). Some even referred to them as manipulated modern-day 'Red Guards' (French 2005) with the CCP 'calling the tune to which the students dance (Cf. Wasserstrom 2005: 60). Zhao (2008: 48) contends many of them 'sided with authoritarian government and harboured a sense of wounded national pride in response to foreign criticism'. However described, a fervent nationalistic outlook, and a positive, even radical, national attitude among university students have been portrayed.

Bearing in mind what has been presented earlier, many would expect a coherent and positive link between the attitude object and attitude subject. However, as will be shown further on, along with the initial positive coherence that resonates with the fervent nationalistic outlook portrayed by many, there is something more complex about the attitude object and attitude subject which, when probed into more deeply, has not been sufficiently captured in usual survey studies. But before going into further detail, it is necessary to lay out the methodological issues concerning this study.

Research method

Taking into account the multi-ethnic situation in China (56 officially recognised ethnic groups), this study focused only on Han students, as the Han people constitute the largest (more than 90 per cent of the total population) and most dominant group within the PRC. The construction and dissemination of 'Chinese-ness' are usually based on the Han people, their history and their culture. Although the government has been making efforts to incorporate the other 55 minority ethnic groups into the big Chinese family and to assert that the Chinese nation includes all PRC citizens regardless of their ethnic background, it would be controversial to assume their Chinese-ness as very few minorities freely chose to be part of China (Dikotter 1996).

Although China has more than 2,000 universities and colleges, with over 20 million students, Han students from elite universities were chosen as the main targeted subjects for investigation, for two main reasons. First, it is usually the elite university students who act at the forefront of any student movement, particularly any nationalistic actions, bringing their non-elite counterparts along behind them (Zhao 2002; Yu and Zhao 2006). This is particularly true in the case of China, as past events have shown. Second, elite universities in China's 'tier one', or major, cities like Beijing and Shanghai have been the normal recruiting ground for the current ruling party, the CCP. So understanding their attitudes and perceptions can also provide a window on China's future elites' national thinking. So, by using purposive sampling/judgemental sampling, a commonly used method in non probability samples (Berg 2007), two of the most prestigious and influential universities (one in Beijing and one in Shanghai) were selected as the sites for investigation.

Respondents were recruited using the approach of probability sampling method. That is, to approach students randomly on campus in public areas such as library, classrooms and university canteens, where a mixture of male and female students from different years, schools and background can be found. This approach was adopted to ensure the chosen sample represents different faculties to which students are attached, as it might be that the kind of discipline a student is studying is relevant to different attitudinal features of the research topic (Bryman 2008). Although less controllable, bearing in mind the danger of generalisation, and assuming different students have their own experience, understanding and attitude towards nation and nationalism, special attention was given to the recruitment of respondents in terms of demographic factors such as their major, age, gender and family background (agricultural vs. non-agricultural) to ensure balance in the section of respondents. Therefore, in order to achieve a representative sample and keep sampling error and sampling bias to a minimum, efforts to avoid subjective judgements on students (i.e. approaching students who appear to be friendly or that the researcher feels more comfortable with) were made, and a variety of time spans and different venues[4] were given to ensure each student in the university has a known chance of being approached (Bryman 2008).

For the purpose of getting students' agreement to be interviewed, when they were approached, I first asked them whether they were undergraduate students in the chosen university. If they said 'yes', I introduced myself to them, (showing them my student card) and briefly explained what I was trying to do. If they showed interest in participating, I then started to explain in more detail about my research and the ethical issues involved. Next, if students gave their consent (verbally) to be interviewed by me, they were asked to sign the consent form. Following this, a printed name card with my contact details was given to

Probing into attitudes and perceptions 73

students so that if they wanted to ask me any questions about the research (now or later) they could contact me. A similar approach was adopted before getting students to fill in the self-completion questionnaire.

Although time-consuming and energy-sapping, given that both chosen universities have a large number of undergraduate students (14,465 in Beijing and 15,306 in Shanghai), access to them was not too difficult, particularly during their free time in the public areas mentioned earlier. As a result, time and cost permitting, a total of 52 undergraduate students majoring in different subjects and from different years, schools and family background were recruited for in-depth interview, and 200 questionnaires were distributed to undergraduate students from different university years, majors, home region and family backgrounds with a return rate of 77 per cent (which can be classified as 'very good' according to Mangione's (1995) classification of bands of response rate) at the chosen universities.

A combination of self-completion questionnaire[5] and in-depth face-to-face interview were employed in the study. Empirical questions asked in the framework that are relevant to this chapter are all associated with nation and nationalism, especially the rising nationalism in contemporary China mentioned earlier. This means the usual and explicit nationalist discourses, including nationalistic expressions and events, such as the 'Say No' books, the 1999 protests against the Belgrade bombing, the 2005 protests against Japan's bid for a permanent seat on the UN Security Council, and the more recent 2008 protests against the Western media's reports of China, were utilised to find out students' attitudes and perceptions towards the rising nationalism expressed in such ways. However, it is important to note here that this investigation was conducted by adopting a reflexive approach, meaning they [nationalist discourses] were only used in 'a supportive role, a background against which the actual research interest ... play[s] out' rather than concerning 'the case per se' (Berg 2007: 291). Furthermore, students' initial responses were not taken for granted but were questioned, challenged, and further probed, which, as shown below, brought out more complex, and even contradictory stories compared to their initial responses.

Aligning with nationalist discourses: a reproduction of 'national habitus'

This section looks into students' initial responses towards certain nationalist discourses sampled in four different yet closely related spheres: national membership, national boundaries (Taiwan as an example), nation vis-à-vis others, and nation in relation to self. While what students said about their nation is vital for the understanding of their attitude towards the attitude object, for the purpose of this chapter, attention is also paid to how they expressed their attitudes and perceptions in terms of scale and reflectivity. By utilising 'national habitus' as an analytical framework, it will show how the seemingly positive national attitude among university students reflected in their initial responses can be interpreted as an automatic reproduction of familiar and taken-for-granted nationalist discourses culturally available to them, rather than a sign of active and self-conscious engagement with the nation as fervent nationalists would be expected to do.

The concept 'national habitus' allows us to examine similarities and differences between countries not only in physical surroundings but also in people's behaviour (Kuipers 2013). By drawing on the notions of habitus, habitudes and habits, and with the examples drawn from Scotland, the UK, India and Mauritius, Edensor (2002) has shown how instilled common sense knowledge – 'rarely the subject of any reflection' – has or can become part of 'a national habitus', which is embedded in things that people usually take for granted and is assumed to be shared by our co-nationals. He notes:

> These are the forms of bodily lexis and social interaction, often criss-crossed with class, gender, ethnicity and age, which are closest to Bourdieu's notion of habits as practical, embodied knowledge.
>
> (Edensor 2002: 94)

Following this, and since nations exist in people's understandings with both universality and particularity,[6] it is not too far off line to say that each nation can build up its own 'national habitus' alongside the universal one. Indeed, Elias argues that a 'national habitus', embedded in institutionalised political collectives, is what sets nations apart (Cf. Kuzmics and Axtmann 2007). Such a national habitus, according to Edensor,

> ...becomes clear when we move to another country and are dumbfounded by the range of everyday competencies which we do not possess, where we come across a culture full of people who do not do things they way we do them, who draw on different practical resources to accomplish everyday tasks.... The effect can be similar when we meet visitors from other nations and try to explain how to accomplish missions when such explanation has rarely been required before. We might struggle for terms to explain the 'obvious', for this is a non-discursive form of popular understanding that we 'just know'.
>
> (Edensor 2002: 93)

It goes without saying that just what the 'national habitus' in a given nation is depends on the national and cultural context in which it operates. Therefore, expressions of certain nationalist discourses may appear to be signs of fervent nationalism only to be embraced by committed nationalists in some nations, but may well have been taken for granted as self-evident national habits, and reproduced without reflection, by uncommitted national members in other nations. As Kuipers notes:

> Habitus is congealed history, absorbed into our bodies – our personal history, which in turn, has been shaped by the history of the society of

which we are part. This larger history determines the ground-tone of our individual history. Thus, our 'self', our self-evident, automatic, yet learned behaviour, is partly determined by the country where we have grown up.

(Kuipers 2012: 20)

Therefore, if 'the category of the nation is taken for granted as a background assumption about the world' (Perkins 2010: 390) as a whole, so can nationalists' discourse of a given nation be taken for granted as a background assumption about the specific nation. To make this argument work, there has to be evidence of taken-for-grantedness of nationalist discourses that students showed their alignment with. This means such discourses are expected to be known and shared by, and indeed, self-evident for, most of the students, if not all. In other words, they have become national habitual thinking within China's national context.

National membership

The defining of national membership – ways of arguing who and who does not belong to the nation – is always an ongoing process (Edensor 2002). Yet, such a process has been often neglected, where common sense assumptions about a given nation are widely shared not only among ordinary people, but also in academic work, even that of 'much ostensibly constructivist academic writing' (Brubaker 2004: 9). In the case of this research, when asked about the Chinese national membership, interviewees were given six options by the researcher: A. The Han people; B. The 56 ethnicities; C. Anyone who loves China; D. Anyone who has a Chinese passport; E. the CCP; and F. Other (with space left for the students to provide their own ideas). With the exception of a few students, who responded with D, E and F, the majority of students responded in a rather uniform and categorically bounded pattern coalesced around the first three choices, which I have re-termed as: the descendents-of-the dragon legend, the 56-ethnic-group-imagination and the anyone-who-loves-China mentality. And although most of the respondents made multiple selections, choice B, 'the 56 ethnicities', appeared to be an indispensable constituent part of the Chinese nation for the majority of students as over 80 per cent of them, including those who also ticked other choices, chose this option as the, or one of the, key constitute parts of the Chinese nation.

Alongside the 56 ethnicities, students also indicated other constituent parts of the Chinese nation, of which 'Han-people' and 'anyone-who-loves-China' stood out as significant. To clarify, although almost half of the respondents ticked 'Han people', a lot (57) of them also included other components in the making of the Chinese nation. Counted separately, only 14 respondents out of 154 made a sole choice of the 'Han people'. On the other hand, by choosing '56 ethnicities', which the majority of respondents did, would automatically have the Han people included. From this, it appears that the pure blood based criteria based on Han people, apparently the descendents of the dragon or the Yellow Emperor, does not resonate widely among students in contemporary China. Indeed, when asked 'What is the most important factor to being Chinese?' more than half of the students suggested the most important factor to being Chinese is to love China.

These relatively uniform and categorically bonded understandings of the nation in terms of membership, shown in the questionnaire, were also apparent among the interview respondents when they were asked the same question but without the provision of categorical answers like those included in the questionnaire. For example, most of the interviewees responded without hesitation about the nation being one big family that constitutes 56 different ethnicities. Although in relatively small numbers (nine out of 52), some of them also talked about the racial/blood based element in defining the nation, which echoes the descendents-of-the dragon legend shown by the questionnaire respondents. They believe blood is the sole criteria to judge whether one is Chinese or not. They hold that people with Chinese blood always remain Chinese even if they emigrate to other countries and give up their Chinese nationality. Just like the Chinese pandas that end up in foreign zoos, these people will remain Chinese for the rest of their lives. Conversely, they believe people with different race or blood, even if they are granted a Chinese passport, will never be true Chinese. Naturally, the notion of Chinese self held by these students extends to include all people with Chinese blood running through their bodies, in every corner of the globe. In contrast to these students, over half of the interview respondents expressed the anyone-who-loves-China mentality and said any others who have a sense of love for China can be included as Chinese, rather than 'the Chinese' – restricted to blood, ethnicity or any other indigenous features. Not only did the interview respondents come up with similar discourses about the Chinese nation, but they also impressed the researcher with the way they talked about the nation: so straightforward, certain and smooth.

The Taiwan issue

Similarly, with regard to the problematic Taiwan issue, students also gave uniform and widely shared responses. Both questionnaire and interview data show that students' responses towards the Taiwan issue largely overlap with the usual Chinese orthodox stance advocated by the regime. When asked for their views on the Taiwan issue, a majority of students strongly expressed the belief that Taiwan should always be part of China or the Chinese nation, and that other countries have no rights to interfere with China's internal and sovereignty issues, a typical diplomatic stance the CCP central government maintains.

In a country where national unity has been given a high profile by the government, and since, as a myth and ideal, it[7] 'still holds enormous appeal' (He and Guo 2000: 33), this outcome was expected. As a matter of fact, according to He and Guo:

> Even those who do not subscribe to the idea of national unity often feel compelled to refrain from voicing opinions in favour of taboo subjects such

as ethnic separatists or Taiwan independence. This partially explains why the majority of people you talk to in China are more likely to agree with their government on such issues as Taiwan and Tibet. Even among political dissidents, including some in exile, few take exception to the CCP's position on territorial disputes, even though they might condemn it for its human rights abuses.

(He and Guo 2000: 33)

Similarly, Weiss (2008) writes that there is widespread and pervasive belief in mainland China that Taiwan is an inseparable part of China, and that the CCP government could be overthrown if Taiwan were allowed to become independent. Nevertheless, this widely shared belief in national place seems to suggest that 'nations stop and start abruptly at demarcated borders' (Billig 1995: 74), but Billig (ibid.) also points out that 'the unity of the national territory has to be imagined rather than directly apprehended'. So the question is how is this comprehension of national territory similar or different to their 'imagination' of national community? To fully understand their attitude and resultant action towards the Taiwan issue, there is also a need to explore their views and feelings about people who live in this territory. Would they regard any citizen who lives there as Chinese including, say, someone with a different racial background who was born there and has been living there their whole life? Students' responses to these questions will be presented later; at this point, what I would like to highlight is the assertive tone students used when they talked about the issue. For example, one male Year 2 engineering student expressed sternly: 'Taiwan is part of China. There is no doubt about it'. Similarly another student said: 'It is an undeniable fact that Taiwan belongs to China'. Another student claimed 'Taiwan belongs to China. That's the end of the story'.

Nation vis-à-via others

Apart from the alignment with basic nationalists' ideas about the Chinese nation in terms of boundary making, further evidence of such alignment is also apparent in students' responses to China's position in the world shown in both the self-completion questionnaire and the in-depth interviewing. For example, when asked to choose their level of agreement to the statement that 'China is now one of the powerful developed countries', over half of the respondents chose to disagree with this view, while about 23 per cent of the respondents were not sure, leaving about one quarter of the respondents choosing to agree with this view. Similar to the questionnaire respondents, the majority of the interview respondents from the two chosen elite universities also rejected the idea that China has risen, or that China has developed itself to be categorised as a developed country. A common response from the students was: *'Cha yuan le!'* meaning China still has a long way to go. They feel China cannot yet be considered as a developed and powerful country when compared with major developed Western countries. Problems listed by students include: the economy in terms of per capital GDP;

too few world-class companies; the gap between rich and poor; lagging behind in the fields of science, technology and academia; military inferiority; and a lack of cultural influence.

Such lines are not unfamiliar within China's national context. Indeed, as an article states in one of China's well-known newspapers, the country has been fighting to maintain its developing country status (Khor 2011). From time to time, especially at times of external pressure for China to act more responsibly and fulfil its international obligations as a developed nation, it is not hard to find – from the country's top political leaders to well-known newspaper headlines – the justifications for China being labelled a developing nation. Alongside the Chinese government's open and repeated stress on the status, this message has also been expressed through other media sources. In a 2010 article from Xinhua, the official press agency of the PRC, just before the forthcoming UN summit on the Millennium Development Goals, 'Is China still a developing nation?', the editor presented voices from different sources to argue for China's developing nation status based on China's per capital GDP and the gap between the country and other developed countries in domains such as social security, health service, public education and world-class brand (Xinhua 2010). Similarly, in the 2011 newspaper article 'China still a developing nation', the editor provided a variety of statistical evidence to argue that 'despite the world media giving it a mighty image, China looks like a very ordinary developing country in terms of per capita indicators'. It states that

> being 92nd in terms of per capita GDP, 101st in HDI and 84th in terms of per capita emission, China is a middle-level or even lower-middle-level developing country, with not only all the developed countries, but also many developing countries ahead of it.
>
> (Xinhua 2011)

Students' responses clearly reflected the discourse of China being a developing nation.

Whether China is a developing or developed nation, as well as the beneficial gains from either status, is an ongoing debate and is not the concern of this study at this point, but what does need to be stressed here is the high proportion of students who share such thoughts. Even the problems they listed are the 'evidence' used by the government and news articles in justifying China's developing-nation status.

However, what contradicts this predominant view is their response to the next question. When asked whether or not China has been well recognised and respected by the world, less than a third of the respondents thought so, while more than half of the respondents believed China's international status does not match its 'big' country image and it deserves a better place on the international stage, a familiar tone articulated by Chinese nationalists. Similarly and paradoxically, while only about 20 per cent of the respondents believed that China has done a great job in dealing with major developed countries, a large number of respondents (72.7 per cent) held the belief that some major powerful countries have the intention of preventing China from prospering and gaining its rightful place at the top of the world system. Such widely shared views are also evident among most of the interview respondents. According to these students, actions taken by different nation-states in international society have their own national purpose, and that purpose is to serve their own national interest. As one female Year 4 student (who was preparing for postgraduate examinations at the time of my fieldwork) expressed:

> The ones without shoes are not scared of those with shoes, but those with shoes are scared of those without shoes. The US now is the one with shoes and China is the one without shoes. The more developed countries such as the US are scared of seeing China rise. They are worried that China will replace them one day and become one of the world's leading countries in the future so they have every purpose and intention to prevent China from developing itself.

Even those respondents who were not sure about foreign intentions towards China's rise believe there is some sort of purpose behind foreign countries' interference in China-related issues. For example, regarding foreign countries' criticism about China's human rights, a male Year 3 student said: 'They are bringing this up from time to time not because they really care about Chinese people's human rights but because they want to make China look bad and make themselves look good'. Similarly, another respondent made the following remark with reference to the Nobel Peace prize winner Liu Xiaobo[8]: 'I don't feel the West truly supports peace. I think they are using Liu Xiaobo purposely to play up China's human rights issue and embarrass China'. When asked why he thought this, the respondent replied: 'Because it is in their interest, and makes their country look better in the international arena, while making China look bad'.

It appears that Chinese nationalists' claim that China deserves a better place in international society has found corresponding resonance here. On the one hand, the students do not think their country has the capacity yet that developed countries have, but on the other hand, they seem to demand an equal footing with world major powers. This is perhaps a good reflection of what scholars such as Levine (1994) and Suzuki (2007) called 'a deep sense of "victimhood"' that the Chinese nationalists suffer from.

These responses have given us a general idea as to how students see their country in the world of nation-states, and preliminary references about their world views relating to China, which are, of course, of great importance for the understanding of their national attitudes in general; however, it would exceed the present purpose of this section to dwell too much on them. What is important to consider here is students' capability to articulate thoughts about their nation in national terms, and against the 'Others' within the contours of nationalist discourses. Not only did students demonstrate their familiarity with nationalist discourses but also aligned and reproduced them in relatively uniform and categorically bounded ways. While it can be argued that 'Uniform and categorically bounded views are in part an artifact of research instruments that implicitly or explicitly provide their respondents with uniform and categorically bounded questions' (Fox 2004: 378–379), it is still worthwhile noting the fact that more than half of the respondents aligned with such nationalist discourses, while they could have chosen to disagree or stayed neutral to such nationalist discourses.

Self and the nation

Alongside the widely shared and straightforward defining of national membership, the assertive stance on the Taiwan issue, and the capable articulation of the nation against Others within the contours of nationalist discourse, students also showed a positive national attitude featured by a strong sense of national identity, attachment and commitment to the Chinese nation. This can be seen by their responses to certain issues such as their feelings and attachment towards their country and their country fellows. By indicating their level of agreement in the questionnaire, the majority of the students expressed that they have particular feelings towards their country and that they are emotionally attached to it, feeling proud of their country's development and ashamed when their country fellows do something bad such as the milk powder scandal. At the same time, more than half of them indicated that if they could help people who are in need, their country fellows will always come first, and that if they have to choose where to live, they will always choose to live in China. Apart from the emotional attachment, more than half of the students also indicated that their own personal goals are closely related to the development of their country, while more than two-thirds of the students believe China's improving status and prestige in international society increases their level of self-esteem. More strikingly, when asked to indicate their level of agreement to the statement 'Being Chinese, I feel it is my duty to assist my country', the majority of the respondents (85.7 per cent) felt they have a duty to their country while only a fraction of them were not sure or did not think so. Corresponding to this morally felt duty, more than half of them claim they often ask themselves what they can do for their country by choosing 'Agree' or 'Agree strongly' in response to the statement 'I often ask myself what I can do for my country'.

Taken alone, such a positive national attitude, characterised by a strong sense of national identity, attachment and commitment to the Chinese nation, makes them appear to be fervent nationalists who regard the nation as an important aspect of their life. Indeed, looking back at how university students have been portrayed, it also seems to mimic well those survey studies of university students' moral and political attitudes conducted by the Chinese researchers, as well as those interpretations of university students being the vanguard of Chinese nationalism. Given that these respondents were born in the years between the late 1980s and early 1990s and went to school at a time when the government's patriotic education campaign was at its height, and when patriotic rhetoric has become a taken-for-granted attitude throughout the whole nation, it is tempting to place this seemingly fervent nationalistic outlook in the broad national context and naturally assume a direct causal link, hence the naturalness of such a fervent nationalistic outlook. Taken at face value, this finding also forms a strong contrast with what Fenton (2007) found about young British people's indifferent and hostile attitudes towards national identity in general and towards British and English identities in particular.

However, bearing in mind the concept of 'national habitus', and taking into account the contradictory responses students gave in responding to other questions included in the same questionnaire, and when further probed (particularly when questions associated with the nation were asked in connection with students' own practical lives, which will be presented later), it is probably premature to draw a conclusion at face value at this stage, because it may give us a false impression of overwhelming national commitment. As Fox has argued, 'A surfeit of nationalist rhetoric and imagery risks exaggerating the degree to which nationalism is actively engaged and negotiated by ordinary people.' (Fox 2004: 365)

Therefore, rather than coming to a conclusion of intensely nationalistic students packed with active engagement and commitment to the Chinese nation, in what follows, I want to show how the seemingly positive national attitude among university students presented above can be interpreted as an automatic reproduction of familiar and taken-for-granted nationalist discourses culturally available to them.

To do this, I look into the objective evidence of the high proportion of respondents sharing the same knowledge shown in both the questionnaire and interview data, and the more or less subjective judgement on the way they responded to questions about nation and nationalism in the interviewing setting. Therefore, looking back what has been presented in this section, when a high proportion of respondents automatically ticked the same nationalist-statement box, it was considered the data is proving part of the evidence required here. In this regard, there is no lack of evidence. Most evidently, this can be seen through questionnaire respondents' responses to nationalist discourses provided by the researcher. Not only did the questionnaire respondents provide relatively categorical and uniform responses, but also with high percentages, suggesting their familiarity and alignment with nationalist discourses, as most of the nationalist discourses (even some controversial ones) attracted more than 50 per cent of the respondents to align with them. What is more, such evidence is also apparent among the interview respondents who also expressed their familiarity and alignment with, as well as their capacity to reproduce, nationalist discourse not being provided by the researcher. Combined together, such evidence of a large proportion of respondents sharing the same attitude towards issues associated with the nation is self-evident of students' taken-for-grantedness of nationalist discourses.

Further evidence of this taken-for-grantedness can also be observed from the way respondents reacted to the issue in question. If there is a lack of understanding of the context in which respondents express their views in a questionnaire setting (Creswell and Clark 2007), it is observable in the interview setting, where respondents' facial expressions and body language are seen by the researcher when they express their views, and are tellingly important. For example, when they talked about the Chinese national membership, they talked about it in such a straightforward and automatic way, with no hesitation, as if the nation is an unambiguous and unquestionable entity. Some of them even threw me an odd look as I, as one of their co-nationals, was mad to ask them such a blatantly obvious question. Similarly, their assertive responses to the Taiwan issue were accompanied by their silent rhetorical question 'Do you, as a Chinese person, need to ask such a question?' Of course, Taiwan belongs to China. Such reaction, on the one hand, showed their familiarity with and certainty of the issues in question; on the other hand, they also suggested respondents' expectation of the researcher, who they assumed to be Chinese (without actually asking), to share such obvious knowledge, as none of the respondents made the effort to explain the issues in question in detail or depth.

Do not such responses and reactions reflect the idea of 'national habitus' that can be instilled and become taken-for-granted, as discussed earlier? Taking their talking about the Chinese nation in terms of membership as an example, whether it is the 56 ethnic-group-imagination or the descendents of the Emperor legend, they are explicitly in line with the usual nationalist discourses of China, the nation, the state, the nation-state, or what Martin Jacques (2009) calls the 'civilisation-state'. Even the 'anyone-who-loves-China' mentality can be traced back to the Confucian thinking of the middle kingdom, and is still popular among cultural nationalists in China. In other words, these seemingly different interpretations of the Chinese nation are easily accessible information within China's national context as, one way or another, the Chinese nation has been predominantly discoursed in such spheres at various times and under different situations. Being born and having grown up in such a national context within which students' primary and secondary socialisation take place, it can be argued, such nationalist discourses of the nation were probably long ago instilled in them. A similar thing can be said about their assertive responses to the Taiwan issue. Obviously, whether or not Taiwan is part of China remains to be debated, yet, with such a high percentage of students resonating with the official standpoint on the issue, it becomes less important whether or not Taiwan is actually part of China. The bottom line here is that the whole discourse of the Taiwan issue has become perceived as natural and objective. Even their emotional attachment and morally felt duties to the nation, when considered alongside the national background as well as students' involvement in the making of the Chinese nation briefly introduced at the beginning of the chapter, are evident of automatic reproduction of national habitus – a habitus of loving and being committing to our nation – as that is what we do in the nation. As mentioned earlier, students, including those participating in the 1989 pre-democracy movement, generally believe they should be 'the embodiment of Chinese patriotism and in the forefront of promoting China's national strength and dignity' (Sullivan 1994: 457).

Therefore, although the nation was explicitly made the subject of enquiry, due to the naturalisation and taken-for-grantedness, students were unthinkingly responding to the questions posed to them in an almost automatic fashion, without much individual and critical thought. This is what Sewell (1992: 22) describes as the 'taken-for-granted mental assumptions', that 'actors normally apply without being aware that they are applying them'. The lack of reflection in respondents' reactions suggest they not only naturalise the ideology of nation in general, but also take for granted the usual ways of imagining and constructing their own nation in particular, within the contours of nationalist discourses.

If the earlier evidence – the objective evidence of a high proportion of respondents sharing the same assumption shown in both the questionnaire and interview data, and the more or less subjective judgement on the way they responded to questions about their nation in the interview setting – are not sufficient enough to support the argument made in this section, students' responses to other questions and further probing into their responses, which will be presented below, clearly suggest this is so.

Probing into 'national habitus': uncertainty, scepticism and complexity

Students' 'taken-for-granted mental assumptions' about nation in general and the Chinese nation in particular, as presented above, do not mean they are uncritical or maintain only simple views about nation and nationalism. By examining the contradictory responses and reactions students gave to different questions included in the same questionnaire and through the researcher's further probing in interview, in what follows, I show that behind the taken-for-grantedness of the usual nationalist discourses of the nation, there are also complex stories about how university students view and articulate nation and nationalism.

Uncertainty, ambiguity and contradiction

In contrast to the straightforward, smooth and simplified alignment with nationalist discourses, as presented earlier, when explored further it became clear that embedded in students there was also uncertainty, ambiguity and contradiction about the nation. Take, for example, the popular mentality shared by a majority of students to include other 'non-Chinese' ethnicities who have a sense of love for China in the big Chinese family: when challenged with questions, such as what is this love, and does it mean that anyone, particularly those amongst the ethnic Chinese within China who do not love China, can be regarded as non-Chinese, many of the respondents became lost and confused in what they were talking about. Although they spoke of this sense of love for China as meaning love and respect for Chinese culture and its people, doing good things for China, making contributions to China's development, or at least not doing anything bad for China and its development, when they were asked about Chinese people who were perceived as *hanjian* (traitors), or about Chinese political dissidents such as

Liu Xiaobo, or about *laowai* (non-Chinese ethnic foreigners) who are said to have love for China and have lived and worked there for a long time, such as Da Shan (a well-known Canadian in the Chinese media who works as a freelance performer in China), many respondents were not certain at all whether to include them or exclude them from the Chinese nation. There were hesitation and frowns on their faces.

Even those students who sternly defined the Chinese nation in terms of blood, when questioned, began to fluctuate. For example, when I asked them what about the minority ethnic Chinese, after a short pause, they defended their initial response: they all indicated that the minority ethnic Chinese are not really Chinese. As a year one male student majoring in Linguistics put it: 'Well, strictly speaking, they [minority ethnic Chinese] are not real Chinese. They are here today as a result of territory expansion from ancient China'. Interestingly, when I asked him 'So, you don't think Chen Luyu[9] is really Chinese?' he was rather bewildered by my question, and was very surprised when I told him that she is from the Hui minority. Tellingly, this student had never had any doubt that this TV presenter was a real Chinese. Similarly, despite their 'talk' about the nation being 56 ethnicities, or their assertive stand on the Taiwan issue, when challenged with questions such as what exactly do the 56 ethnicities refer to, for example, whether they are constrained to the Chinese living within the borders of China or include Chinese people located all over the world; or in the latter case, whether they would regard any citizen who lives in the territory as Chinese including, say, someone with a white racial background who was born in Taiwan and has always lived there, students showed a lot of uncertainty. This can be seen from their hesitant responses to the researcher – many comments like, 'er…, yeah, it should be … but I am not sure', 'hmm, this is the question', and 'oh, I've never really thought about it'.

Accompanying this uncertainty, when delving deeper, there was also ambiguity and contradiction in students' talk about their nation. For example, their initial 'talk' about the 56 ethnicities being equal brothers and sisters, and their inclusion of anyone-who-loves China into the big Chinese nation seem to suggest the nation has greatly transcended ethnic and racial divisions among students, yet more questioning revealed this was not the case. When asked about their thoughts on the 'special beneficial policies' that minority groups enjoy under Chinese law, such as exemption from the one-child policy, easier access to higher education, and more favourable tax laws, most of the Han students expressed their support by reasoning that the strong should be assisting the weak. Such responses not only break down students' claims that all 56 ethnic groups are equal, but also revealed a hierarchical view towards the minority groups. Indeed, a few students openly expressed a perceived 'backwardness' of minorities, or as one female student put it: 'they are remote and impoverished'. Nonetheless, by suggesting minorities are weak and in need of help, students were also implying the strength and domination of the majority Han group. Surely there are marginalised weak Han people who need help and special beneficial policies too, but such concerns do not seem to have occurred to the respondents.

According to Jacques (2009: 266), there is generally 'a lack of recognition of other ethnicities, which are seen as subordinate, inferior, and not deserving of equal respect', among the Hans.

Similarly, alongside their inclusion of *laowai* (non-ethnic Chinese) into the Chinese nation, when probed, students also implied their discomfort when imagining non-ethnic Chinese as Chinese, especially those of a different skin colour. One female Year 2 student majoring in Management in Beijing expressed the opinion:

> I think race is an important factor in the making of Chinese self. Although, in theory, I have no problems with foreigners becoming Chinese; in reality, I'd be lying to say I don't feel uncomfortable when a white or black person is introduced to me as a Chinese. You cannot stop thinking about the differences, as their appearance is so different from Chinese. So I think it is easier to accept people like the Koreans and the Japanese as Chinese. This doesn't mean that I am against white and black people. I have no problem socialising with these people. So long as we can comment and get on with each other, factors like nationalist and race do not matter.

Similar feelings were also expressed by some other students who come from both urban and rural backgrounds. They contend that they can accept the idea of integrating people from other racial backgrounds into the big Chinese family, just like some Western countries have included people with different racial backgrounds into their nationality; yet, they concede it would feel different and strange. Here, while expressing politically correct and multicultural Western ideas about including non-ethnic Chinese in their nation, students were also implying a sense of special, unique feelings that they maintain about their nation and their national members. Skin-colour defined race appeared to be one such feeling. A sense of discomfort when people of a different colour skin were said to be Chinese suggests that the Chinese nation really constitutes only people who were born with yellow skin, dark eyes and black hair, and that, although we can accept you in our home, you can never be part of our family. So the willingness to bring 'outsiders' in does not necessarily lead to the breaking down of cultural and racial barriers.

In summary, all this uncertainty, ambiguity and contradiction further suggests that when students talked about the Chinese nation in the first instance, as presented earlier, they did not really think it through, but, as argued in the previous section, were reproducing the usual nationalist discourses about their nation that they are so familiar with and have taken for granted. And because of the familiarity, they were unselfconsciously pouring out the information stored within them rather than displaying thoughtful engagement.

Scepticism, disdain and much more

While the pro-China street demonstrations and nationalistic publications that have appeared since the 1990s have been taken by many as a sign of rising nationalism in contemporary China, China's future elites had their own thoughts regarding such phenomena. Alongside the usual reproduction of standard lines such as 'a way of defending national sovereignty and dignity', 'a way of showing national solidarity to the outside world', 'a way of attaining and maintaining justice' and regarding them as 'patriotic actions which any Chinese should join in', students also expressed sceptical and even disdainful views about such nationalism-in-action for a variety of reasons. For example, one student noted:

> I support all kinds of demonstrations but I won't take part in any of them. Patriotism is good in itself, but it can be used as peace-harming militarism, and will then be very harmful.

The implications hinted at by this sceptical student were addressed more directly by another student:

> I support demonstrations to defend China but I don't take part in them because the government selects which are allowed and which are not, so they are used by the government to express its voice.

Tellingly, both students were actually supportive of patriotism and demonstration to defend their country but sceptical of being used by the state and government. In fact, the second student was sure of the Chinese government's involvement in these demonstrations and that was what put him off taking part in demonstrations. This view was also expressed by another student who described these demonstrations as 'ridiculous' as 'they were controlled and selectively permitted by the government'. Similarly, another student said:

> Demonstrations are a tool for the state. The media is a political tool. If there is time, more attention should be paid to China's own political, economic and social structures. You should not have a rich state but poor people.

Not only were there sceptical thoughts regarding demonstrations and media, implied here were also dissatisfaction with China's political, economic and social structures, and criticism of the '*guo fu min pin*' (rich state but poor people) situation.

Unlike these students, whose sceptical thoughts pointed to the state and government, another female student directed her scepticism at the Chinese people:

> I don't have anything to say regarding what other people do but I won't take part in anything like this or do anything for safety reasons as I don't love my country that much.... In addition, the so-called rising nationalism in contemporary China, in my opinion, is in some people merely anti-Japanese or anti-South Korean feelings, while at the same time they are deeply in love with Japanese cartoons and South Korean film stars ... I feel the Chinese people are becoming more and more narrow-minded and sensitive.

Similarly, another student remarked,

> I believe the initial thoughts behind some demonstrations are good but I am not sure about the way some demonstrations are carried out. Many people join in not because they have sufficient background knowledge about demonstrations but merely because they are stirred up by a nationalistic atmosphere, which sometimes leads to ugly violent scenes.

Alongside these sceptics are those students who openly expressed their disapproval, even disdain, towards such demonstrations for different reasons. Some of them objected to these demonstrations for pragmatic reasons; they simply saw such demonstrations as 'useless'. For example, one Year 3 male student majoring in car engineering commented: 'I don't understand why people do these things [street demonstrations]. To me, such actions are meaningless with no real effect whatsoever'. Another student majoring in Chinese language and literature described the demonstrations as 'angry youth action – another symptom of self-abasement, and of no real significance'. Similar views are also apparent among the respondents who filled in the questionnaire. They suggested in different ways that demonstrations that have occurred in recent years were a waste of time and could not solve any real problem. Some of them even viewed the demonstrations as 'a signal of discomposure from within, and having no real meaning to them'. One student commented:

> To me, such demonstrations are nothing more than impulsive populism, radical, and not very sensible. If these people really love China, they should know the first task for China now is to calmly work on developing the economy rather than running to the streets and carrying out demonstrations that have no effect whatsoever.

Another student made this point even more explicitly:

> I don't know what those national fellows were thinking – as soon as they heard something, they rush to the street to protest, behaving crazily – why can't they do something more useful for our country? I think if one can do whatever one is supposed to do, that is the best thing we can do for our country.

Embedded in the last two students' comments there was not only disapproval of the demonstrations and pragmatic thinking, but also a challenge questioning the demonstrators' real love for China and a proposal of their own sense of love for China and understanding of nationalism, as well as how such love should be put into practice. In other words, they were not merely criticising; they were also proposing a competing vision of nationalistic or patriotic thoughts and deeds for China. One female student openly remarked: 'These are not true patriotic demonstrations. These people need to know China and themselves better'. Another male Year 3 students noted in the questionnaire:

> Nationalism is important for a nation but it has to be appropriate. Otherwise it becomes a double-edged sword that could constrain the nation. So we should be more open-minded about certain criticisms and let nationalism work as an important political motivation for greater objectives.

Similarly, a third male student majoring in Medical Science expressed it thus:

> There is no single country in the world that can become the world overlord overnight, especially when it has only just managed to get itself a begging bowl. If these people really have time and energy, why don't they just say less and do more ... do more useful things.

In this regard, some other students also expressed the view that the best way to love one's country is to do one's job well. They maintain one's love for one's nation or country does not have to be carried out at full volume, that is, via loud speeches and fervent nationalistic writings. As students, they believe all they should do is to work hard and learn as much as they can, so that they can contribute to the building of their country in the future. In the current peaceful internal and external atmosphere, even occasional demonstrations against activities carried out by foreign countries are not an attraction for these students. Many students in this category generally believe that demonstrations against foreign countries may have some spiritual merits, but they fail to solve problems and usually end up being a waste of time. Hence they feel their time and energy would be better spent on realistic works to aid in the development of China.

While such lines sounded convincing, taking into account the cultural norm of being Chinese, as Davies (2007)[10] has discussed (that is, being Chinese means being responsible for the Chinese nation), and the belief of being 'the embodiment of Chinese patriotism and in the forefront of promoting China's national strength and dignity' that China's young people, especially those from elite universities, are supposed to hold (Sullivan, 1994: 457), this argument of what is the best way to love and serve China should be treated with caution. Indeed, such arguing over what is the best for China in the name of patriotism/nationalism is a common nationalist rhetoric in China, and has appeared before. For example, with reference to the 1989 Tiananmen students protest, Zhao notes:

> It was ironic that pro-democracy demonstrators in Tiananmen Square, while confronting the government, claimed that patriotism drove them to take to the streets in the Spring of 1989. Most people who were involved in the demonstration, both the students and their supporters, also equated promoting democracy with patriotism. Urging the government to stop corruption, to protect citizens' rights and to start political reform was considered a most patriotic action.
> (Zhao 1998: 289)

Similarly, when Chinese intellectuals criticised Chinese history and tradition, they were speaking of what they thought was the best for China. As Zhao (1997:

526) remarks, 'their [intellectuals] critique or even cynical treatment of their own past was one way of yearning for the re-creation of China's national greatness'. In the case of this study, students' thinking of implicit national action to do one's job well, and hence contribute to the development of China, if genuine, has more profound meaning for China and its future, and implies that these students seriously care about what is best for China. However, it can also be argued that students who gave such views are merely interested in developing themselves, but because there is pressure to be patriotic in the wider national context, they have to run with the crowd to achieve their own personal dreams, but under the guise of serving their country. Or it could be the case, that 'in the presence of someone [the researcher] they perceive as an insider, respondents may feel disproportionately encouraged to provide answers consistent with dominant thinking within the group' (Hodkinson 2005: 140). So, anything they say and do is decorated in the colour of patriotism/nationalism. As Swidler notes, when individuals come to act in culturally informed ways, it is not necessarily because their values are shared, but because 'they must negotiate the same institutional hurdles' (Swidler 1995: 36).

In whichever case – either embracing such nationalist discourse on one's own initiative or feeling pressured to accept it – it is clear that the majority of the students appeared to acknowledge the cultural norm of the nationalist moral order for being Chinese, or even, at least on the surface, espouse the cultural norm, and believe as members of the Chinese nation, they should take the nation as an important category in their lives. In reality, their thoughts may not be followed up with relevant actions, as even for those students who expressed a supportive attitude towards pro-China demonstrations, there were different and more complex stories behind their support. For example, one student indicated in an interview that she was fully supportive of all kinds of what she perceived to be patriotic demonstrations that have taken place in recent times, but when asked whether she would stand up and do something similar for her country, she replied: 'No'. When asked why, she said, 'My parents will not allow me to do so'. At other times, students who expressed a supportive attitude also indicated why they would not follow up for different reasons such as 'I don't have the right kind of personality', 'I am a low key person', 'I am not that kind of person', and 'It may not be legal'. This suggests, as studies carried out by LaPiere (1934) and others have shown, attitudes do not necessarily lead to corresponding behaviours. But these results would not have been brought to light if no further probing had been carried out. So if LaPiere had further looked into those 'No' replies by 92 per cent of his respondents, he probably would have found that some of the 'No' replies are not exclusively defined. They might be given, as in the case of this study, unreflectively, as a result of the national context at the time, in which the Chinese race was negatively received by the Americans.

Nonetheless, others objected to the idea of demonstrations because they believed actions like this do more harm than good to China. One Year 2 female student in the law department said: 'such actions are chaotic and if managed badly can destabilize society, and cause more trouble'. Another Year 2 female student said: 'I think these kinds of demonstrations are neither beneficial to resolve issues nor good for the image of China that is held by other countries. I think they make Chinese people appear irrational'. A third male student wrote in the questionnaire: 'Demonstrations like these make it worse for the public to know what is going on. It is not good for the resolution of the issues at stake'. Still others held a disdainful attitude and commented on the demonstrations with a very negative tone, either describing them as 'radical', 'very stupid', 'very naïve actions', 'tomfoolery', 'not sensible and inadvisable', or targeted to 'instigate people who have no background knowledge' and conceived as 'inappropriate actions taking place at the wrong time'.

While we have seen abundant reasons why students would and would not stand up and speak out for their country through the discussion of their attitudes towards previous demonstrations, the category of students who when asked about their future action answered 'It depends' needs some elaboration here. Overall, these students are relatively more reflexive on such issues. To start with, they viewed different demonstrations taking place in recent times separately. Depending on how they view the background of each demonstration and how demonstrations were carried out each time, their views swing back and forth between being supportive and disapproval. For example, regarding the 1999 US bombing of the Chinese Embassy in Belgrade, the majority of the respondents who knew about this event and the follow-up demonstrations showed their firm support for these demonstrations, while indicating their disapproval regarding the 2008 boycott of French products and the supermarket chain Carrefour. In this respect, demonstrations that took place at different times for different reasons have been given different meanings by these students. It is clear that the 1999 demonstrations are seen as a fight for justice against hegemony and necessary defence of China's sovereignty, while the 2008 boycott of French products is seen as radical angry youths' actions that not only damaged China's international image but also harmed the lives of Chinese people. As for the worldwide demonstrations against the Western media's reportage back in 2008, again, a lot of students held a sceptical attitude, while some openly showed their disapproval, as they believe any media has the rights to report what they think is the truth, and Chinese people should not have been so sensitive about the remarks made about their country. As one student stated:

> Nationalism shouldn't become chauvinism. Loving a country does not equal loving its government. When viewing foreign countries we should treat their governments and their people in a separate way because the two notions [government and state] in foreign countries are not as closely bound together as they are in China.

While there are a number of students who firmly support different demonstrations against Japan, others believe issues (such as the Japanese history textbooks, its bid to join in the Security Council of the UN, as well as its territorial dispute with China regarding the Diaoyu Islands) that have provoked all kinds of demonstrations should be left to the government to resolve.

It is also worth mentioning here that even for those students who indicated a possibility of standing up to demonstrate for their country if a China-related conflict such as the 1999 bombing of the Chinese embassy happens again, when asked whether they would have a clear objective that they wished to strive for by demonstrating, many of students shrugged and suggested it would be a way of expressing their anger, which sounded more like an emotional reaction towards the conflict itself rather than anything 'anti-foreign' as portrayed in the literature.

While the reportedly bestselling nationalistic books – such as *China Can Say 'No'* and *China is Unhappy* – have been said to represent nationwide feelings and have gained popularity specially amongst young people in China, which has been referred to as evidence of China's rising nationalism, they do not seem to have attracted as many of China's future elites as one would have expected. More than a third of students from two of China's elite universities had not even read them, not to mention giving their support to the advocated key themes in the books.

Without doubt, there were students in the group who side with 'China's leading nationalist' Wang Xiaodong and his radical thoughts regarding China's future actions towards foreign countries. Taking out the 49 respondents who did not read the book, the re-calculation shows only about 12 per cent of respondents who had read the book aligned with the key themes put forward by Wang and his co-authors; while the majority of the students were not sure about, and some openly rejected, Wang's views and suggestions for China's diplomatic strategies and thought him too radical. This is even when they were not asked to be physically committed but to merely comment upon. On the contrary, they stressed peace, and were against all forms of conflict, violence and instability. As one student remarked, 'nationalism is necessary for a country, but one shouldn't be nationalistic just for that reason. One certainly should not be affected and controlled by a fervent nationalistic atmosphere'. Similarly, another student noted, 'demonstrations can work as a way of expressing our attitudes and feelings, but they shouldn't be used to stir up emotions and lead to chaos and violence'.

In short, while many have been worrying about the implications of so-called rising Chinese nationalism, in the eyes of many students in elite universities such rising nationalism is no more than 'an illusion', reflecting only 'the discomposure from within' and has little significance. In other words, the so-called rising Chinese nationalism is, in the eyes of China's future elites, 'not true enough' but filled with 'empty and unrealistic bubbles', a view coinciding well with Pye's (1993, 1996) observation of Chinese nationalism in general two decades ago, and is also very suggestive of students' own sense of nationalism.

Conclusion

By exploring university students' attitudes and perceptions towards nation and nationalism in contemporary China, this chapter has demonstrated that attitudes and perceptions can become taken for granted as a second nature embedded in people's mind and reproduced without much reflection when asked directly. Yet, when explored in a less direct way and with some probing, more complex and even contradictory stories can be revealed. Considered reversely, this finding has important implications for the study of attitude in general and attitude towards nation and nationalism in particular. To elaborate this, if attitudes and perceptions have become taken for granted and naturalised over time, it not only suggests they are deeply entrenched but also implies the lack of questioning or reflexivity. This means direct questioning of such attitudes and perceptions can only generate what Mann and Fenton (2006:10) have described in the case of nation and nationalism as 'flat, formulaic and ordinary responses'. Such data have their own value in different regards, i.e. showing the overall picture of people's attitudes towards certain attitude objects, and such taken for granted attitudes can play a role in the mobilisation of people's behaviour in reality, if not always resonating with it; yet they lack detail and depth, and more importantly, have the tendency to overexaggerate. In the case of LaPiere's study, while the data showing that 92 per cent of the respondents replied 'No' to his survey question 'Will you accept members of the Chinese race as guests in your establishment?', is informative in the regard that it reflects the overall picture of the American people's general negative attitude towards the Chinese race at that time, judging by what happened in reality, it clearly enlarged and exaggerated the picture of racial prejudice and concealed more complex stories. Of course, LaPiere could have designed his question differently, in a less direct style; yet due to the nature of the survey method, it is not easy to gain great detail and depth via this one-dimensional approach. Therefore, in order to gain a fuller and more balanced picture, it is the contention of this study to suggest a more qualitative method to probe into people's initial attitudinal responses rather than taking them for granted, and at face value.

Notes

1 Also see *China Can Still Say 'No'* (1996), and a follow-up version *China is Unhappy* (2009), written by the same authors.
2 Demonstrations such as the 1999 protests against the Belgrade bombing of the Chinese Embassy, the 2005 protests against Japan's bid for a permanent seat on the UN Security Council, and the more recent 2008 protests against the Western media's reports of China.
3 'Mao fever' (*Mao re*) refers to the reappearance of Mao souvenirs, such as Mao's 'Little Red Book' and Mao medallions, in Chinese cities in the 1990s.
4 I spent several weeks at each of the selected universities, visiting everyday early in the morning (to meet students having their breakfast) till evening (when after supper, students started their self study in public areas). A variety of venues on campus were visited at different times of a day during my visit there.
5 The quantitative method, a self-completion questionnaire survey, used in the research is quite modest – mainly for collecting data rather than analysing them in a quantitative fashion, i.e. testing for relationships. Therefore, although the whole research adopted the tenet of a mixed methods approach, it leant substantially towards a semi-structured qualitative in-depth interview method.
6 See Billig, 1995.
7 According to Fitzgerald (1995: 84), China's national identity itself is rooted in the 'historical consciousness of a unitary state'.

8 Liu Xiaobo is Chinese political dissident who was awarded the Nobel Peace prize shortly before my fieldwork commenced in October 2010.
9 Chen Luyu, a well-known television presenter in China, is from the Hui minority but has no obvious physical features of a minority people.
10 According to Davies, educated Chinese elites commonly share an attitude of 'cultural defensiveness' – a sensibility to the Confucian value of taking responsibility for their nation. This, as Davies argues, has become part of 'being Chinese' (2007).

References

Berg, L. 2007 *Qualitative Research Methods for the Social Sciences*. Boston: Pearson Education.
Berger, P.L. and Luckmann, T. 1967 *The Social Construction of Reality: A Treatise in the Sociology of Knowledge*. London: The Penguin Press.
Bernstein, R. and Munro, R. 1997 'The coming conflict with America'. *Foreign Affairs* 76 (19).
Billig, M. 1995 *Banal Nationalism*. London: Sage.
Broudehoux, A. 2004 *The Making and Selling of Post-Mao Beijing*. New York and London: Routledge.
Brubaker, R. 2004 *Ethnicity without Groups*. Cambridge, MA: Harvard University Press.
Bryman, A. 2008 *Social Research Methods*, 3rd edition. Oxford: Oxford University Press.
Carlson, A. 2009 'A flawed perspective: the limitations inherent within the study of Chinese nationalism'. *Nations and Nationalism* 15 (1) pp. 20–35.
Chang, M. 1998 'Chinese irredentist nationalism: the magician's last trick'. *Comparative Strategy*, 17 (1) pp. 83–100.
Chen, J. 1995 'The impact of reform on the party and ideology in China'. *Journal of Contemporary China* 9 pp. 22–34.
Chen, Z. 2005 'Nationalism, Internationalism and Chinese Foreign Policy'. *Journal of Contemporary China* 14 (42) pp. 35–53.
Creswell, J. and Clark, V. 2007 *Designing and Conducting Mixed Methods Research*. Thousand Oaks, London, New Delhi: Sage.
Davies, G. 2007 *Worrying about China: The Language of Chinese Critical Inquiry*. Cambridge MA: Harvard University Press.
Dikotter, F. 1996 'Culture, "Race" and Nation: The formation of national identity in twentieth century China'. *Journal of International Affairs* 49 (2).
Edensor, T. 2002 *National Identity, Popular Culture and Everyday Life*. Oxford, New York: Berg.
Fenton, S. 2007 'Indifference towards national identity: what young adults think about being English and British'. *Nations and Nationalism* 13 (2) pp. 321–339.
Fitzgerald, J. 1995 'The nationless state: the search for a nation in modern Chinese nationalism'. *The Australian Journal of Chinese Affairs*, No. 33 (January 1995), 75–104.
Forney, M. 2008 'China's loyal youth', *New York Times*. Available at www.nytimes.com. Accessed on 26 April 2008.
Fox, J. 2004 'Missing the mark: nationalist politics and student apathy'. *East European Politics and Societies* 18 pp. 363–393.
French, H. 2005 'By playing at "rage", China dramatizes its rise'. *New York Times*. Available at http://query.nytimes.com. Accessed on 11 September 2009.

Friedman, E. 1997 'Chinese nationalism, Taiwan autonomy and the prospects of a larger war'. *Journal of Contemporary China* 6 (14).

Karl, R. 2002 *Staging the World: Chinese Nationalism at the Turn of the Twentieth Century*. Durham and London: Duke University Press.

Guibernau, M. 2004 'Anthony D. Smith on nations and national identity: a critical assessment'. *Nation and Nationalism* 10 (1/2) pp. 125–141.

Guo, Y. 2004 *Cultural Nationalism in Contemporary China: The Search for National Identity under Reform*. London and New York: Routledge.

He, B. and Guo, Y. 2000 *Nationalism, National Identity and Democratization in China*. Aldershot, Brookfield USA, Singapore and Sydney: Ashgate.

Huang, Y. 1995 'Why China will not collapse?' *Foreign Policy* 99 pp. 54–68.

Huntington, S. 1996 *The Clash of Civilization and the Remaking of the World Order*. New York: Simon and Schuster.

Hodkinson, P. 2005 '"Insider research" in the study of youth cultures'. *Journal of Youth Studies* 8 (2) pp. 131–149.

Israel, J. 1966 *Student Nationalism in China: 1927–1937*. Stanford, California: Stanford University Press.

Jacques, M. 2009 *When China Rules the World: The Rise of the Middle Kingdom and the End of the Western World*. London: Penguin Group.

Khor, M. 2011 'China is still a developing nation'. *China Daily*, 25 November 2011, p. 9.

Kuipers, G. 2013 'The rise and decline of national habitus: Dutch cycling culture and the shaping of national similarity'. *European Journal of Social Theory* 16 (17).

Kuzmics, H. and Axtmann, R. 2007 *Authority, State and National Character: The Civilizing Process in Austria and England, 1700–1900*. Hampshire and Burlington: Ashgate.

LaPiere, R.T. 1934 'Attitudes vs. Actions'. *Oxford University Press* 13 pp. 230–237.

Lee, J. 2006 'The revival of Chinese nationalism: perspectives of Chinese intellectuals'. *Asian Perspective* 30 (4) pp. 141–165.

Lilley, J. 1996 'Nationalism bites back'. *New York Times*, 24 October 1996.

Luo, X. 2004 'Farewell to idealism: mapping China's university students of the 1990s'. *Journal of Contemporary China* 13 (41).

Lutz, J. 1967 'December 9, 1935: Student nationalism and the China Christian Colleges'. *The Journal of Asian Studies* 26 (4) pp. 627–648.

Lutz, J. 1971 'The Chinese student movement of 1945–1949'. *The Journal of Asian Studies* 31 (1) pp. 89–110.

Mangione, T.W. 1995 *Mail Survey: Improving the Quality*. Thousand Oaks, CA: Sage Publications.

Mann, R. and Fenton, S. 2006 'Everyday articulations of national identity: methodological considerations'. Paper prepared for the Mobility, Ethnicity and Society Conference, 16 and 17 March 2006.

Perkins, C. 2010 'The banality of boundaries: performance of the nation in a Japanese television comedy'. *Television and News Media* 11 (5) pp. 386–403.

Perry, E. 2001 'Challenging the mandate of Heaven: popular protest in modern China'. *Critical Asian Studies* 33 (2) pp. 163–180.

Pye, L. 1993 'How China's nationalism was Shanghaied'. *The Australian Journal of Chinese Affairs* 29 pp. 107–133.

Pye, L. 1996 'China: not your typical superpower'. *Problems of Post-Communism* 43 (4) pp. 3–16.

Rosen, S. 2009 'Contemporary Chinese youth and the state'. *The Journal of Asian Studies* 68 (2) pp. 359–369.

Seckington, I. 2005 'Nationalism, ideology and China's "Fourth Generation" leadership'. *Journal of Contemporary China* 14 (42) pp. 23–33.

Sewell, W. 1992 'A theory of structure duality: duality, agency and transformation'. *American Journal of Sociology* 98 (1) pp. 1–29.

Shen, S. 2007 *Redefining Nationalism in Modern China: Sino-American Relations and the Emergence of Chinese Public Opinion in the 21st Century*. New York: Palgrave Macmillan.

Sullivan, M. 1994 'The 1989–89 Nanjing anti-African protests: racial nationalism or national racism?' *The China Quarterly* 138 pp. 438–457.

Suzuki, S. 2007 'The importance of "Othering" in China's national identity: Sino-Japanese relations as a stage of identity conflicts'. *The Pacific Review* 20 (1) pp. 23–47.

Swidler, A. 1995 'Cultural power and social movement'. In Johnston, H. and Klandermans, B. (Eds) *Social Movements and Culture*, London: UCL Press.

Wang, H. 2009 'A study of the education of university students' rational nationalism'. *Legal System and Society*. June 2009.

Wang, L. and Cai, L. 2009 'A discussion about the evaluation and construction of Chinese youth values – starting with doubt and reflection on the "worsening generation"'. *Chinese Youth Studies* 12 pp. 79–82.

Weiss, J. 2008 'Powerful Patriots: Nationalism, Diplomacy and the Strategic Logic of Anti-Foreign Protest in China'. PhD Dissertation, University of California, San Diego.

Wasserstrom, J. 2005 'Chinese students and anti-Japanese protest, past and present'. *World Policy Journal* Summer 2005.

Wu, X. 2007 *Chinese Cyber Nationalism: Evolution, Characteristics, and Implications*. Plymouth: Lexington Books.

Xi, J. 2006 'Introduction to Chinese youth'. In Xi, J., Sun, Y. and Xiao, J. (Eds) *Chinese Youth in Transition*. Hampshire/Burlington: Ashgate Publishing Limited.

Xinhua 2010 'Is China still a developing nation?' Accessed online at: http://news.xinhuanet.com/english2010/indepth/2010-09/20/c_13521680.htm. On 8 March 2012.

Xinhua 2011 'China still a developing nation'. Accessed online at: http://news.xinhuanet.com/english2010/indepth/2011-11/25/c_131269386.htm. On 8 March 2012.

Xu, Y. 2008 'The Carrefour event and Chinese nationalism'. *Weekly Comment* May 2008.

Ye, S. and Zweig, D. 2007 'Energy challenges: the view of Chinese university students'. Paper presented at the conference on the 'Future of US–China relations'. University of Southern California, Los Angeles, CA, 20–21 April 2007.

Yu, Z. and Zhao, D. 2006 'Differential participation and the nature of a movement: A study of the 1999 anti-U.S. Beijing student demonstrations'. *Social Forces* 84 (3).

Yuan, J. 2008 'Nationalism in China: Domestic discourses and impact on relations with the neighboring countries'. Paper prepared for delivery at the 49th Annual Meeting of the International Studies Association. San Francisco, CA, 26–29 March 2008.

Zhang, H. 2002 *America Perceived: The Making of Chinese Images of the United States, 1945–1953*. Westport: Greenwood Press.

Zhang, M. 1997 'The new thinking of Sino-US relations'. *Journal of Contemporary China* 6 (14) pp. 117–123.

Zhao, D. 2002 'An angle on nationalism in China today: Attitudes among Beijing students after Belgrade 1999'. *The China Quarterly* 172 pp. 885–905.

Zhao, S. 1997 'Chinese intellectuals' quest for national greatness and nationalistic writing in the 1990s'. *The China Quarterly* 152 pp. 725–745.

Zhao, S. 1998 'A state-led nationalism: the patriotic education campaign in post-Tiananmen China'. *Communist and Post-Communist Studies* 31 pp. 287–302.

Zhao, S. 2000 'Chinese nationalism and its international orientations'. *Political Science Quarterly* 115 (1) pp. 1–33.

Zhao, S. 2004 *A Nation-state by Construction: Dynamics of Modern Chinese Nationalism*. Stanford, CA: Stanford University Press.

Zhao, S. 2005 'Chinese nationalism and Beijing's policy toward Taiwan: the making of the anti-secession law'. *Institute of International Relations English Series* 53.

Zhao, S. 2008 'Olympics and Chinese nationalism'. *China Security* 4 (3) pp. 48–57.

Zheng, Y. 1999 *Discovering Chinese Nationalism in China: Modernization, Identity, and International Relations*. Cambridge: Cambridge University Press.

Zhou, Y. 2005 'Informed nationalism: military websites in Chinese cyberspace'. *Journal of Contemporary China* 14 (44) pp. 543–562.

4 Attitudes to housing tenures among young people in transitional China

Chen Nie

> At current rates of construction, China can build a city the size of Rome in only two weeks. In the decade leading up to 2010, China built houses equivalent to roughly twice the total number of houses currently in Spain or the UK, or about the same number as Japan's current total housing stock.
> (The Economist Intelligence Unit 2011: 1)

> This week, Harvard University released a report on real estate in the US. Home construction is way off. And the housing market is deeply depressed. One bright spot of the report: Lower rental-vacancy rates. Renters are back. In China, it's quite the opposite. Homes are going up everywhere. And people are buying.
> (Marketplace 2011)

After the end of the Second World War, home ownership rates grew significantly in many developed societies, especially in English-speaking countries, such as Great Britain, the United States and Australia. These societies, whose overall tenure structure has been gradually dominated by the owner-occupied sector, are considered to be typical home-owning societies. In the 1980s and 1990s, the creation of home-owning societies became a more widespread phenomenon, through housing reform characterised by commercialisation and privatisation in many post-socialist societies, such as Eastern and Central Europe countries and China.

Against the background of the increasing popularity of home ownership across those different countries, opinion or attitude to home ownership is becoming a research hotspot. However, much academic research in terms of preference of owner occupation mainly focuses on English-speaking home-owning societies, or other developed countries. Recently, comparative housing research has started to include Eastern and Central Europe post-socialist societies. Although China, as the second largest economy after 2010, has also emerged as a home owning society with the rate of home ownership reaching nearly 90 per cent in 2012, it has largely been neglected in the discussions of home-owning societies. Meanwhile, a large amount of existing English-language research literature relating to the Chinese housing system focuses on the economic dimension, and prefers a more or less top-down perspective, or relies on statistical data mainly released by official bureaus. The individual perspective, in terms of ordinary people's attitudes and expectations to different housing tenures, has long been neglected.

Although post-socialist societies tended to abandon the central planned economy and embrace a market-based economy, the successful reform and continuous economic growth has made China's developmental trajectory different from other transitional societies. Following a gradualist approach of housing reform which began in the early 1980s, China entered an era of unprecedented housing construction, accompanied by unprecedented home purchase activities (Deng, Shen and Wang 2009), in contrast to an underdeveloped housing market in many Eastern and Central Europe transitional societies. In this process, China, a developing society with a very different political regime, experienced perhaps the most rapid increase in home ownership in the world (Wang and Murie 2011), the home ownership rate increasing to nearly 90 per cent by 2012, from less than 20 per cent at the beginning of the 1980s. Within the context of the neoliberal turn, its post-reform housing system and housing market shares some features with English-speaking home-owning societies (Nie 2015).

> On the one hand markets are desired to be as heavily profit-determined as possible while on the other, the consequences of this are that the state is pressured to construct a set of safety-net provisions. These are kept as negligible as possible to discourage their use.
>
> (Kemeny 1995: 9)

In this way, both the Chinese housing system and the housing market offer a valuable case-study within which to discuss the attitudes and behaviours of an emerging home-owning society, particularly as existing research in this area is often focused on developed English-speaking societies and European transitional countries. While most of the literature in terms of Chinese housing research paid attention to the structural level or contextual issues, such as evaluations of gains and losses in housing reform, the relationship of the housing sector with national economic growth, or whether house price bubbles exist in a booming Chinese housing market, this study is focused on the more individual level, for example, the attitudes of ordinary Chinese people to different housing tenures, against the background of the transformation of housing policy. It not only investigates the attitudes of Chinese people to different tenures in different time periods, but also considers how these attitudes form or change.

Qualitative research methods rather than statistical analysis are employed in this study. I view attitudes as 'general, socially shared, evaluative beliefs (opinions) of a group' or 'specific, organized clusters of socially shared beliefs' (van Dijk 1998). I argue that fragments of attitudes are indirectly and directly expressed in people's subjective dialogues and experiences; furthermore, I believe quantitative examination is often hampered by understandable personal sensitivities, deep meaning and complexities of these data. Thus, qualitative research methods, such as interviews, are better in capturing fragments of attitudes. Meanwhile, most English-language literature targeting the housing system and housing market within the context of transitional urban China has employed quantitative methods and has relied on official statistical data. In order to fill the gap, the qualitative research method cannot be neglected as a useful strategy to expand the academic debate in this area.

Research into attitudes to housing tenures in the West

Kemeny (1992) suggests that, regarding the process of the rise in home ownership in Western countries, a comparative study of housing forms in different societies and more individual aspects of housing need to be considered for further study rather than merely as tools for policy and market analysis. In this way, meanings of and understandings around different housing tenures, especially social representation of home ownership, have gradually become a research key topic, not only in the area of housing research, but also in diverse disciplines and interrelated subfields, against the background of popularity of home ownership across different societies. Attitude as an important example of social understanding of housing tenures also attracts much attention. Before turning to the reviews of discussions on housing attitudes, the fundamental question of whether attitudes exist within context is briefly discussed further on.

The word 'attitude' can have complex meanings, as we saw in Chapter 1. There are many arguments around the definition of attitude. Traditionally, attitude can be an evaluative belief of particular objects, events or ideas, ranging from extremely negative to extremely positive. However, the transitional notion of attitudes is seen as anti-cognitivist by some social psychologists. For them, 'attitudes' as opinions are verified in languages within situations and contexts. Thus, they are reduced to some kind of rhetorical structure with contextual variation. Meanwhile, attitudes 'cannot be observed or measured' and therefore do not exist.

> Traditional social psychology largely ignored the crucially discursive and social nature of attitude construction and manifestations, and underplayed the contextual variation of attitude expression.
>
> (van Dijk 1998)

Although van Dijk (ibid.) admits that the critique of the traditional notion of attitudes in some ways makes sense, such as the perspective of the social constructionist, he disagrees with the denial of the existence of attitudes. He clarifies the notion of attitudes and changes of attitudes. For him, although a person participates in or shares a social representation, individual opinions are not referred to as attitudes. Only a cluster of socially shared particular opinions can be 'attitudes'. Despite the fact that group-shared opinions or evaluative beliefs are not fixed, they do gradually form and change, thus remaining relatively stable across several situations and contexts. Moreover, van Dijk claims, the fact that an attitude is 'non-observable' is not a good reason to deny the existence of attitudes. If it was true, many general beliefs, such as commonsense knowledge and rules, would be thrown out. Van Dijk emphasises the real consequence of 'attitudes':

> ...they explain how and why people can 'meaningfully' and 'purposefully' act and talk. They explain very powerful commonsense self-observations: people know they think, they know they know things, and they know they 'have' opinions, whether or not they express them, and even if they express them differently in different situations. People know that often they agree with others, and may thus share opinions as members of a group.
>
> (Ibid.)

The development and debates regarding conceptions and analytical frameworks of housing attitudes mainly follow the argument attitudes. One notable early proposition dominating housing attitudes research is made from a psychological perspective, in which home ownership is usually portrayed as a universal human need or a force coming from the internal rather than the external context. For example, Weil (1955) states that private property is 'a vital need of the soul' (cited in Duncan 1981: 112). Cooper (1974) claimed that the house is a symbol reflecting how man sees himself. For Canter (1977), a home with a physical form of place represents to some extent, a psychological place. Within the context of the growth in home ownership in Finland, Ruonavaara (1996: 101) argued that 'some sort of change of mentality among people has also taken place' and 'now people are more prone to value a home of their own as a worthy goal in life'. Linked with the 'spirit of capitalism' of Max Weber, Ruonavaara (ibid.) pointed out that preference to home ownership made the efforts required to become a homeowner subjectively sensible to people.

Later, this psychological perspective of housing attitudes focuses on a behavioural explanation based on an 'individualism approach', in which 'all social explanations must ultimately be framed in terms of individual attitudes, motives and desires' (Duncan 1981). The social factors and institutional limits tend to be neglected while home ownership is seen largely as a function of demand. From this perspective, entering owner occupation becomes a rather important step in many people's lives in Western societies (Mulder 2006; Saunders 1990). The ideal of home ownership is also often thought to be an essential ingredient of 'the American Dream'. Living in a single-family, owner-occupied dwelling unit is central to the American conception of a secure and successful life (Fannie Mae National Housing Survey, 1994). In Australian values, home ownership also expresses 'the Great Australian Dream' (Kemeny 1981). Physically, home ownership provides better quality housing and environment than rental accommodation (Megbolugbe and Linneman 1993). Financially, home ownership is considered to be an investment, offering financial security and part of the process of the accumulation of wealth (Saunders 1990; Megbolugbe and Linneman 1993; Thorns 1995). Psychologically, home ownership increases mental health, life satisfaction and self-esteem (Rohe and Stegman 1994b; Rossi and Webber 1996; Hirayama and Hayakawa 1995; Balfour and Smith 1996). Clark, Dieleman and Deurloo (1994) summarised that home ownership not only means a stable shelter and a psychological haven, but a piece of property also has the potential to increase in value, and offers the owner increased participation in political activities and community building. For Saunders (1989), home ownership is a key factor influencing a sense of identity, and to own a home fits with people's aspirations and values. According to survey data in the UK, Saunders (1990) also argued that home ownership displays the 'innate and natural desire' of individuals and offers 'ontological security'. Compared with renting, home ownership is more strongly associated with pride, warmth, autonomy, relaxation and identity. In terms of the contribution of home ownership to a sense of ontological security, Saunders (1986) disagreed with Gidden's position (1989, 1991) where ontological security has been undermined by the rapid changing nature of the modern world. He suggests that ontological security can be maintained in the built environment rather than only being derived from nature. Based on this proposition, he suggests:

> Home owners more readily associate positive images of home with the house they live in; they speak readily of a pride of ownership; they associate home more strongly with values such as personal autonomy; they are more likely to see the home as a place where they can relax and 'be themselves'; they are much more strongly attached to the houses they live in; they express choice in selection of where they live; and they derive satisfaction from working on their homes – a satisfaction which appears not to be inherent in the labour itself but which is, to a large extent, dependent upon the feeling that they are improving their own personal property.
> (Saunders 1989: 188–189)

However, this individual perspective, although widely cited, has been extensively critiqued as a traditional notion of 'attitudes,' because of an apparent neglect of structural factors, and for selecting an 'over universal' view. For Forrest et al. (1990), the rise of home ownership was not only caused by consumer individual preferences, but also by the decisions of those involved in the production of housing, including the government. They also disagreed with Saunders for his insistence on the universal benefits of home ownership, and because his empirical base refers to only one specific set of circumstances at a time of economic boom and soaring house prices. As Saunders attempted 'to ground the pattern of predominant tenure preferences on a 'natural' basis' (Ronald 2008: 33), his assertions were later criticised by Ronald (2004, 2008), who claimed that Saunders neglected the role of the state in enhancing the advantages of home ownership. Meanwhile, Ronald's critique pointed out that Saunders's suggestion ignored diversity in the constitution of households, as well as gender differentiation within the space of the home. Mandic and Clapham (1996) disagreed with Saunders's analysis of his ambiguous treatment of culture and context. They emphasised the importance of social factors and identified that evidence in Slovenia does not support the view of a universal desire or preference for owner occupation. Rohe and Stegman (1994a) studied the home ownership of low income families in centre of the city of Baltimore in US. They argued that purchasing a house has no significant impact on personal self-esteem, and suggested that an assumption of a positive relationship may need to be qualified. In terms of methodology, Gurney (1999b) suggests that Saunders's work, which is based on positivist research methods, appears to be too blunt to adequately reveal the multiple meanings of tenure.

Another contrasting perspective emphasised the effect of structural elements and context; this has gradually dominated the debates around housing tenure preferences, especially following the development of comparative housing studies. The seed of this contextual perspective is the work of Friedrich Engels. Engels (1935, 1975) felt that promotion of home ownership among workers negatively affected their class consciousness because of an essential contradiction: their class allegiance was neither with tenant workers nor with the capitalist class. Hence, working class homeowners have been seen as victims of false-consciousness, while the promotion of home ownership by the political right has been viewed as a strategy to construct a conservative hegemony and to create a stabilising force in capitalist societies. The theoretical assumption has been that preference of home ownership stimulates market practices, reinforces household dependency on wage labour and private property relations, and promotes political conservatism (Ronald 2008). Harvey (1976), for example, pointed out that worker mortgage schemes and the promotion of owner occupation within the working class construct a pillar of social stability.

Home ownership by workers has an ideological as well as an economic function meaning 'chronic indebtedness ties individuals into the job market and into society in general in a most repressive way' (Castells 1977: 185) and fosters a back-to-the-land ideology (Castells 1977). Lambert, Paris and Blackaby (1978: 169) drew attention to 'the style of urban managerialism as having a potent ideological force in shaping and reinforcing the dominant pattern of power, influence and profit'. Forrest (1983) suggests that the values and ideas surrounding owner-occupied housing have been claimed to be the epitome of conservative values and a 'bulwark against bolshevism'. For Marcuse (1987: 251), this character of home ownership restricts the opportunities and even desire of homeowners to participate in public affairs. For Kemeny (1981, 1992), home ownership is closely linked to increasing privatism with a growth in lifestyles centered on the home rather than the workplace and public actions. He identified home ownership as having been politically sponsored to sustain a stabilising effect in civil society by offering a stake in a 'property owning democracy'. Furthermore, he attempted to develop a general theory which aimed to explain different housing systems in English speaking societies and countries with integrated rental markets. In this way, Kemeny (1984, 1992, 1995, 1998, 2001, 2005, 2006) reveals, first, a constructed preference for home ownership fostered by a dualist housing system in which non-profit rental has been prevented from competing with home ownership and profit-oriented rental in the open market; and second, a negative relationship between the rate of home ownership and the extent of social welfare. His concept of policy constructivism has been used to elucidate the diverse nature of housing policy and social structures in different societies. Saunders (1990) summarised five reasons underpinning critical views on home ownership: ideological conservative effects of home ownership, creating or enforcing divisions within the working class, tying the working class into long-term debt and thus wage work, withdrawing the working class from collective life, and reinforcing contemporary consumption.

> The preference for owner-occupation, then, is not the product of genuine choice. It has been massaged by government housing policies and molded by commercial pressure.
>
> (Saunders 1990: 66)

However, many of the above analyses of attitudes to home ownership have been criticised, mainly from two positions. The first criticism suggests that the conservative interpretations of home ownership should be limited to certain contexts, historical times and even specific geographical areas. Occupational inequalities have been lessened because of a general social change in which class conflict, one of the important pillars of Marxist theory, has been progressively displaced by multiple lines of social cleavage of lesser salience (Dunleavy 1979). Moreover, home ownership rates have greatly increased and indeed dominate the cultural and economic landscapes of many societies, especially in English-speaking societies such as Britain and Australia. The traditional concern, a fragmentation of the working class into housing classes, seems to be a hard fact. Hence, transformation, diversity and the localisation of social contexts should be considered in studying home ownership ideologies.

The results of Gilderbloom and Markham's confirmatory factor analysis (1995), based on data from the annual General Social Survey conducted by the National Opinion Research Center (NORC) from 1990 to 1993, have critiqued the traditional belief in the conservative impact on home ownership. They found that home ownership rarely has an impact on political attitudes. They explained that the widespread theory of the conservative influence on homeownership has ignored its contexts:

> A full understanding of the impact of homeownership on political beliefs can only be acquired through a knowledge of the context in which the theory was shaped and by an awareness of how current circumstances differ from those in which the theory was forged.
>
> (Gilderbloom and Markham 1995: 1603)

Ronald (2004, 2008) also argued that due to the changing nature and role of home ownership through fundamental social shifts, the traditional associations of home ownership are no longer adequate in capturing the complex relationships between private housing consumption and socio-ideological practices. Home ownership has taken on a new salience in mediating relations among individuals, families, works and welfare, the market and the state.

The second critique of traditionally critical structural approaches is that the individual was presented as a passive agent of a top-down hegemonic force. Its version of over-determinism and a simply structural explanation indicates that the efficacy of human actors was largely denied. Early criticism, such as those of Agnew (1981), pointed out that the 'social being' of Marxist theory must be constructed in a much wider and more flexible sense because of a transformed reality. A single and direct dominant attitude surrounding home ownership appears to be one that needs to be challenged (Ronald 2008). Following a great social change, the diversity, complexity and fragmentation of relationships between social structure and the individual should also be considered.

As well as Agnew's (1981) focus on 'over-determinism', Duncan (1981) also pointed out that the individual is seen as a passive agent of an external force. Saunders (1990) considered that critical ideological views have been too dismissive of empirical research into preferences for owner-occupied tenure. According to survey results, such as data from 'a withdrawal from collective life' and data on 'membership and participation in different kinds of voluntary organisations', Saunders (1990) expressed his disagreement concerning the notion that home ownership produces a privatised life style or that owner occupation undermines working class solidarity. Ronald (2004, 2008) was also critical of the premise of structural approaches to housing attitudes for being largely determinist and for over-emphasising the actions of the state and the relationships between social classes.

According to the questions of the above two perspectives or dichotomies between structural and individual elements, recent research into housing attitudes has begun to take into consideration new frameworks of structure and individual interaction. Both forces from a structural level and an individual, internal level have been emphasised. As Duncan (1981) claimed, there needs to be a model combining both structure and consciousness, aiming at providing a balanced perspective of the relationship between housing, social structure and identity. Adopting Foucault's notions of power and the exercise of power, Gurney (1999a) analysed the disciplinary power of home ownership in terms of hierarchical observation, the normalising judgement and the examination. Through a comparison of discourses concerning the three main tenures (home ownership, private and public rental sector) in policy documents and in-depth interviews involving working class homeowner households in Bristol, Gurney found a tenure prejudice from a normalising judgement in the way the word 'home' is used. He states that 'this judgement does not suggest that home – with all the significance this word implies – only exists for home owners, but it does suggest that home exists in a much more meaningful way for those in home ownership' (1999a: 172). Moreover, together with his interviews, Gurney reveals a 'normalising discourse of home ownership concerning a raft of specific values of pride, self-esteem, responsibility and citizenship' (ibid.), and 'the power of natural behaviour as normalising discourse of home ownership' (ibid.). In this process, attention has turned to the constructed process of 'normal' home ownership and the bias against rental tenure. The approach of interactions has indeed overcome the drawbacks inherent in structural and the individual perspectives. However, it does not mean the end of the question of the relationship between society and the individual, not only in housing research, but also in social theory in general.

First, based on critics of the dominance of positivism and structuralism in housing research, social constructionism is selected to explain the process in which housing attitudes form. As one of the social theories aiming to challenge the conventional view of empiricism and positivism, that knowledge is based on objective and unbiased observation (Burr 2003), social constructionism is a growing influence in housing research. Many scholars argue that housing research has been oriented to empirical case studies with a heavy policy-salient emphasis:

> It has remained a bastion of traditional postivism, heavily influenced by stucturalist explanations and strongly oriented toward the use of quantitative methods, including the use of official statistics and the collection of additional data through large-scale interview surveys.
>
> (Kemeny 2004: 50)

As such, emphasis is placed on the legislative and institutional structure of the housing sector, while government policy is an important determinant of housing outcomes; government or media-determined definitions are unreflexively accepted as fact-like. Most housing studies within a Chinese context followed the same route. Two major criticisms can be made of the approach: over-determinism and an already changed context. First, top-down determinism takes actors merely as passive receivers and neglects how their behaviour, attitudes and perceptions react and interplay with structure. Second, in Jacobs *et al.* (2004) and Clapham's terms (2002, 2005), the context of housing has altered significantly while government has a less important role in the housing sector. For King (2009: 42), policy focus presents 'only a partial picture of housing phenomena and artificially restricts the field of housing studies'. Clapham also critiqued other positivist approaches including neo-classical economics, and geographical and sociological approaches in the housing field. Clapham (2005: 18) asserted that the existing approaches share similarity and problems because 'only one truth or only one rational way of looking at things is problematic' in a contemporary 'post-modern' society. For the neo-classical economic and geographical approach, 'they are assumed to have simple and universal attitudes and motives' (Clapham 2002). For the sociological tradition, which includes the Marxist or Weberian approaches discussed earlier, more attention has been paid to constraints on choice rather than the process of choice.

> In general it is assumed that households are rational and instrumental in their approach to housing decisions and that there is little empirical work to investigate and attempt to understand how different households perceive and react to the housing context facing them.
>
> (Clapham 2005: 10–11)

Overall, Clapham (2002, 2005) points out that approaches to housing research have failed to keep up with recent developments in sociology, which have taken this individual/structure interface as the focus of their attention. Kemeny (1992) also suggests that due to a narrow empiricism, housing studies has been left behind by the advances in social sciences over the last 20–30 years.

Thus, social constructionism is 'viewed by its adherents as providing a richer and more sociologically informed analysis of the policy process than traditional explanations. It develops from the prior existence and more recent emergence of more explicit theories derived from positivist traditions' (Jacobs et al. 2004: 2). 'In particular, Kemeny has encouraged a considerable body of work in the area of social constructionism and discourse analysis' (King 2009: 44). The significance of the work is that 'it begins to take seriously the role of human subjects in housing processes rather than concentrating on structures and impersonal forces' (ibid.). Ronald (2008: 38) suggests that the development of social constructionist approaches to housing research 'essentially rejects claims to objective measures of facts and redefines the scope of social scientific investigation within the limits of social interaction, discourse and representation'. There is a fundamental assumption that social life is constructed by people through interaction, and people playing an active role in constructing and enacting their own realities of 'the common sense world of everyday life' (Garfinkel 1967: 35). This provides some important insights into belief and attitudes surrounding housing practices (Kemeny 1992; Jacobs et al. 2004), although the social constructivist perspective has been used in a number of different ways in housing studies. The approach 'marks an attempt to broaden the scope of housing studies by relying upon a different conception of reality from the one advanced by positivism' (Ronald 2008: 38). For example, Clapham (2005) develops a valuable tool from the perspective of social constructionism: the housing pathway to overcome limitations of a dominantly positivist orientation in the housing field. Based on social constructionism, his approach pays attention to the 'social practices of a household relating to housing over time and space' (Clapham 2005: 34). As such, it effectively deals with the relationship between structure and action in housing in postmodern societies.

Second, in order to overcome poorly developed theory in housing research area, and also for establish a integrated resolution of the debates of relationship between structural and individual level, housing studies has begun to take into consideration developments of grand social theory. Theoretical contributions of Giddens and Bourdieu have been introduced in research of housing attitudes. Giddens's structuration approach aims to offer a resolution to the dichotomy between structural and individual factors. His approach suggests a recursive process that individuals are constrained by and also experience the rules and resources of structure, and structures are reproduced or transformed by individuals' actions. As Franklin claims,

> Structure has an abstract and recursive quality, and is not fixed in either time or space. Human action, on the other hand, is necessarily situated in time and space, and thus action helps to fix structures and social systems, both in the here and now, and through constant reproduction as actions are repeated or re-created anew. For this reason, the settings of action are important to Giddens, providing the contextuality of social life in both time and space.
>
> (Franklin 2006: 15)

Giddens's approach is heavily influential in theory development in housing research, especially in the areas of social attitudes towards different housing tenures. For example, Ronald (2004, 2007 and 2008), according to Giddens's approach, develops a useful analytical framework in solving the question of structural and individual factors in housing attitudes research. Ronald differentiates between the concepts of home ownership ideologies and homeowner ideologies, and suggests that consideration of homeowner ideologies constitutes the basis for the appreciation of home ownership ideology. Ronald (2008: 9) states that 'the former denotes ideological relationships that represent discursive practices of power and legitimation with regard to social production, and the latter, discourses and systems of values related to the consumption of, and dwelling in, owner-occupied housing.' From this perspective, he focuses on the interaction between individual factors related to dwelling and housing consumption practices and discourses, and structural factors including socio-historical contexts of housing policy, housing system development and policies, and policy related discourses.

More recently, the work of Bourdieu is widely employed in empirical housing research. His central concept, 'the habitus', is particularly relevant and useful when exploring people's attitudes to housing tenures, locations and so on, as a mediating factor between structure and individual practices, and their practices with his theory of capital and field. 'The habitus' refers to an individual's disposition which influences the person's attitudes and behaviour within a given field, which allows 'individuals to know how they should act in a given circumstance, and in a way that accords with social norms and institutional precepts (thus reproducing them)' (Franklin 2006: 16). Using Bourdieu's approach, Butler and Robson (2003) and Bridge (2001, 2006) make contributions towards the analysis of the housing attitudes of different social classes towards locations and neighbourhood.

Of course, this is not the end of debates between structure and the individual, between the macro and the micro, between objectivity and subjectivity. While social constructionist approaches offer important insights into comparative housing research across different societies, there are important criticisms of social constructionism: it tends to negate the significance of society at the macro-level (Collin, 1997), and it 'does not question whether things exist or not, or whether there is a "real world", but rather that reality is constructed by discourse' (King 2010: 94). Giddens and Bourdieu still 'remain closer to the objective than the subjective end of the epistemological tradition of sociology' (Franklin 2006: 17). The processes of decision-making and negotiation among individuals tend to be neglected. Thus, many scholars are trying to find better solutions for debates on effects of social structure and individual elements regarding peoples' attitudes and practices, through re-classifying factors or defining new levels at which to work. For example, Lowe (2011) focuses on institutional factors at the meso-level aiming to explain housing attitudes and behaviours.

However, these fierce debates over attitudes to housing tenures rage within developed English-speaking societies, such as Britain, the USA and Australia, and in other Western developed societies, such as Sweden (Lundqvist 1998) and Finland (Ruonavaara 1996). It is necessary to develop a theory of home ownership ideology within a more diverse context. Although there is a growing interest in the societies of East Asia, the focus is still limited to developed societies, such as Japan (Forrest *et al.* 2003; Ronald 2004, 2007, 2008) and Hong Kong (Lee 1999). However, the meanings of home ownership in developing societies in East Asia, especially in transitional societies with a high rate of home ownership such as China, where housing tenure has changed from the previous socialist rental system to privately owned, have been under-researched. Compared to European transitional societies, the continually upward trend in house prices and the booming primary and secondary housing markets in urban China have created different contexts which affect people's attitudes towards different housing tenures. Although Chinese post-reform housing systems share many features with those in English-speaking home-owning societies, experiencing the great structural changes of the housing system from a planned public-rental to market-oriented private owner occupation means that the Chinese housing system and housing market offers a valuable case-study within which to discuss the relationship between structural and individual elements in the process in which attitudes to housing tenures form.

Another aspect relates to differentiated home ownership ideology shared and developed by fragmented homeowners, which has received little attention in the research of attitudes towards housing tenures. According to van Dijk (1998), people from different groups display different social attitudes to the same attitude object. As home ownership becomes increasingly diverse, homeowners tend to be highly fragmented (Forrest *et al.* 1990). Hence, it is useful to consider different beliefs shared by differentiated social categories, such as age, gender and race, and to consider different social-economic conditions rather than a common 'attitude' shared by a general social group. In this way, within the Chinese background, young people will be selected as a target group for this study. First, young people as homeowners share many social features. They experience particular stages of transition in their life course, such as from education to employment, from living in the family home to independent living, aspects which are shared by many young people globally. According to Forrest (1989: 3), 'there are particular features of the experiences of young people which occur regardless of class, culture or location'.

A series of studies of the housing careers of young people by Ineichen (1975, 1977, 1979, 1981) also discussed how young people as owner-occupiers and council tenants develop as groups with contrasting social characteristics. Second, young people, especially those of the post-1980s generation, face a more or less similar housing system to that in English-speaking societies, with an increasingly mature housing market and powerful market forces. Their parental generation lived under a public housing system dominated by public rental housing, or a transitional housing system with a mix of public and private housing, and could access home ownership in a variety of ways, such as buying public housing at a relatively low price because of heavy subsidies, self-built or commodity housing; for young people, however, housing has ceased to be a welfare entitlement and the 'most heavily subsidized commodity' (Huang 2004). Thus, it is more appropriate to apply theory of attitudes to housing tenures established in Western contexts to young people within China.

The cultural and historical origin of Chinese owner occupation

Although technologies improving at rapid and exponential rates allow a gradual adaptation of culture, it (culture) is still a solid foundation in structural elements. As a collective social phenomenon shared by a cultural community, 'cultural knowledge is the basis of all group-specific belief' (Van Dijk 1998: 37). He goes on, 'cultural knowledge is also the basis of all evaluative beliefs including socially shared opinions, attitudes and ideologies' (ibid.). In other words, specific group beliefs presuppose culturally shared knowledge, and group values should presuppose a culturally shared moral order. Therefore, as a common ground, culturally-based housing knowledge in China needs to be reviewed before scrutinising attitudes to housing tenures in China.

Many publications mention the Chinese cultural desire pertaining to owning land and property. For example, Li and Yi (2007: 342) suggest that 'for centuries, Chinese people have believed in the value of possessing land and housing'. Huang (2004b) asserted that housing with land had, for thousands of years, been considered by the Chinese as the best investment that a family could depend on. According to Chinese housing culture, Chinese people have been zealous, throughout their history, in their efforts to purchase land and build their own houses. The adage 'resident has his own house, and cultivator has his own land' (*ju zhe you qi wu, geng zhe you qi tian*) can be considered as the key ideology that guided household and housing practices (Zheng 2007). 'Cultivator has his own land' means that the cultivator or tiller can have his/her own land, rather than being a tenant farmer. Consequently, 'resident has his own house' indicates that residents have own their houses rather than pay rent. Chinese culture and traditions imply that the home has not only been treated as a place of living, but as a sign of wealth, a symbol of well-being and of social status (Huang 2004b; Yao, Luo and Loh 2011). However, most of these papers only simply explain the existence of the notion of the desire to own a house, and the perception of other tenures being viewed inferior, as a cultural phenomenon in contemporary Chinese society. But the origin of this cultural phenomenon has remained unexplored. In addition, other structural elements, such as policy change and individual elements, have been neglected. I cannot explain these origins in every detail here but will briefly discuss where the cultural desire to own housing came from, as a base for the analysis of attitudes to housing tenures in current Chinese society.

China has been an agricultural society for thousands of years. Thus, the significance of an agricultural economy is an essential factor in understanding Chinese history, society and character. Land played a very important role in the agricultural society. Land privatisation is a result of an interaction with policy changes, rather than from an 'innate rights of man' ideology, in Chinese history. Since the middle of the Tang Dynasty (after AD 755), the government ceased to enforce the system of state-supervised land allocation because of sheer economic necessity. The implications of this were, first, that the equal-field system (*jun tian zhi*) completely collapsed as the government lost centralised control over land allocation; second, land privatisation, land transactions and land annexations were legalised. As a result, large areas of land were concentrated in the hands of powerful property owners. The peasants lost land and became tenants or hired labourers for their rich neighbours. As such, possession of landed property meant not only a means to subsist and a symbol of wealth, but also signified an independent identity and powerful status. Lewis (2009) described 'the accumulation of wealth to establish local power and influence as an ultimate springboard to political power' (2009: 124) and 'an object of aesthetic contemplation and literature' (ibid.). Against the backcloth of extreme land concentration in the history of China, Liang (2005), based on his experience and fieldwork in North China, asserted that some tenants had the right of permanent tenancy. It seemed that tenants had parts of land ownership. Besides the owning of land, the possession or holding of land has been one of the most important features in forming the foundation of social structure of villages. In this way, for the majority of people in the agricultural society, what they can achieve is not ownership of land, but a stable income and a sign of settling down from a right of relatively permanent tenancy.

There are a number of idioms and proverbs which associate positive attitudes with settling down, such as the idiom *an ju le ye*. *An ju le ye* originates from the seminal text of Philosophical Taoism 'Laozi', which was written around the sixth century BC by the sage Laozi and strongly influenced other schools such as Neo-Confucianism. The literal meaning of the idiom is that 'one has a place to live and one can work in peace and contentment'. It reflects a traditional Chinese aspiration of settling down in order to have a happy life. There are also negative attitudes associated with similar idioms; for example, the literal meaning of *piao bo bu ding* is 'drifting from place to place'. It suggests that a life without putting down roots, or settling down permanently, means a family perishing in the agricultural society. In addition, being rooted in Confucian philosophy and embodied in the context of an agricultural society for thousands of years, it is argued, has resulted in the conventional and conservative personality of the Chinese. Recalling Liang's argument (2005), this conservatism can be seen to inform another of the perceived characteristics of Chinese culture, which is valuing the past over the present, lacking an adventurous spirit, preferring the routine of normal life and being reluctant to leave the place where one has lived for a long time (*an tu zhong qian*). The evidence of these characteristics can be seen perhaps in the fact that the Chinese prefer living in a place for generations. Moving away and not settling down was perceived as an abnormal situation, occurring only as a passive, miserable response to disasters such as flooding, famine and war (Fei 1985). Thus, from a historical perspective, ownership of land is not necessarily what Chinese preferred in the agricultural society. What they want is a site of constancy which could function as a secure base, a place for living in for a long time. People's positive attitudes are not towards land per se, but their preferred meanings, such as a stable income and settling down, could be achieved by holding land. In other words, as an agricultural society for thousands of years, the Chinese cultural origin is not a desire of owning land, but of settling down, living a stable life and being reluctant to move.

Preference of public rental before and during housing reform

During the pre-reform period in urban China, the publicly owned housing system seemed to be inconsistent with the culture of a desire of owning land discussed by some scholars. However, public housing tenants 'enjoyed far superior rights over their dwellings than traditional tenant rights. Once they had access to a dwelling in the public sector, they could occupy it as if they owned it' (Huang 2004b: 780). They could live in public rented accommodation as long as they wanted, but only if they were employed in the same work unit. They only paid nominal rents, bills and even maintenance fees. As discussed in the last section, the cultural propensity towards settling down and living in a place for long time, chimed with this situation. In this way, within the background of a housing policy fitting with the cultural common ground, the positive attitudes towards the public rental sector had been formed, while private ownership was viewed as inferior or unavailable.

The structure of housing system and attitudes to tenures in China has experienced a zigzag path in the last 60 years because of the dramatic changes in ideology and political economy. The housing system has changed from mostly private rental housing in the early 1950s, to virtually all public rental housing after the socialist transformation (1956–1966) and the Cultural Revolution (1966–1976); additionally, there has been rent reform since 1979 and a mix of increasing home ownership and decreasing public rental housing since the housing reforms launched in 1988.

Before 1949, there was effectively no housing policy in urban China because of the government's long involvement in wars. The major housing tenure was the private rental sector, while a few large landowners owned most housing in urban China. The housing problem was very severe. There were considerable housing shortages and substandard housing conditions but despite this, there were dramatically high rents (Zhang 1997). During this period, a privately owned house was obviously a symbol of wealth and prestige (Huang 2004b). In the early period of Communist China, the principle function of political ideology was to socialise the entire population of the Chinese continent. It was an anti-capitalist and anti-market revolution. The change from private ownership to public ownership was the major instrument of the revolution (Zhang 1997). However, the Chinese Communist Party (CCP) chose to implement detailed policies gradually rather than immediately, such as the implementation of the housing policy during this period, because impoverished economic conditions prevented the government from drastically redistributing properties or making adequate investment in improving housing conditions (Lim and Lee 1990). During this period, private housing still remained the major housing type and renting was the major housing choice in urban China (Huang 2001). According to the document *Report on Urban Private Housing Property and Suggestions for Socialist Transformation* from the CCP Central Committee (1956), most of the housing stock still remained in private ownership in many cities in 1955, 53.9 per cent in Beijing, 66 per cent in Shanghai, 54 per cent in Tianjin, 61.3 per cent in Nanjing and 80.3 per cent in Wuhan.

Private ownership and inequality in the housing sector was contradictory to the socialist ideology, which led to the Socialist Transformation that began in the second half of the 1950s. The ideology of socialisation was translated into practical policy and influenced housing policy. As an example of the superiority of Communism over capitalism, housing was recognised as a welfare benefit that should be provided solely by the nation and rents should be extremely low (Lim and Lee 1990). The government began to nationalise most of the urban housing stock in modest ways, such as government purchase, rather than confiscation (Zhang 1997). Work units were encouraged to increase their housing construction in urban areas in the first half of the 1960s. The state gradually took on the responsibility for urban housing provision, allocation, maintenance and management through local municipal housing departments or work units. Housing distribution was based mainly on the status of the household head, and his or her job rank and seniority in the work unit (Lee 2000). In 1966, public rental housing became the dominant form of housing, while private rental housing only accounted for 5 per cent. The housing market had almost disappeared. Housing was no longer regarded as a commodity but as a component of state welfare. The government had reached its political and ideological targets through the Socialist Transformation (Zhang 1997). Although privately owned homes were still allowed, owner occupation was not encouraged or rewarded. Most households had few options but to wait for the allocation of public housing (Huang 2004b).

Attitudes to housing tenures 113

The Cultural Revolution that followed continued the elimination of private ownership under the ideology of class struggle and equality. Given the influence of this radical ideology, a large amount of private housing was confiscated by the state and government agencies. The 'bourgeois' practice of maintaining existing private housing was discouraged (Lim and Lee 1990). The purchase of private housing became illegal (Kirkby 1985). Against this backdrop, private ownership was inevitably a target of attack. Most landlord-owned housing properties were transferred into public housing, and the individual families, such as professionals and officials who owned private housing in urban areas, were classified as reactionaries by radicals. As a result, their houses were often confiscated while they were sent to the countryside. At the end of the Cultural Revolution, privately owned housing accounted for only about 10 per cent of the total housing stock in urban China (Whyte and Parish 1985) and less than 4 per cent in some cities (Yang 1992). During the period of the Cultural Revolution, the Chinese housing policy can be termed an anti-home ownership policy (Lim and Lee 1990). 'By the end of 1970s, the housing stock in urban China was characterised by the dominance of public and rental housing and very limited private housing for owner occupancy' (Huang 2001: 11).

In summary, under the socialist ideology, public rental housing provision formed part of the socialist welfare system, which also included basic education, free medical care, pensions and lifetime employment (Zhang 2000; Zhao and Bourassa 2003). The freedom of housing choice and owner occupation was abolished and replaced by exclusively public rental housing that served political and social purposes. State controlled housing production had been incorporated into the national economic plan through governmental financial appropriation. It was the responsibility of work units and the local housing bureau to supply and maintain housing, and the market had been (almost) completely excluded. The practice of allocating housing in the form of material distribution was considered a socialist welfare benefit based on the number of working years and employment rank.

For the government during this period, home ownership meant not only the epitome of exploitation and inequality but also an obstacle to pure socialism. In contrast, public housing allocated by work units signified socialist advantages and the removal of the ravages of landlordism. It was the way to display socialist equality, because a factory's party secretary, an engineer, and a canteen cook may live side by side in the same building. Second, urbanisation and a growing population would be easier to manage without the private housing market. It was easy for the work unit to convene employees to hear government decrees and for political study, to approve or mediate employees' marriages and divorces, and organise 'one-child' programmes. In addition, it was a very practical method for government to control population strictly between urban and rural areas, and to manage the *hukou* system, discussed in Chapter 2 (Whyte 1983). Farmers could not find housing in the urban areas and this would discourage non-planned rural–urban migration. Furthermore, a work-unit based quasi-clan housing system was supposed to produce employees loyal to the state owned enterprises (SOEs) and to the state (Zhang 2000). As such, public housing as a reward to employees of work units could stimulate an ethos of hard work (Zhang 1997).

For individual owners, under the top-down control mechanisms, home ownership was no longer regarded as a sign of wealth or high social status but represented a stigma that often resulted in political persecution. Meanwhile, during the period, home ownership provided worse quality housing and environments than public rental accommodation. 'What remained in private hands was typically small and of poor quality, because the best private housing had always been at the highest risk of nationalization ... it (private housing) had unavoidably deteriorated' (Zax 1997: 379). Huang compared the living conditions of homeowners and of public tenants:

> Housing usually consisted of bungalows built before 1949 or former suburban farmhouses, thus they were often in poor condition with few modern facilities such as running water, gas or a private bathroom. In contrast, public housing newly built by work units and the government – mostly multi-story apartment buildings – is equipped with these facilities, although still at a modest level.... Moreover, owners and their family members usually did not qualify for subsidized public housing, as they already had their own housing. Thus, living in privately owned housing in socialist Chinese cities often meant poor conditions and severe crowding.
>
> (Huang 2004b: 780)

Moreover, homeowners in pre-reform urban China did not enjoy much more beneficial property rights than public tenants. Home ownership only meant the right of use and control by owners in the period. Under policy restrictions in socialist urban China, profiting from housing, which was considered to be gaining without working and exploiting the working class, was not permitted. Housing trading, described as '*tou ji dao ba*' (speculation), was a criminal offence. In contrast, public housing tenants 'enjoyed far superior rights over their dwellings than traditional tenant rights. Once they had access to a dwelling in the public sector, they could occupy it as if they owned it' (Huang, ibid.). It was the state or work units' responsibility to invest, build, allocate, maintain, repair and generally manage public rental housing. As such, rents and bills had become merely a nominal charge. In the early 1980s, public housing rents were only equivalent to 1 per cent of household income (Zhu 2000; Chan 2008). Water and electricity fees only took 0.97 per cent of household expenditure in 1981 and 1.14 per cent in 1983 (Kirkby 1990). In the housing reform afterwards, tenants could enjoy heavy subsidies when they purchased their own living spaces.

Although there are many critical positions, Zhang described the residents' attitudes to housing during the period from one particularly interesting perspective:

Attitudes to housing tenures 115

> There was little demand for housing. This could only be explained by the spiritual magic created by Mao Zedong. The spiritual satisfaction in the process of socialist construction overwhelmed personal physical needs. The old Chinese saying that 'there are houses made of gold and silver, but I would rather stay in huts' best described the people's attitudes towards the housing situation at that time.
>
> (Zhang 1997: 442)

After the Cultural Revolution, investment in public housing increased significantly to improve housing conditions and to mitigate a severe housing shortage (Huang 2001). The ideological climate in China had veered further towards the concepts of market guidance and market regulation in the planned economy (Kirkby 1990), which has resulted in profound changes in every aspect of Chinese society, including the provision and consumption of housing. In 1980, an article by Xing Su was published by the CCP's theoretical journal, *hong qi* (Red Flag), which attempted to develop a theoretical case that under the socialist system, housing could be a commodity (Kirkby 1990). Though enlisting Engels to his cause, Su's article signified the gradually changing attitudes to housing and home ownership:

> In a socialist society, housing is an individual consumer item and remains a commodity. What is different is that here it is no longer a transaction between individuals; instead, the state, representing the system of ownership by the people. rents or sells the house to the individual laborers, making this a form of the principle of his labor...
>
> (Su 1980 cited in Kirkby 1990: 303)

Many scholars, such as Bao (2002), Li (2003) and Zhang (1990), believed that Deng Xiaoping, the most powerful leader of the Chinese Communist Party (CCP), was the principal architect of China's housing reform. In 1978 and 1980, two significant talks by Deng laid the foundations of urban public housing reform: (a) urban residents may construct their own houses; (b) not only old houses but also new houses can be sold to individual households in instalments; (c) rent needs to rise to market levels to encourage ownership. Wang and Murie (1996) contended that Deng's statement paved the way for the subsequent housing reform measures. Lin (1989) further discussed the plan and the task of China's housing reform: China's housing reform, sponsored and implemented by the central and local governments, aimed at resolving the problem of the housing shortage, reducing the financial burden of government and SOEs, eliminating dissatisfaction in housing allocation, and creating a sound circulation for housing investment, production and distribution. Xu (1993) pointed out that, in planning terms, housing commercialisation as a goal of housing reform was hoped to be achieved and specified as: (a) the State redefines its economic relationship to its employees through increasing salary and allowing them to assume responsibility for housing their families; (b) the State becomes a housing developer and owner (rather than a non-profit superintendent or supplier) through selling and renting housing, and reinvesting money from sales and rent to build more houses for the rising demand in the market; (c) individuals make their own housing decisions according to their intention and financial capacity; (d) the overall social consumption could be rationalised when tremendous stress had been placed on supplying electric appliances because people gained more money than before and proposed to spend it on household appliances.

The ideology of the reforms of the 1980s was the utility of the market as a solution to situations in which supply was hopelessly outmatched by demand. In 1983, the State Council (SC) issued an important policy paper: *Ordinance on managing urban private housing*, which officially recognised the role of private housing in meeting housing needs: the state will protect citizens' rights over their private housing. However, it was still forbidden to trade houses between work units and individuals, and among individuals. In 1988, the policy paper: *Implementation plan for a gradual housing scheme reform in cities and towns* was published by SC in order to provide a clear direction of housing reform: 'one of the main objectives of housing reform is to let people buy housing'. In the same year, the government recognised the economic and social benefits bought by housing reforms in the National Housing Reform Conference. Since 1988, housing reform has completely reversed the housing policies and ideology of the Socialist Transformation and the Cultural Revolution (Huang 2001). Housing marketisation became the overall objective of central government policy, through continually lifting rents to competitive levels and beginning implementation of the sale of public sector housing. Chen and Wills (1997) explained that the initial phase of housing reforms intended to create a housing rent market while selling public houses with great subsidies. Ye *et al.* (2006) divided the stage of housing reform from 1979 till 1994. They noted that housing reform went hand in hand with reform of the economy and named the period as the double-track system stage. During this time, there was a gradual transition from welfare housing to the marketisation of housing. They explained that the policy of this period was characterised by the experiment of housing reform, and by the parallel existence of public rental housing and a market mechanism for housing distribution. The reform included the sale of public housing without profit-making; encouragement of housing construction by the private sector and increasing both the rent and housing subsidies of public housing.

However, the experiment of the initial stage failed to increase incentives for home ownership because not only were the purchasing prices too high for most families, but also because benefitting from public rent housing, as mentioned earlier, residents had little desire to own houses under the double-track system stage. Chen and Wills (1997) described how, because of insufficient rent increases, affordability problems, rudimentary housing loan systems and work unit responsibility for maintaining public rents, the raised rent policy did not trigger a great demand for home ownership. Lee (2000) also emphasised that initiatives of rent increases in the 1980s for promoting home ownership were not entirely successful because of the low wage system, such as the 'Yantai[1] model' and the issuing of vouchers to offset the increased rent. As a result, SOEs had to take on new financial burdens. The goal of reducing SOEs' burdens had not been achieved due to housing sales with the large subsidies, although officially banned in 1988, which were still common in many municipalities. In addition, much of the housing stock was seriously under-maintained, which meant that the work unit retained the responsibility for maintaining this old low-quality housing. Exacerbating the problem, financial instruments for housing remained rudimentary. For example, unrealistically high household saving rates discouraged ownership, and low interest rate housing loans caused inflationary pressures, while interest subsidies were not financed by explicit taxes on others. Although 'the process of housing commoditization ... has evoked a desire for private property ownership that has long been suppressed by socialist ideology' (Chu and Kwok 1990: 664), another major obstacle was that SOEs which had many older workers were reluctant to change their existing benefit position enjoyed in public rented housing unless there were obvious new benefits to be derived from owner occupation. In other words, home ownership was still less attractive than public rent during the period despite higher rents. According to interview materials collected in Yantai in 1986, Ren Min Wang (People's Daily Online[2]) (2008) offered evidence supporting how owner occupation was a less attractive tenure in the beginning of housing reform. Interview excerpts in Yantai in 1986 below indicate two key points. First, at the initial stage of housing reform, private housing was still stigmatised as it was still influenced by socialist ideology. Second, home ownership was still inferior to public rental housing because tenants could enjoy more benefits. Besides, for the respondent, even with a subsidy, it was difficult for her to have access to a flat of about 70 square metres. It cost RMB20,000[3] when her monthly salary was RMB52:

> Buying a house means you owning private property. Dare you buy it? Moreover, in public rental housing, not only the rent is low, but also when the water pipe broke down they would repair them for us, when a light bulb was not working they will change it. Why would I need to buy house?
>
> (cited in Ren Min Wang 2008)

The reforms could not be expanded because of a lack of support and follow-up action by the central government (Chen and Wills 1997), and the implementation of the 1988 housing reforms slowed down due to rising inflation as well as political instability[4] (Wang and Murie 1999). Without comprehensive reform of the economic structure and financial system, desire for home ownership could not be successfully created. Only 8.6 per cent of respondents bought a public rental house between 1980 and 1990 (Ren Min Wang 2008).

In the 1990s, following lessons learned from the failure of the initial stage, as well as insight gained from a number of successful trials in selected cities, the CCP government announced further housing reforms as part of the whole country's economic reform progress (Chen and Wills 1997; Lee 2000). Many financial support measures were established in order to help individual house purchase. Encouraging home ownership became an important aim of housing policy in urban China. The State Council (SC) (1991) published the policy document *Continuation of urban housing reform in a stable manner*, reconfirming continuous rent growth aligned to market price with reduced rent subsidies and the selling of public housing. Practically, SC endorsed the Shanghai Housing Reform Plan in May 1991 and encouraged other cities to follow the Shanghai model: based on the previous subsidy model, reform was characterised by such innovative devices as the Housing Provident Fund (HPF),[5] rent subsidies, and housing bonds (Li 2003). Lee (2000) illustrated the model in detail: (a) raise rents to cover costs of basic construction, maintenance, repair and management; (b) solve overcrowding problems in cities; (c) deal with dangerous housing; (d) improve urban living standards; (e) rationalise and standardise constant housing investment to sustain housing production. There were clear statements that housing reform should keep the same pace with improvements in living standards, and the housing finance burden should shift from state and SOEs to individuals.

In 1994, the SC took further measures in order to promote private home ownership in a new housing policy document entitled: *Decisions on deepening the urban housing reform*, which further indicated that the state or work-unit in the role of sole housing provider was to be gradually diminished, and funds from multiple sources were to be made available for housing construction, management and maintenance. Meanwhile, home ownership was expected to shift from the public to the private sphere in various ways, such as selling public rental housing to sitting tenants and building Economic Comfort Housing (ECH)[6] for families with limited purchasing power. Housing finance also diversified. Mortgages offered by banks and the HPF as a cornerstone were reaffirmed in order to enhance the employee's purchase power and replace the state or work-unit as the entities responsible for housing finance (Lee 2000). The figures indicated that between 1981 and 1997 the state's contribution to investment in the housing sector decreased significantly from 28.1 per cent to 2.8 per cent (Zhu 2000). The statistical data addressed showed, in 1996, housing investment was 26.6 per cent of total fixed asset investment and achieved 9.06 per cent of Gross National Product (GNP), compared with an average 1.5 per cent of GNP before 1978 (Ye, Wu and Wu 2006). In 1997, the average building area per person reached 17.66 square metres, and the home ownership rate reached 63 per cent. Clearly, the public housing allocation system was gradually being replaced by a new housing system. The diversified house mortgage product would prove to be a key element in allowing the middle class to bridge the housing affordability gap (Rosen and Ross 2000). However, Zhang (1998) argued that home ownership is not what people cared about most; rather, it was the fear of continual rent increases that caused the drive towards home ownership.

In 1998, China's housing reform entered a new era, characterised by the end of welfare housing and the establishment of a multiple housing supply system in which housing units were expected to be acquired through market mechanisms (Ye, Wu and Wu 2006). Home ownership was supposed to have positive effects on economic development. The policy paper: *A further step on deepening housing reform and accelerating housing construction in urban areas* was published by SC in 1998. It defined the guiding ideologies of housing reform as housing commercialisation in order to establish a housing market, and a social welfare housing system to separate housing from work units, aiming at constructing 'housing property as a new pillar supporting economic growth'. All work units had to stop offering housing or providing rental housing, and gradually a system to distribute housing through cash had to be instigated (SC 1998). The ECH was defined as a 'secure housing project' for middle and low-income groups based on government-issued guiding prices. The Low Rental Housing (LRH) scheme was launched for very low-income groups (SC 1998; Wang 2000).

Lee (2000) made several comments about the housing policy in this period; namely, the monetarisation of housing policy was regarded as the most important factor in China's macroeconomic transformation. 'It involves a whole new set of national accounting methods, shifting resources from housing construction and management to various pecuniary measures based on local government and community needs' (Lee 2000: 66). Ye *et al.* (2006) noted that, starting from this period onwards, the housing industry had become a new engine of growth for the economy: between 2000 and 2004, average annual investment in the housing industry grew to RMB745.8 billion, representing an annual growth rate of 24.9 per cent, 6.9 per cent of Gross Domestic Product (GDP). The average urban living space increased from 18.7 square metres in 1998 to 24.97 square metres in 2004 (National Bureau of Statistics of China (NBS), 2005). The ownership rate reached 80.77 per cent in urban areas. Figures such as these serve to illustrate that China is indeed becoming a home-owning country, and a homeowner class is emerging (Huang 2004; Huang and Li 2006). However, Huang (2003, p. 103) argued that 'in the late 1990s while private housing is becoming an important option, renters who can access public housing are still more likely to choose public housing because of heavy subsidies'. Only disadvantaged groups not qualifying for public housing had to buy housing in the new housing market. Lee also described the 'last through train' phenomenon in 1998 that indicated attitudes towards the end of welfare housing allocation:

News of the imminent implementation of the housing monetarisation policy in early 1998 triggered off what has come to be termed the 'last through train' phenomenon. In anticipation that the new policy would halt all welfare housing programmes by the end of 1998, many young people rushed to get married on the assumption that a certificate from the marriage registry would guarantee them a last welfare housing allocation. It was assumed that after housing monetarisation, housing benefit would never be the same again. Some couples went as far as to divorce, simply to allow another spouse to be entitled to qualify for another welfare housing allocation, this time with a view to obtaining one more set of subsidized rental housing for their sons or daughters who will be unlikely to get welfare house allocation in the new housing regime in 1999.

(Lee 2000: 62)

New problems emerged in this new period. Although free housing distribution had been banned, SOEs were allowed to cooperate with private land agents, and practices such as offers of free land, or directly purchasing houses from the market then selling them to employees at discounted prices, developed. The creation of housing cooperatives was another strategy tried by SOEs. Housing was built on spare land under SOE control (in order to save the cost of purchasing land) while the building cost was mainly from collected money from qualified employees. Meanwhile, SOE applied strict controls to building costs and aimed to lower the housing price to match what employees could afford (Wang et al. 2005). In this way, many eligible employees of resourceful work units could access home ownership not only by purchasing existing welfare housing with a heavily-subsidised price, or by buying commercial housing from the market, but they could also choose newly-built housing sold by work units at discounted prices. In this way, the incremental transformation displayed a high degree of path dependence. SOEs were still involved in housing provision but had more autonomy than before, in line with the government's plan. As a result, the quality of living conditions among staff varied, shaped mainly by the financial status of work units, while many SOEs were faced with limited capacity and deteriorating financial conditions to improve housing for their employees. At the same time, the pre-reform cleavages between households headed by officials and managers and those headed by production workers became more pronounced during the same process.

In addition to these issues, a kind of a double track housing system emerged: 'a public housing system and a newly created market system', which 'aggravated inequities in the allocation process' (Lee 2000: 75). Although housing conditions have improved and ownership has been promoted because of the multiple housing provision policy, housing reform also marginalised millions of households which are below the national standard (Lee 2000). Li (2003) listed many aims of the housing reform which have not been achieved: the housing shortage is a long standing issue; the problem of housing affordability has worsened with dramatically increased housing prices in recent years, especially for those on low incomes. Also, the removal of poorly maintained buildings and the clarification of property rights have not been successfully achieved. Zhu (2000) argued that the aim of establishing a market-oriented system of housing development and investment with clear property rights needs to be much more fully realised.

At present, many publications in English tend to focus on the gains and losses of China's strategy for creating a home owning society. The ways in which China can develop into a fully-fledged housing market have been discussed; for example, Chen 1996; Chiu 1996, 2000a, 2000b; Lee 2000; Lee and Zhu 2006; Li and Yi 2007; Logan, Fang and Zhang 2009; Michael and Kwong 2002; Tang and Tse 2005; Sato 2006; Wang 2003; Wang 2000, 2005; Wang and Li 2003; Wu, 1996; Zhao and Bourassa 2003.

Due to rocketing house prices nationwide after the housing reforms, it is very difficult for the majority of residents in China, especially young people gradually emerging as the main body of house purchasers, to move into home ownership.

However, few studies focus on individual housing values and practices at a time when the overheated market has gradually become the only source of housing for the majority of urban dwellers, and when subsequent development indicates that social welfare housing performs no more than a cosmetic function. It is, however, important to study how individuals and households fare in this rapidly changing environment (Li and Huang 2006). Huang and Clark (2002) also noted that, with some exceptions (Li 2000a, 2000b), the majority of existing research is policy-oriented and focused on macro aspects of the housing system, such as housing policies, housing problems and housing reform. Although the micro foundations of the housing market emerge as an essential cornerstone of housing analysis at all spatial scales (Gibb 2012), there has been much less research at the micro-level within the Chinese background.

Recently, a small number of housing studies at a micro-level and set in the Chinese context have gradually emerged (e.g. Li 2000a, 2000b; Li and Huang 2006; Li and Yi 2007; Huang and Clark 2002; Forrest and Izuhara 2012). This research has begun to recognise the complexity of tenure attitudes and choices. However, most of these studies placed emphasis on the outcomes of a process of choice, rather than on a detailed understanding of perceptions and attitudes of common people. There has been little insight into the reasons behind the choice of one housing tenure over another within the context of the altered housing policies and the emerging new housing market.

Moreover, most of these contributions targeting the individual within the context of transitional urban China employed quantitative methods. For example, in order to examine housing tenure choice, Huang and Clark (2002) used a survey and a multi-level modelling technique. Based on a sample in Guangzhou, China, Li (2000b) also used a multi-level logic analysis to explore the housing allocation process and housing decisions. Considering the complex causes of and values around housing tenure choice, as well as the changing context after house reform, a qualitative research method cannot be neglected as a useful strategy to expand the academic debate in this area.

In addition, except for Forrest and Izuhara (2012), the studies focusing on the micro-level have paid attention to the housing behaviours of residents nationwide or in particular cities, but have neglected specific age groups, such as young homeowners or young house buyers. Young people in China, as the first generation to face a more or less mature housing market with marginalised public welfare housing, have begun to play an increasingly important role in the housing market. While most lived in public rental housing in their childhood, currently, buying a home in the housing market seems to be the only option to access home ownership. What they think about housing tenures and the values they associate with them, deserves to be explored.

Further, most housing studies in urban China, whether at macro-level or micro-level, are in favour of evidence-based policy analysis, which has been challenged in contemporary housing research, as explained in the Review section. Therefore, beside the theoretical contribution on debates of structural and individual elements in housing research, the empirical contribution in this study is to fill these gaps in the existing housing research literature focusing on urban China. It will explore the attitudes of young people towards housing tenures in contemporary urban Chinese society, with the analysis targeted at their individual housing values and practices, with the background of the now transformed housing policies and the booming housing market. This will be achieved mainly by qualitative methods, which will be discussed in the next section.

The research method

The main data in this study is qualitative discursive data, which expresses young people's perceptions towards and housing tenures. For investigating these data, official statistics data tend to be unreliable or unavailable, because direct quantitative investigation is often hampered by understandable personal sensitivities, deep meaning and complexities of these data. Thus, more qualitative research methods were employed. As discussed, their subjective dialogues and experiences may indirectly and directly express fragments of attitudes and vice versa. In this way, this research aims to capture attitudes through analysing the discourse used by a group of young people. Discourse analysis is an approach for the analysis of qualitative data, based on a way of creating and sustaining reality that focuses on the implicit meaning of the text or image rather than on its explicit content (Denscombe 2007). As Gill (2000) suggests, discourse, as a way of constituting a particular view of social reality, is a focus of enquiry itself, and not just a means of gaining access to the aspects of social reality that lie behind it. Affected by the context that he or she is confronting, discourse involves 'establishing one vision of the world in the face of competing versions' (ibid.: 176). Thus, in order to account for the subjective and discursive dimension of attitudes among young people, a direct empirical investigation of young people with different housing experiences is necessary.

Among qualitative research approaches, the interview is an important tool used to depict the story behind the interviewees' experiences (McNamara 1999). It is almost certainly the most suitable method when the researcher needs to gain insights into opinions, feelings, emotions and experiences (Denscombe 2007). Therefore, semi-structured, in-depth interviews were the most appropriate means of collecting data in the fieldwork. The task of the in-depth interviewer is not the collection of data, but the collection of ideas (Oppenheim 1992).

The city of Beijing was the fieldwork location. As the capital city, Beijing is significant in policy design, issues and implementation. Along with other metropolises, such as Shanghai and Shenzhen, Beijing has attracted a variety of housing purchasers including a large number of young people, developers, investors and speculators. As the national capital, Beijing had a classic socialist housing system (Huang and Jiang 2009), and it was a pioneer in social welfare housing development in China (Wang and Murie 2011). It is also at the forefront of the transformations in the housing market in China. With a diverse group of people, Beijing offers an excellent context within which to explore the meaning of tenures and living arrangements.

The semi-structured, in-depth interviews were carried out in Beijing. In this research, young people, including first-time house buyers and tenants mainly from the post-80s and post-90s generation, were selected as a target group and as representative of housing tenure choices. As discussed earlier, first, according to a large number of media reports, young house buyers, especially from among the post-80s generation, have started to play an important role in housing consumption (Kang *et al.* 2009). For example, the *Beijing Morning Post* (Beijing Chenbao) (2009) reported that, according to interviews with loan institutions in Beijing, young buyers under the age of 30 currently account for 70 per cent of first-time house purchasing loans. An analytical report of second-hand trading in Beijing, conducted by the China Everbright Bank and the market research department of the Beijing Homelink Housing Agency in 2010, found that the average age of first-time homebuyers is 27. Second, unlike their parents, who lived under a transitional housing system with a mixture of public and private housing, and who could access home ownership in a variety of ways, such as buying heavily subsidised public housing from work units, self-building their own properties or purchasing commodity housing on the open market (Huang 2004), young people in China, especially those of the post-1980s and post-1990s generation, have to face an increasingly difficult housing market and powerful market forces. The most practical way for them to achieve their goal of home ownership, as young people in English-speaking home-owning societies, is to seek home ownership on the open market (Ye and Wu 2008).

Preference of home ownership among young people in contemporary urban Chinese society

Positivity and economic motivation

After the housing reforms, the housing sector was seen as a pillar industry of economic growth, especially at a local level, largely because its boom provided a substantial benefit to GDP growth and the fiscal revenue of local governments. Therefore, housing consumption has been treated as an effective means of stimulating and maintaining economic development. Home ownership became a core principle of the post-reform ideology, as well as a core aim of the housing system. In contrast, the social welfare housing system has been neglected due to its lack of direct economic benefit. A housing system displaying features of a dualist-housing model of English-speaking societies has been constructed in China (Nie 2015). Meanwhile, a profit-seeking but 'dysfunctional' private rental housing market emerged. When it is not policy emphasis, the sector becomes unregulated and only offers poor quality private rental accommodation in urban China, which cannot meet multi-level requirements (Chen 2005). As a consequence of policy constructivism, the population is now encouraged, and also obliged, to seek home ownership on the commercial housing market.

When considering the attitudes to different tenures, the economic aspect is always critical.

> In societies dominated by owner-occupier housing market, the most salient aspect of public and individual discourse has been the augmented significance of privately owned housing as an asset, as a property in a market and its general monetization as a commodity.
>
> (Ronald 2008: 53)

Investments discourse and asset building discourse have been increasingly applied to explain the positive attitudes to home ownership, especially within the context of the booming housing market and substantial house price inflation. In urban China, the housing reform has meant that access to housing has become increasingly market-oriented. Soaring house prices are a factor in the discourse of Chinese young people, which displays an association between owning property and specific economic advantages. However, the evidence from interviews in the Beijing fieldwork indicates that young people are more concerned with use value rather than profit expectation from a later sale. The role of intergenerational transfer of wealth seems partly to do with their attitudes to owner occupation. Against constantly rising house prices, this intergenerational transfer of wealth allows young people to climb onto the property ladder. Thus, young people are often not making decisions about housing independently.

Li is single and did not have any plans for marriage in the near future; nevertheless, he bought his house in October 2009 because of his perception of house price inflation. He suggests that soaring housing prices are an external force pulling him into owner occupation:

> I decided to buy a house because of high house prices. I bought it in October of last year. I experienced the radically increased house price in 2007, 2008 and 2009. I thought 'I have to buy it'. In Chinese tradition, a house is necessary sooner or later ... I have to buy it before house prices reach the peak ... I estimate the house price will keep its upward trend. I cannot follow the rule. I cannot wait to buy it when I get married. Because I estimate I could not afford it when I get married in future.
>
> (Li)

The discourse of M5 represents many of the housing perceptions of young people. After housing reform abolished the public housing system and promoted the development of the market system, the context of constantly soaring house prices can now be seen to shape attitudes and further motivate the housing practices of young people. The context model, as Van Dijk argues, is not based on objective facts but 'how they see and construct themselves in general or in the current social situation'. It is 'part of the interface between social shared representation and personal talk ad text' (1998: 212–213). The context of soaring house prices then, contributes to young people's subjective understandings of home ownership. It further affects the discourse and the ways in which the ideologies of home ownership are constructed among young people. For example, Li said that he 'experienced the radically increased house price in 2007, 2008 and

2009'. Then he interpreted the context as 'the house price will keep its upward trend'. So he decided to 'buy it before house prices reach the peak'. In this way, Li's interpretation shaped his perceptions and actions in the housing market. Home ownership is perceived as an insurance against house price inflation.

Wang experienced dramatically increasing house prices in Beijing. He offered details of constantly rising house prices and, as a response, his ongoing discourse regarding owning property:

> It was 2002 when I entered my university in Beijing. There is a newly built community near the campus of my university. The price for its commodity housing was RMB3,000 to 4,000 per square meter in 2003. At that time, I thought it was none of my business. I went there to have a look in 2005 when I was a junior student only because my dad said we may consider buying an apartment. It was RMB6,000 per square meter. Compared to that in 2003, I thought it was too expensive. I saw a flat which is about 100 square meters costing more than RMB800,000. I thought it was not worth it at that location. Now the price is around RMB20,000 per square meter there. At that time, I just thought it was not worth it.... At the end of 2007, I went to see an apartment in a community where it is said house prices were cheap. The house price there was about RMB9,000 square metre. I still considered it was too expensive and not worth to buy it. My parents hesitated about it as well. Then I went back to my hometown for Chinese New Year. When I returned, the price in the community was surprisingly RMB14,000 per square metre. It was just after one month. It jumped from RMB9,000 to 14,000 in only one month. I did not know why. Nothing happened. This caused terror to us. The growth trend was too horrible. We should buy it in a hurry ... it seemed that your money is sinking if you did not buy it.
>
> (Wang)

The interview material mirrors the process of his transferred attitudes to house prices through his ongoing interpretation. At first, he thought house prices were 'too expensive' and 'not worth it'. However, seeing house prices rise dramatically made him reconsider house purchasing, taking the position now, 'we should buy it in hurry' because 'the growth trend is horrible'. In this way, there is an ongoing critical negotiation between the changing financial aspects of the housing market and the perceptions and traditional assumptions regarding the meaning of home ownership. Home ownership is treated as an insurance against house price inflation. Consequently, a huge demand in the housing market has been created and has resulted in further house price increases. This pattern is repeated and exacerbated as more and more young people attempt to enter the housing market, feeling compelled to do so by the rapidly rising house prices.

Zhao's narrative associates home ownership with an insurance against not only house price inflation but also general inflation and the high risks of the financial markets, such as the stock market and the funds market. Owning property is perceived as a devaluation of mortgage payments by inflation based on discursive ongoing constructions from much complex information. It involves a complex interaction between shared social understandings ('they said'), contexts, personal experiences, beliefs and knowledge in terms of not only the housing market but also the financial markets and markets in general. This process of interpretation shapes young people's discourse of home ownership and further strengthens their beliefs that home ownership is a useful hedge against inflation; while other financial strategies, such as buying stock and investment funds, are perceived as highly risky. The formed ideology of home ownership monitors their housing practices. These discourses reveal the complexities of owning property in urban China and challenge determinist perspectives regarding home ownership ideologies, as well as assumptions that the desire to be a homeowner is simply innate:

> When we bought it, the house price was already high. It was around RMB20,000 per square metre. But you had to strive to buy it as soon as possible. People around me said that house prices in Beijing would catch up that in Hong Kong.... If you have money, it is not sensible to buy stock. It means high risk. I do not have specific knowledge about the stock market. For investment funds, they have the same risk with buying stock.... Currently, facing serious inflation, there is no way to keep your money, except by owning property. Comparing home ownership with stock and investment funds, it is a much better way.
>
> (Zhao)

The private rental market is mentioned by Hong, referencing the idea that home ownership is always preferable to renting when rent and house prices both increase. This comparison between different experiences in different tenures seems to account for her positive attitudes towards home ownership. Meanwhile, Hong shares with other interviewees the desire to 'not lose money', rather than prioritising home ownership as a good future investment:

> Housing prices have continued to increase in Beijing.... Following it, the rent I paid also constantly increases. Why not buy a house when I can afford it. At least you would not lose your money.
>
> (Hong)

Surprisingly, my interview data do not reveal a meaningful link between accessing home ownership and investment opportunities. Although they have capital gains more or less already benefitting from soaring house prices, based on the perception of continual house price inflation, few of the interviewed young people perceived home ownership as an effective investment. They do not expect that their paper profit would be transferred to cash. In this way, there seems to be less concern over the fluctuation of house prices after buying a house compared with anxieties before owner occupation. Wang's interpretation represents a frequently occurring attitude to housing in terms of it being an investment.

He explained that his apartment is for living in, rather than an investment. He emphasised the use value of the home. His narrative indicates that the possibility that housing as a financial investment may be a practice more typical of other groups who own more than one house:

> If you only have one house it is definitely not an investment. You need to buy another house to live in if you sell it. You have to put your money into another house again. Thus, for a person as a first time home buyer and only has one apartment, it is just for living. If he owns more than one house, his demand of living has been satisfied. One of the other houses could be an investment.
>
> (Wang)

Liu expressed a similar point of view, even though the value of her house has doubled:

> Compared with the price I paid, the value of my house has doubled. But when I consider it from perspective of living, I will never sell it even if the price keeps upward. It is my home.
>
> (Liu)

In China, the intergenerational transfer of wealth plays a critical role in allowing young people access to owner occupation. All interviewed homeowners received family financial assistance from their parents as they purchased houses. Clearly this is a key behaviour, and equally clearly a behaviour on the part of parents, grandparents and the wider family, rather than of the young people interviewed. Zhang explained his feeling that this intergenerational transfer of wealth was a rational choice against the soaring house prices.

> I agree with the view that young people currently accessing home ownership depends on parental financial resources rather than their own. You can work very hard. You can try your best. However, while you are saving up for your deposit, the house prices continue to go up quickly.... Therefore, relying on your own resources is not a rational choice.
>
> (Zhang)

This notion of transfer can make it impossible for young people to decide independently on the saleability of owned property. Rooted in traditional familism, many consider home ownership as wealth accumulation for the next generation. Duan is married but without a child when interviewed. He expressed the meaning of home ownership as an intergenerational transfer of wealth to the next generation.

> I will consider the next generation, you know, children I may have.... According to parental advice, my house will be an accumulated wealth for

the next generation. It could be a kind of insurance which I can offer for the next generation.

(Duan)

Meanwhile, parents help their children into home ownership because those parents believed that becoming homeowners was a 'natural' development in life's course. They felt that helping acquire a house for their young people was for 'living', rather than for investment. Zhang's interview reflects this position. As a first time homebuyer, home ownership is viewed as 'a necessity of life' rather than an investment because 'how can you sell your only house?' Renting and living in hotel is excluded as an unacceptable through the use of this rhetorical question. The meaning of investment was attached to a 'second, third house'. In other words, in order to profit from the booming housing market, it is perceived as being necessary to buy a second house, which may, of course, further contribute to increased demand and add to house price inflation.

> You know, home ownership is a necessity of life. For a kind of necessity, you would buy it in hurry if it had a clear increased trend.... However, for our generation, home ownership is needed to provide the necessities of life. For older generations, they may consider housing as an investment. They could estimate the trend and wisely buy their second, third house.... The reason for still paying attention to house prices is not checking current housing value but thinking about the right time to buy a second house. You can say the first house is an asset. But you cannot turn that kind of asset into cash. If you could not liquidate an asset, it is dead. As a first time home buyer, how can you sell your only house? Would you rent a place to live or you live in a hotel?
>
> (Zhang)

Ying's discourse reflects negative attitudes to home ownership in terms of investment. In her discourse, the group-defining word 'ours' was used in order to claim that housing as a financial investment is very rare. Conversely, others in the out-group 'sell the necessary house' are perceived negatively as 'in serious financial problem', illustrating some of Ying's ideological assumptions in regard to housing practices.

> The families like ours, it is very rare to sell a house in order to gain profit. Only if you were in serious financial problem, you would sell the house that is necessary for you.
>
> (Ying)

Positivity: settling down, security and control

Home ownership is supposed to have an effect on individual households in terms of an increased sense of freedom, security and control over life. Within the context of the contemporary Chinese housing system, attitudes towards home ownership have been strongly differentiated from other tenures because it is perceived to provide stability, security and control. The different characteristics attached to tenures also contribute to the attraction of home ownership as a perceived 'normal' carrier for home and 'standard' tenure in one's life course. However, the different meanings or advantages associated with home ownership are not eternal truths but socially constructed through mutual definition with other tenures in terms of shared discourses, experiences, assumptions, expectations within historical, economic and cultural contexts. Hence, it is necessary to explore how people regard groups living in other forms of tenure.

Stability seems to be the most important advantage to home ownership voiced by the respondents, especially by those from outside Beijing. Hong and Jing both pragmatically saw home ownership as conferring stability. Their narratives reflect the practical meaning of home ownership as a physical shelter where they were able to settle down and live permanently:

> Since then (buying a house), it is never necessary to deal with estate agents. I hate dealing with estate agents. And I do not need to move constantly from one rental to another. Moving made me tired.
>
> (Hong)

> I can live here permanently. I do not need to move frequently.
>
> (Jing)

The perceived advantages of home ownership are formed through a comparison with renting. In their narratives, home ownership is matched to a permanent way of living and opposed to 'moving constantly' and 'moving frequently', which they experienced as tenants. This idea of permanence emerges from a context of previously having had to move; that is, ideas of permanence regarding home ownership are shaped by a positive comparison to the negative experience of moving home frequently in other tenures.

From this it can be inferred that these young people equated home ownership with emotional and psychological stability and security; a sense of settling down. Their narratives stressed a subjective and emotional understanding regarding their owner occupation. Zhang abstracted the feeling of settling down as a sense of belonging. His discourse conceives of homeowners in Beijing as a group of young dream seekers. He emphasised that, especially for those from outside Beijing, home ownership creates a homely sense of belonging:

> From my personal feeling, I get a sense of belonging from home ownership. Our hometown is not Beijing but we work and live in Beijing. Thus, we are called as Bei Piao[7] (dream seekers in Beijing). We are a group of 'drifters'. We did not have a home and did not have a place for our heart before owning a house.
>
> (Zhang)

Yang offered a similar emphasis. She conceived home ownership in terms of psychological security and safety and settling down. In her discourse, the tenure of owner occupation represents an ideal. Home ownership and home are seen as virtually interchangeable terms:

> Before owning the house, I really expected that we could cook at home. I desired to have a feeling of home. Then we could wash clothes at home or we could do housework at home. We could experience the warmth of home.
>
> (Yan)

Actually, their narratives indicate that the meaning of owner occupation seems to 'kidnap' the concept of home although its process is subtle. Home ownership signifies home in a way that other tenures systems do not for this group. The meaning of home and a sense of belonging surrounding home ownership seem to be formed through discursive personal experiences and shared group beliefs. For Zhang, the desire to become a homeowner is the shared and interactive experience of a group of dream seekers in Beijing. For Yan, a shared social experience regarding home and home ownership also contributes to her image.

Fang's narrative indicates that the sense of settling down can be discursively constructed from daily experiences. In her discourse, the feeling of settling down is revealed in the use of metaphors of the nest. As birds come back to their nests, she felt that settling down in the house she owned gave her a secure feeling every day:

> It has a feeling of settling down. It is very important. For example, after busy work every day, you come back to your own nest.
>
> (Fang)

As discussed, in traditional agricultural society, Chinese people were reluctant to leave the place where they had lived for so long. The alternative explanation is that the strong sense of settling down and perceived stability is rooted in a common cultural ground. Under the pre-reform publicly allocated housing system, the sense of settling down and stability was continually attached to public rental housing. As Huang (2004b) argued, residents could live in public rental housing as long as they wanted but only if they were employed in the same work unit. On the one hand, this mobilised mass support. On the other hand, it further extended the sense of stability as 'natural' meaning surrounding mainstream tenure. The discourse of Dan reflects this point. Chinese residents lived in public rental housing and despite this housing not being owned, the notion of settling down in public housing was very much apparent. Therefore, the process through which home ownership ideologies have formed is a complex interaction between shared social beliefs and cultural and historical contexts:

During my childhood, my family lived in a public house allocated by the work unit.... During that period people had a stable place to settle down. That is why they did not seek home ownership.

(Dan)

Moreover, control is another main advantage attached to home ownership. Compared with experiences of private rental, control, autonomy and freedom have also been demonstrated to be a crucial and exclusive meaning attached to owner occupation. For Richards (1990), the control in terms of owner occupation has two aspects, one negative and one positive. The negative one is that no one can put you out, and the positive one is that you can make the place 'yours'. The positive aspect of control can be interpreted as settling down, as mentioned earlier. The term 'you can make it yours' indeed stresses the sense of autonomy and independence that young homeowners derive, as well as voicing a sense of their gaining individuality, despite often needing family help.

Jie stated that her quality of life improved because owner occupation offers the freedom for her to buy more furniture and electrical appliances. When she rented, she would never have considered buying such items:

Because it is my own home, I have bought a lot of things which I would never buy if I was in private rental, such as a table, sofa, water dispenser and so on. In this way, your living quality has been improved.

(Fang)

Negative attitudes to the private rental sector

During the socialist transformation in China during the 1950s, the private housing sector, conflicting as it did with socialist ideology, was completely removed, and privately rented housing was changed into a public, government controlled housing. In the socialist ideology, landlords were treated as social outcasts and viewed as exploiting the class below them by taking money through rent, rather than by earning it through having their own labour or skills. Through socialist purchase, most private housing was transferred to public ownership. The housing market almost disappeared, and the private rental sector declined dramatically from about 17 per cent in 1949 to 5.3 per cent in 1963; since then it has remained below 5 per cent. The remaining privately owned houses were mainly for self-occupancy rather than for profit (Huang 2004). The responsibility for urban public rental housing provision, its allocation, maintenance and management, was tied to the state and its work units as a part of the state's political and ideological goals (Zhang 1997). The empirical analysis of Huang (2004) indicated that, during the reform period, those living in the public rental sector were less likely to move from renting to home ownership as there were many advantages to renting public housing created by the government's housing policies.

The national housing reforms begun in 1988 have led to an increasingly privatised housing system. Private home ownership has become a popular choice in

China (Lee and Zhu 2006). As discussed, there is now a housing system with the dual features of state controlled social housing and privately rented housing. One consequence of China's powerful economic growth is that there has been rapid and dramatic industrialisation and urbanisation in the country, which has acted to stimulate the growth of rented housing, which is necessary to support the growing urban migration. Renting privately in urban China began to play a significant role in providing either a transitional tenure or residual housing to this mass influx, especially to those who could not afford to buy a home, and could not access social housing because of the stricter eligibility criteria. Zhao (2007) pointed out that urban migrants, migrant workers, those who have to move because of the reconstruction of the old city and those living in 'new living modes' (such as changes in family structure, divorce or independence of young people) constitute the main consumer groups for privately rented housing in urban China. However, from a migrant worker's view, the evidence of Wang, Wang and Wu (2010) suggests that private rental housing in 'urban villages' offers cheap and affordable housing in a less intimidating environment. Although for young educated people working in large cities, the private rental arrangement seems the only feasible way to live before becoming homeowners or moving into social housing, such low-quality rental housing is mainly provided for rural to urban migrants (Logan et al. 2009; Wang et al. 2012). The interview below with an estate agent suggests the importance of renting privately to young people:

> There are a large number of graduate young people choosing private rental.... At the beginning of their career, they cannot earn as high a salary as they may have expected.... Against the current house prices in Beijing, it is impossible for most of them to achieve their own home ownership without any family help.... They have to rely on the private rental sector if they prefer to work in Beijing.
>
> (Estate Agent)

However, within the context of transitional urban China, the private rental sector and its association with owner occupation has remained under-researched while, Kemeny (1995, 2001, 2006) argues, most housing research focuses on the empirical nature of the argument and an Anglo-Saxon dualist rental paradigm. Home ownership has been perceived as inherently more attractive than renting for a long time. But, from the perspective of policy constructivism, Kemeny (1995: 152) emphasised that in fact, as a result of dualist housing policies, a great many households are forced into owner occupation. He argues that

> with its high insecurity of tenure, rents that gravitate towards a return on the current market value of property, and often high levels of landlord selectivity from among potential tenants and interference in domestic matters, create a housing system in which the only form of housing that offers security of tenure and at least an element of non-profit extraction is owner occupation.
>
> (Ibid.: 152)

This section, then, aims to offer empirical evidence in order to clearly explore the relationship between attitudes to owner occupation and the private rental sector and the process through which these attitudes are forming.

Ambiguity: perceived advantages of renting privately

In my fieldwork, nearly all the interviewed young people from outside Beijing have experience of renting privately in the short and long term, although most described it as a temporary or transitional tenure. These personal experiences of renting play an influential role in their attitudes to tenures and then their housing practices.

Most of the young people interviewed offered practical explanations of their decisions to rent privately. They emphasised that the main advantage for choosing private rental housing over owner occupation was its short distance to their college or working place. It is understandable that young people prefer living near their working places so that they do not waste time and energy in commuting; however, they most often cannot afford to buy a home near their places of work. Hence, renting privately is a viable, low cost housing choice which can help facilitate young people's careers and improve their quality of life, rather than immediately choosing to buy expensively in the same area. Their explanations actually reflected the short-term cost advantage and location advantage of private rental:

> My rental was located around the north 4th ring road. It was near to my working place ... I rented it because I could not afford owner occupation (around the area).
>
> (Wu)

> I rented a one bedroom flat before buying my house ... it was in the Hepingli community, near the city centre ... it is an old building built in the 1970s ... it was very cheap at that time, RMB1,300 (for monthly rent).
>
> (Zhou)

> In terms of my rented place before (having my own house), it was within the 3rd Ring Road of Beijing. I always prefer a rental location near my working place.
>
> (Hong)

Moreover, flexibility is another advantage young people enjoyed as tenants. As discussed previously, the young people interviewed preferred to live near their places of work so that they could avoid the inconveniences of commuting. Renting made it easy to move to other areas, for example, following a change in their working location. Short-term rent contracts enabled them to move quickly from one rented accommodation to another. The interview data from Wang and Fei highlight the flexibility of renting privately. Wang could move to accommodation near her work place. Fei similarly described the convenience of being able to live near his place of work or study:

I moved to a new rented place because my previous living place was too far from my working location ... I never lived here before. I prefer rental housing here only because my work is here...

(Fei)

Since 2005, I had rented for two years ... I changed my rented place three times. At the beginning, I rented a place near my university. Normally, I chose private rental not far from my study place. After graduating from my previous university, I prepared for the postgraduate entrance examination of the Beijing Film Academy. So I moved to a private rental place near the Beijing Film Academy.

(Wang)

Negative feelings: long-term financial loss

Although there are some pragmatic advantages within the short-term which the interviewees identified from renting privately, they still perceived this as the less desirable tenure. In terms of the perception of the cost of renting privately, it is interesting to note that the respondents had some very unhappy associations with renting privately, such as the constant rent increases, although rent growth ratio is slower than that of house prices. They expressed the point of view that the economic benefits of renting privately were only short-term ones. While rocketing house prices with constantly increased ratio of price to rent provided the resources of being used in the application of epistemic evaluation, young people gave subjective interpretations of context based on personal and shared social knowledge. They considered renting privately to be expensive only when they compared rent prices with house prices. In their discourse, expensive rents connoted not only a high cost in the present, deducted from their disposable income, but also a high cost in the future, as it was money not being spent in order to buy a home, and in the context of soaring house prices, it would be imperative to buy as soon as possible. Therefore, renting privately was not seen as a long term option. Ostensibly, increases in rent pushed the interviewees into leaving privately rented accommodation; however, an ideological evaluation of the cost of rent is an important element influencing their attitudes to the private rental sector. In this respect, the narrative of the young people interviewed appeared to be central: a mortgage was perceived as buying something rent payments did not. Fang and Hong explained that it is not worth paying more and more rent:

The rent goes up so rapidly (in Beijing). Compared to rent in June of 2009, rent increased by about 50%. That is you have to pay RMB1,000 more. Before, I paid RMB2,400 for a flat with two living rooms. Now it requires more than RMB3,000, around RMB3,500.

(Hong)

> We considered that we needed to pay more money as rent in every month. We might as well pay a mortgage monthly as pay the landlord.
>
> (Fang)

This response evidences how rents in the profit-dominated private housing market push the tenants out; nonetheless, the point needs to be explained more clearly. On the one hand, the dualist housing policy is significant. Landlords can charge rents at the current market value and do not need to worry about competition from other tenures such as social welfare housing. Young people have to rely on the private rental market in order to access accommodation. On the other hand, against soaring house prices in transitional urban China, paying more rent is understood as 'wasting' money. Influenced not only by personal experience and knowledge but also shared social beliefs, the interviewees preferred to become homeowners as soon they could in order to avoid financial loss in the long-term as house prices continued to rise.

Moreover, young people's generalised inference to private rental sector is built not only on what they were engaged in but also what they repeatedly witnessed, heard or read. Zhao's hometown is Beijing. She had never had any personal experience of renting privately. However, she had a negative perception of the private rental sector in terms of rent being expensive, rising rents, and unregulated rent payment terms which she had heard from her colleagues:

> Compared to rental, the cost of owning a home is the major advantage. For my colleagues, they have to move when the rent increases. Our company does not offer very high salaries. You had to move to another place (with cheaper rent) in case the rent increases. In Beijing, landlords sometimes ask you to pay half-year rent or whole year rent at a time in advance. It is very difficult to spare so much money all at once. They prefer paying RMB200 more every month rather than paying half-year rent or whole year rent once.
>
> (Zhao)

Negative feelings: instability and insecurity

After China's housing reform with neoliberal urbanisation (Lee and Zhu 2006), the private rental market was transformed into a profit-making free market. There were no effective regulations to restrict landlords, housing agents and tenants. In this way, the landlord became a powerful figure in the private housing sector, and experiences of renting privately seem to depend on the behaviour and practices of the landlord. Most young people interviewed complained that it was difficult to find good quality privately rented accommodation for the time period they required it. As tenants, the insecurity of their positions disturbed them, and they experienced a lack of control over their tenancy, as well as conflicts with landlords or housing agents during the process of renting.

The majority of interviewees expressed negative attitudes to landlords and housing agents and the private rental market. These negative perceptions seem to be widely shared among other tenants in Beijing and throughout China. As a consequence of a dualist rental system, 'housing provision on a non-profit basis is cut off from the rental housing market through being socialised and controlled by a bureaucratic set of rules that limit public access to the non-profit rental housing stock' (Kemeny 2007: 2). While the Chinese housing system shares some features of the dualist housing system, the private rental sector does not face competition from publicly rented housing. This has led to the 'free' private rental sector being free for landlords rather than free for tenants. Tenants in privately rented accommodation have weak or non-existent security of tenure. The unregulated, profit-oriented private rental housing market has directly shaped the personal experiences of young people. Their unhappy personal experiences in privately rented accommodation fuel their desire to become homeowners.

Zheng and Mei, a couple, perceived renting privately as insecure because they were asked to move out during the rental contract. It seems that their security was dependent on the landlord himself rather than rental contract.

> The previous landlord told us he would sell his flat when our contract was not due. We had no idea. He paid us a penalty sum and asked us to move out.... We did not know whether his story was true. The only thing we could do was look for another rental place...
>
> (Zheng)
>
> Just feel insecurity.
>
> (Mei)
>
> Just like you lived here, you had to leave when the landlord asked you to move out.
>
> (Zheng)
>
> You just cannot live in a place for long.
>
> (Mei)
>
> Interviewer: Even within the rental contract period?
> Yes. Even during the period of rental contract, there is no guarantee that you can live here.
>
> (Mei)

While effective competition from social welfare housing has been suppressed, the private rental housing becomes a particular resource of the landlord. Controlling the particular resources can help the landlord and housing agent to acquire as much profit as possible. The tenants have a rather poor bargaining position. The interpersonal interactions between powerful landlords (with housing agents) and relatively powerless tenants have gradually constructed the interviewees' attitudes to private rental housing. Hong's negative opinion of renting privately was formed from personal experiences with housing agents. Her response indicates that not only can the duration of the tenure be insecure, but also the deposit is not guaranteed to be returned:

> In Beijing, it is difficult to rent an apartment directly from a private landlord. Normally, their apartments have been rented by small 'black' house agents. Then they rented it out for earning more money. For me, the main disadvantage of private rental housing in Beijing is the result of these landlords and house agents. There is very much a lack of regulation.... You paid a deposit and just never got it back. It was impossible. He could invent any excuses, this is not good, that is not good, or delayed returning it forever. There are uneducated hooligans to do this business (rented from landlord and then sublet to tenants).... Once we rented directly from a landlord. He was a rascal as well. Before we moved out, he checked everything and said all was well. He always says everything is fine, even now. However, it has been half a year since we moved out. I have not received my deposit. He always says he is outside Beijing for business and so on.... To such people, I cannot help but say sorry to myself. What can I do? For RMB2,000, will I sue him? It is too much bother ... There are weak regulations controlling them.
>
> (Hong)

Moreover, even though some young people did not have unhappy rental experiences, they still had negative attitudes towards the private rental sector because they had been largely influenced by the perceptions of others with regard to renting privately. M19's negative opinion was not based on his personal experience but from listening to his friends' experiences. In his narrative, the feeling of insecurity is associated with private rental housing, and he frames the negative experience of renting privately as 'common':

> For myself, I did not have any unhappy experience (in private rental housing). But I just knew I had to suffer it before renting. One of my friends, they rented a flat at good price. However, the landlord did not give real details of the flat. After moving in, my friends found there were many pipes under the floor. So it was too noisy to go to sleep at night. Of course, they got gypped. It was enough to make anyone jumpy if this kind of thing happened many times. But it is common.
>
> (Zhang)

According to the interview data of M4, it seemed to be a common experience that landlords would not keep to the terms of the rent contract if they could increase their profits. This made tenants feel powerless and insecure, and without any recourse of action.

> It is obvious that rental is different from owning housing. You are really anxious about the landlord. For example, the rent around the area is soaring

at the moment. You would be informed that your monthly rent would increase by RMB300. If you disagreed, ok, you would be asked to move out.... He would say my relative would come to live here or I would sell the flat you rented.... He could invent any excuse.... You know, the contract is simply not reliable.

(Zhou)

Negativity: low quality and inconvenience

In addition to the more direct interactions with a profit-oriented 'free' private renting market, this section explores more complicated aspects of the process of constructing the meanings attached to renting privately. It examines the pragmatism in the responses of the interviewees rather than only emphasising constraints from the supply side. The fieldwork in Beijing found that young people were a relatively vulnerable group in low-paid and unstable work and tended to rent housing with a relatively low rent. Moreover, in order to live near their places of work or to commute easily, they rented relatively cheap private housing which tended to be of low quality in terms of poor building quality and badly furnished living areas. This housing was also often in undesirable neighbourhoods. Negative attitudes to private rental have emerged from negative personal living experiences in private rental housing. Thus their generalised inferences construct value to the private rental sector as the lower rung of a hierarchical tenure ladder.

First, most young people attributed their negative attitudes to the low quality of private rental housing. In the fieldwork, young people with rental experience preferred low rent, convenient private rental housing, at the expense of quality. In this way, poor housing quality plays a crucial role in forming negative perceptions of private rental. Wending indicates his repeatedly observed specific event in private rental housing. The negative label 'old' and 'dirty' has been attached to private rental. Wang complained about the size, facilities and furniture in privately rented accommodation. His personal experience led him to think of private rental housing as 'shabby':

> I rented a one bedroom flat between the north 3rd ring road and the 2nd ring road. The rent was RMB1,800 per month. The size of the flat was 40 square metres. It was very shabby. The elevator stopped on every third floor. You had to climb up the stairs if the elevator did not stop on your floor. It was too old and shabby. And the elevator did not work after 12 p.m. I lived on the 12th floor. I had to climb up the stairs if I got back late. I had a dog at that time. In winter, when I finished work very late, I had to climb up to take the dog downstairs for a walk. Then I had to climb up again. Anyway, it was very shabby. Only 40 square metres, one bedroom and the all furniture was broken.

(Wang)

> The room I rented was old. It had wooden floors, but there were cockroaches. Especially in winter, the cockroaches were under the wooden floor. I felt it was very dirty ... I lived there only because it was cheap, only RMB800 per month.
>
> (Wending)

In turn, the low quality housing young people rented reinforce the 'free state' of the private rental market from the tenant aspect. Tenants would not maintain low quality rented housing in a good condition. In order to seek maximum profit, landlords would also neglect the refurbishment of low quality housing. Han and Zhu revealed the 'hidden rules' of the private rental market; there is a striking contrast in terms of attitudes toward private rental housing and owner occupation. Privately rented accommodation is not well maintained, but if the landlord himself wanted to live there, he 'would refurbish and even renovate his apartment'. The outcome is that the label of lower quality attached to private rental housing is further reinforced:

> It is unregulated here.... It may be a formal rental contract (between landlord and me).... No one would strictly follow it. When you moved out, it was no problem if there were any small damages in his flat. The landlord himself knew it would not be maintained well when he wanted to rent it out. He would refurbish and even renovate his apartment if he wanted to live here.
>
> (Han)

> I never signed any contract with landlords. It was in China.
>
> (Zhu)

> It was a mere formality. Nobody would care it as long as you did not go too far.
>
> (Pin)

> As long as you did not pull down the wall in the room, everything would be fine. As for the landlord, he did not at any time come here to check everything. Sometimes the landlord never comes here as long as you paid rent on time. He will renovate it when he wants to live in it. The landlord has earned enough money for renewing and redecoration. But normally, he just leaves it.
>
> (Zhu)

Second, it seems common that young tenants tend to share an apartment in order to save money in Beijing. Most young tenants prefer renting one bedroom in an apartment and share the kitchen, bathroom and living rooms with other tenants. Consequently, there has been much 'inconvenience' emerging in their daily lives. Although shared private rental housing only occurs as one kind of low cost living arrangement, the young people, especially those who only had personal experience in shared rental housing, use the word 'inconvenience' to express their discontent with private rental. In other words, their negative perceptions formed discursively in shared private rental housing have been attached to the whole private rental sector. In their discourse, they indicated that they are dissatisfied with the subordination of their personal goals in shared rental housing. Interview data indicates a desire to 'do things as they wished without considering others'. To some extent, this individualist tendency plays an important role in pulling young people out of the private rental sector.

Li had moved several times before owning a house because of 'inconvenience'. His negative attitude was formed after being disturbed by the improper and immoral behaviour of other tenants:

> You cannot constrain other tenants' behaviours. You had no way in case they played until 2 a.m.... Nobody would clean the common areas, such as kitchen and toilet. They were always in a mess. Even though I cleaned them, it would be in a mess again next week.... But compared to renting an apartment, it (renting one room) was cheap.
>
> (Li)

Li lived in rented accommodation for approximately one year before buying a home. Her complaint was a result of feeling discomfort in the public areas and feeling that her privacy was invaded. Her negative perceptions of the private rental sector gradually built up from her daily interaction with other tenants.

> There are too many inconveniences when you choose sharing-renting, such as no privacy, and inconvenience when cooking. You just do not know who would share with you. You have to fit in with them. You have to sacrifice many things.
>
> (Li)

> Interviewer: What is the privacy you mentioned? What are your things you have to sacrifice? Could you give me some examples?
>
> The concept of privacy is too general. It mainly means inconvenience in daily life. For example, it was inconvenient when a friend visited me and we talked with each other. Or in summer, it was inconvenient when wearing very casual clothes. Or when other renters' friends came, we had to talk with them although we did not wish to do that. There were all tiny things. The sacrificed things were, as I like to sleep late or I wanted to play music loudly, but I might be disturbed by or disturb other tenants.
>
> (Li)

Before owning a house, Zhu had always lived in a shared rented apartment. Perhaps because he lived with his friends, he never mentioned the improper or immoral behaviour of other tenants. Nonetheless, he mentioned that his lifestyle had been negatively impacted. In this way, 'too many inconveniences' were associated with the private rental sector:

> There are too many inconveniences, too many in private rental housing. Everyone has different habits and lifestyle, different sleeping times, such as someone works at night so he had sleep in the daytime.... We had to queue to use the toilet. Every morning, we all left for work around 7 a.m., 8 a.m. For the toilet, that was a busy time. We were all tired after the last day's work. Nobody wished to get up early.
>
> (Zhu)

Makeshift lifestyles and a feeling of 'homelessness'

Financial loss in the long-term, the feeling of insecurity and low quality living environments have contributed to the interviewees' perceptions of the private rental sector. Through repeated observations and experiences of sharing and interacting with other tenants, landlords and housing agents, young people have gradually formed a perception that the private rental housing is a transitional tenure. The outcomes are that, on the one hand, young tenants had a pragmatic attitude towards private rental housing; on the other, a prejudice towards renting privately has been constructed, in that private rental housing cannot be considered 'home', but owner occupation can and is. Gurney (1999a) has argued that 'home' is frequently used to differentiate between the dwellings of householders in owner occupation and those in rented accommodation; the dwellings of those in owner occupation are imbued with 'the warmth and security of "home", whilst renters are accorded a more Spartan language to describe their dwelling' (1999a: 172). The word 'home' has been used less frequently, less evocatively and less emotionally in relation to private rental than to home ownership. In Gurney's fieldwork in Bristol in the UK, 39 of the 52 respondents considered that 'ownership did make a difference to their feeling about the home' (1999b: 1713).

In transitional urban China, the interviewed young people expressed similar prejudices in terms of the relationship between home ownership and renting privately, but more distinctly and pragmatically. At the very beginning of entering private rental housing, nearly all of them treated the tenure as only temporary accommodation before owning their own home. Among the young people interviewed, there is ample evidence in terms of managed lifestyle in private rental housing. They tended not to do any decoration or buy any unnecessary things in privately rented accommodation because it was only a transitional place before owning a home. Their narratives attribute their pragmatic attitude to a feeling of 'homelessness' in private rental.

Yan gave a representative impression of rented accommodation. In her narrative, private rental housing was matched to the rough concrete floor and a few of pieces of simple furniture. She developed the sense of a makeshift lifestyle while living in low quality privately rented accommodation. Private rental housing was treated as 'not our house' and 'not a permanent solution':

> The advantage of rental was that I did not need to clean the room. There were only two of us. The floor was rough concrete without any covering.

> The only thing we had was a double bed in the room. Then we bought a simple wardrobe. We picked an old desk thrown out by my husband's company.... During the period in rental, the only thing we bought was the wardrobe.... The disadvantage was that it is not our house. I did not feel as if I was settling down.... It is not a permanent solution.
>
> (Yan)

Fei draws on a familiar stereotype about these temporary places and a 'have to self-manage' lifestyle. Because of a feeling of 'makeshift' in private rental, she tried to 'not to buy any unnecessary things' and to live 'as simply as possible':

> I felt I did not have a home. I would not buy anything for the rented apartment although I really wanted to buy them. I always swallowed my desire. I was afraid it would be too much stuff to move. The only thing I bought was a refrigerator. It was so necessary for me ... I tried to not to buy any unnecessary things in my rental accommodation. It was as simple as possible.
>
> (Fei)

More ambiguity: attitudes to social welfare housing

Although the system of public housing provision came to a close at the end of the 1990s, the government aimed to develop a social welfare housing system in order to solve the affordability problem most residents in urban areas faced. The housing reform targeted most urban residents while only the higher-income households were expected to purchase newly built commercial housing in the housing market. In Beijing, The Low Rental Housing (LRH) scheme is designed to make housing accessible to low-income groups who had the Beijing *hukou*; the Economic Comfort Housing (ECH) scheme and 'Two-Limitation' Housing (TLH) programmes were designed to enable middle and low-income groups with the local *hukou* to own their own property after they had lived in it for five years. Within the context of the neoliberal turn, it is clear that the primary goal of these housing policies was to stimulate housing consumption in order to promote economic growth for central government and for local governments to profit from land sale. Decentralisation has facilitated the creation of a housing model in China with several similarities to housing models in English-speaking countries. As a result of the housing policy reform, social welfare housing has been marginalised. The original goal of social welfare housing system has been not achieved. There is evidence of a reduced proportion of ECH and insufficient LRH housing available, partly as a result of the decentralisation of housing policy and soaring land prices. Local governments are able and willing to sell more land for financing local use rather than freely allocating land for social welfare housing.

From a quantitative perspective, the evidence of the home ownership rate reaching nearly 90 per cent in 2012 with a constantly decreasing proportion of social welfare housing indicates that China indeed shares features with a dualist housing model demonstrated in English-speaking home-owning societies. One of the important characteristics in a dualist housing system is the stigmatisation of marginalised social welfare housing. As Gurney (1999a) argues, a normalising discourse embedded within home ownership has stigmatised private and social rental in a home owning society. In this way, the stigmatisation of social welfare housing and desire to escape the negative aspects of private renting play a crucial role in the process of creating positive attitudes for home ownership. Surprisingly, the interview data do not show meaningful associations between the social welfare housing sector and stigmatisation in urban China, despite the social welfare housing sector being marginalised in terms of its proportion in tenure structure. Although a few of the young people interviewed expressed their negative attitudes towards social welfare housing, the attitudes of most young people towards social welfare housing tend to be positive, while they complain about why they can not access it.

Prejudice against social welfare housing

From an analysis of the fieldwork interviews in Beijing, it is clear that all interviewees do not have any direct personal experience of accessing social welfare housing, such as ECH, TLH and LRH. Considering their attitudes to the sector, a few of them express prejudice against social welfare housing. Zhang's narrative indicates his negative perceptions of the neighbourhood of social housing, even though he used the word 'objectively' to try to qualify his negativity. He explains, 'you would never wish your child to grow up in this kind of neighbourhood'. His discourse reveals a desire to distance himself, his identity and his family from the negative connotations of social welfare housing and social housing tenants:

> From my personal perspective, I have not considered applying for ECH at that time. It has been said of old, Meng Mu San Qian, Ze Lin Er Ju (Mencius' mother had moved her house three times before finding a location that she felt was suitable for the child's upbringing[8]). Objectively, I have an impression that there are some problems in environments and groups who purchased ECH. You would never wish your child to grow up in this kind of neighbourhood. It is very important to raise children in a good environment. Buying housing in a decent environment is an important thing in your life.
>
> (Zhang)

Positive attitudes to social welfare housing

For most of the young people interviewed, their focus is on reasons why they could not access it. The following extract illustrates how strict the entry requirements are, including the requirement that applicants have a local *hukou* and proof of a low income. There are currently five million people in Beijing, that is,

29 per cent of Beijing's total population, who do not have a local *hukou*, and are therefore ineligible to apply for social welfare housing. For Wu and Fang, the requirements of the household registration system were the main barrier to accessing social welfare housing, even though the income of Wu and her boyfriend met the entry criteria for ECH:

> You know, only residents with a Beijing *hukou* are qualified to apply for social welfare housing. It was impossible for me to apply for any kinds of social welfare housing because I did not have a Beijing *hukou* at that time.
>
> (Wu)

> The length of employment and a Beijing *hukou* are key criteria. At that moment, I just graduated from the university. My boyfriend had worked for only one year. We may meet the income criterion of applying for ECH. But for the other requirement, it was difficult to meet it. For example, he did not have a Beijing *hukou*.
>
> (Fang)

Two interviewees used the word 'sandwich class' to describe themselves as marginal households who were penalised by the strict eligibility criteria for social welfare housing, in relation to their family asset and annual earning being below a certain amount and the affordability problem of buying a home. They explained that it is impossible for them to access social welfare housing because of the strict eligibility criteria. However, the increasing housing prices also make it difficult for them to become homeowners:

> In terms of ECH, you know, we belonged to a sandwich class. I mean we fell in between applying to ECH and being able to afford commodity housing. We could not reach both sides. So what could you do? Finally, we had to buy commodity housing on the housing market because we could not access social welfare housing ... I had read the regulations of requirements. My situation was just over their restriction a little bit. But what could I do? What do you think I should do? Those are rigid regulations. Nobody can stretch a point for me.... If I met the qualifications, I would definitely apply for it. I know its location is far from the city centre. For young people, it does not matter.
>
> (Qiao)

> I had considered applying for it. But I found I was not qualified. For ECH, it's necessary that your age is over 30 if you are single. Or it has income limitations if you are married. For example, the annual income of your family is below a certain amount of money. We cannot meet them. We are just like a sandwich class who cannot reach the lower side of ECH and cannot afford to buy a house on the market.
>
> (Jie)

Interview data from Mei shows the decreasing possibility of gaining access to welfare housing. Although it was very difficult for her family to buy a home, she never attempted to apply for social welfare housing. She believed that there is little possibility of accessing it, given the application experiences of her colleagues. She explained that although 'the numbers of social welfare housing applicants are increasing, compared to the number of demands, there is still be a gap between them'. This reflects the effect of marginalised social welfare housing in terms of it being largely inaccessible in urban China:

> It's like this. It is difficult to gain access to them. One of my colleagues, he gained it in 2008. At that time, it was not too difficult to access it. Before him, another two colleagues have actually accessed ECH around Li Shui Qiao.[9] That sounds good. However, after them, it needs a long long time to gain it. Another colleague had waited for it for a long time, finally having to buy an apartment on the housing market ... you have to wait and wait. You can see whether you wish to spend ages waiting. You know, at present, more and more young people are graduating from universities. Thus, more and more qualified applicants are joining and will join the list. The numbers of social welfare housing applicants are increasing that much. The Government announced that ten million units of social welfare housing will be constructed in this year. But compared to the number of demands, there will still be a gap between them.
>
> (Mei)

It is interesting to explore ambiguous attitudes towards the social welfare housing sector. First, the issue of fragmentation among groups of young people should be considered. When further analysing the background of young people holding negative attitudes to the sector, it indicates that they are from more wealthy families who support their housing purchase or have well-paid jobs, such as bank managers. As homeowners, or being able to access home ownership in a good neighbourhood, they want to distinguish themselves from residents living in social housing. For the majority of young people from ordinary families and at a weaker position in the labour market, their positive attitudes reflect pragmatism. It seems they are pushed to enter the housing market rather than being offered initiative to escape from the social housing sector. Social housing schemes offer an economic way to achieve home ownership because, based on housing polices, they are able to own their own property, such as ECH and LRH, after they have lived in it for five years.

Second, the important role played by policy in the process in which positive attitudes to the social housing sector are formed should be re-emphasised. As discussed, according to social housing policy, only groups who have the Beijing *hukou* are qualified to join the queue to apply for social welfare housing. It means that the groups at the lowest position in the labour market, such as migrant workers, are excluded. Meanwhile, companies, institutions, ministries and commissions are allowed to collect funds from their qualified employees for cooperative house-building. Based on social housing policies, this kind of fund-raising building qualifies for parts of the national ECH scheme. In this process, qualified employees are allowed to enjoy tax cuts and a discounted price or cost price, while their company will offer the construction land and pay other related fees and tax. In this way, only employees working for companies with better benefits or institutions with good financial revenue are able to reach the 'welfare housing'. Thus, the tenants in this kind of 'welfare housing' as a group of social elite make a contribution to the attraction of quantitatively marginalised social welfare housing.

Conclusions

I have attempted here to promote an understanding of attitudes to housing tenure attitudes among young people in transitional China, which has experienced a rapid growth of home ownership, and shares features of the housing system in English-speaking home-owning societies. I have discussed the effects from both structural and individual elements during which the 'attitudes' form, focusing on the micro level and using a qualitative approach. I have chosen the young as a target group for this discussion since they play an important role in the contemporary Chinese housing market, in the context of a more or less mature housing market and a fragmentation among various groups regarding housing practices.

Through analysing the cultural origins of attitudes to housing from a historical perspective, I offer a criticism of the 'taken for granted' desire of owning land as an explanation for the current preference of private ownership, and I offer explanations of a cultural common ground in terms of tenure: the desire to settle down and the reluctance to move. Based on this cultural common ground, I argue that there was a preference for the public rental sector rather than owner occupation during the era of top-down socialist housing policies; this cultural common ground played a crucial role in shaping housing attitudes when ordinary people had limited choices. Based on the interview materials, I explore the attitudes of young people towards different tenures in the post-reform housing system.

Following the housing reform, which has significantly changed the Chinese housing system from being centrally planned to being market-oriented, people have achieved more freedom in housing tenure choices. Their feelings include positive attitudes towards owner occupation, negative attitudes towards the private rental sector and rather ambivalent attitudes towards social welfare housing; these feelings have been formed through comparing their direct or indirect experiences in these tenures. However, it does not mean their attitudes are discursively formed only from the process of social construct. The positive attitudes to owner occupation and negative attitudes to the private rental sector are constructed by the dynamic process of policy transformation within the market situation, and within a cultural situation where substantial intergenerational transfers occur. In other words, people compare their experiences in different tenures, construct their beliefs to tenures and share their tenure attitudes. But in this process during which their attitudes are constructed, their positive attitudes appear not to be towards 'owner occupation' per se, but towards the perceived advantages such as 'not losing money' against the background of a booming housing market, and toward that 'settling down', which I have explained as arising from a cultural common ground. My perception is that attitudes have been formed through an interactive process between personal tenure experiences, and meanings constructed by policy pertaining to these tenures.

Notes

1 A housing reform trail was initiated in *Yantai* (a prefecture level city in northeastern Shandong province, People's Republic of China) between 1982 and 1985 that combined economic rents and housing vouchers in order to encourage housing sales.
2 People's Daily Online is a key news website in China constructed by *People's Daily*, one of the world's top ten selling newspapers.
3 RMB, short name for Renminbi, also known as Chinese yuan, is the official currency of China. The average middle exchange rate between British pounds sterling and RMB during the period from August 2006 to February 2012 was: 1 pound=RMB12.0808. At the 1 March 2012, the middle exchange rate between British pounds sterling and RMB was: 1 pound=RMB10.0356. The data is from the official website of People's Bank of China (www.pbc.gov.cn/publish/zhengcehuobisi/637/index.html) [accessed 2 November 2012].
4 Mainly caused by the Tiananmen Square incident in 1989. Moreover, some leaders also questioned whether encouraging private housing ownership would alter the existing social structure and contribute to social inequalities.
5 Through learning from Singapore's Central Provident Fund and Hong Kong's management system, the Shanghai HPF was established in 1991and the contributions to the fund were managed by the Shanghai Housing Provident Fund Management Centre with the Bank of Construction as its fund manager (Lee 2000). The system required both employer and employee to make a contribution to the employee's housing saving fund. The initial rate of contribution was set at 10 per cent of an employee's salary (shared between employers and employee). The fund could only be used for housing purchase or repair or for other purpose when the employee reaches retirement age (Wang *et al.* 2005).
6 Another name is Affordable Housing; the kind of housing for which buyers only need only pay for the production costs (SC 1994).
7 The literal meaning of the word is 'drifter' in Beijing. It normally represents the group of young migrants in pursuit of dreams in Beijing. The word drifter means that, physically, the group of young people migrate to Beijing; psychologically they lack a sense of belonging.
8 Mencius was a Chinese philosopher who was arguably the most famous Confucian after Confucius himself. His mother is often held up as an exemplary female figure in Chinese culture. The story of moving three times indicates the importance of finding the proper environment for raising children. Zhang used this story to indicate that the neighbourhood of ECH was improper for raising children.
9 *Li Shui Qiao* is a community located outside the north 5th ring road. Compared to other ECH projects which are far from the 5th ring road, it is close to the 5th ring road. It also mirrors a gradually marginalised process of geographical distributions of social welfare housing in urban China.

References

Agnew, J. 1981 'Home-ownership and Identity in Capitalist Societies'. In Duncan, J.S. (Ed.) *Housing and Identity*. London: Croom Helm.
Balfour, D. and Smith, J. 1996 'Transforming lease-purchase housing programs for low income families: towards empowerment and engagement'. *Journal of Urban Affairs* 18 (2) pp. 173–188.

Bao, Z.H. 2002 *Residential Housing and Property*. Beijing: China Building Industry Press.

Bridge, G. 2001 'Bourdieu, rational action and the time-space strategy of gentrification'. Transactions of the Institute of British Geographers NS 26 pp. 205–216.

Bridge, G. 2006 'It's not just a question of taste: Gentrification, the neighbourhood and cultural capital'. *Environment and Planning A* 38 pp. 1965–1978.

Burr, V. 2003 *Social Constructionism (Second edition)*. Sussex: Psychology Press.

Butler, T. and Robson, G. 2003 *London Calling: The Middle Classes and the Remaking of Inner London*. Oxford: Berg.

Canter, D. 1977 *The Psychology of Place*. New York: St. Martin Press.

Castells, M. 1977 *The Urban Question: A Marxist Approach*. London: Edward Arnold.

Chan, C.K., Ngok, K.L. and Phillips, D. 2008 *Social Policy in China: Development and Well-being*. Bristol: The Polity Press.

Chen, J.J. and Wills, D. 1997 'Development of urban housing policies in China'. *Construction Management and Economics* 15 (3) pp. 283–290.

Chen, W. 2005 'Urban planning and real estate industry in scientific development review (*Yi kexue fazhan guan kan chengshi he fangdichan*)', *Urban Studies (chengshi fazhan yanjiu)* 12 (1) pp. 14–18.

China Everbright Bank and the Beijing Homelink Housing Agent. 2010 'An analytical report of housing loan market of second-hand house in Beijing' (*Beijingshi ershoufang fangdai shichang fenxi baogao*) S*ina Dichan*, Accessed at http://news.dichan.sina.com.cn/2010/08/26/204626_all.html on 27 August 2010.

Chu, K.Y. and Kwok, R.Y. 1990 'China'. In Vliet, W.V. (Ed.) *International Handbook of Housing Policies and Practices*. New York: Greenwood Press.

Clapham, D. 2002 'Housing pathways: a post modern analytical framework'. *Housing, Theory and Society* 2002 (19) pp. 57–68.

Clapham, D. 2005 *The Meaning of Housing: A Pathways Approach*. Bristol: The Polity Press.

Clark, W.A.V., Dieleman, F.M. and Deurloo, M.C. 1994 'Tenure changes in the context of micro-level family and marco level economic shifts'. *Urban Studies* 31 pp. 137–154.

Collin, F. 1997 *Social Reality*. London: Routledge.

Cooper, C. 1974 'The house as a symbol of the self', in Lang, J., Burnett, C., Moleski, W. and Vachon, D. (Eds) *Designing for Human Behavior: Architecture and the Behavioral Sciences*. USA: Dowden, Hutchinson & Ross.

Denscombe, M. 2007 *The Good Research Guide: For Small-scale Social Research Projects (Third Edition)*. Berkshire: Open University Press.

Deng, L., Shen, Q. and Wang, L. 2009 *Housing Policy and Finance in China: A Literature Review*. Washington, DC: US Department of Housing and Urban Development.

Duncan, N. 1981 'Home Ownership and Social Theory'. in Duncan, J.S. (Ed.) *Housing and Identity*. London: Croom Helm.

Dunleavy, P. 1979 'The urban basis of political alignment: Social class, domestic property ownership and state intervention in consumption processes'. *British Journal of Political Science* 9 (4) pp. 409–443.

Engels, F. [1935] 1975 *The Housing Question*. Moscow: Progress Publishers.

Fannie Mae 1994 Fannie Mae National Housing Survey 1994. Washington DC: Fannie Mae.

Fei, X.T. 1985 *Rural China (Xiangtu zhongguo)*. Beijing: Sanlian Chubanshe Press.

Forrest, R. 1983 'The meaning of home ownership'. *Society and Space* 15 (1) pp. 205–216.

Forrest, R. and Izuhara, M. 2012 'The shaping of housing histories in Shanghai'. *Housing Studies*. 27 (1) pp. 27–44.

Forrest, R. Kennett, P. and Izuhara, M. 2003 'Home ownership and economic change in Japan'. *Housing Studies* 18 (3) pp. 277–293.
Forrest, R., Murie, A. and Williams, P. 1990 *Home Ownership: Differentiation and Fragmentation*. London: Unwin Hyman.
Franklin, Bridget. 2006 *Housing Transformations: Shaping the Space of Twenty-first Century Living*. Oxon: Routledge.
Garfinkel, H. 1967 *Studies in Ethnomethodology*. NJ: Prentice-Hall.
Gibb, K. 2012 'Housing market', In Clapham, D., Clark, W. and Gibb, K. (Eds) *The Sage Handbook of Housing Studies*. London: Sage.
Giddens, A. 1989 'A reply to my critic'. In Held, D. and Thompson, J.B. (Eds) '*Social Theory of Modern Societies: Anthony Giddens and his Critics*'. Cambridge: Cambridge University Press.
Giddens, A. 1991 *Modernity and Self-Identity*. Stanford: Stanford University Press.
Gilderbloom, J. and Markham, J. 1995 'The impact of homeownership on political beliefs', *Social Force* 73 (4) pp. 1589–1607.
Gill, R. 2000 'Discourse analysis'. In Bauer, M.W. and Gaskell, G. (Eds) *Qualitative Researching with Text, Image and Sound*. London: Sage.
Gurney, C. 1999a 'Pride and prejudice: Discourses of normalisation in private and public accounts of home ownership.' *Housing Studies* 14 (2) pp. 163–183.
Gurney, C. 1999b 'Lowering the drawbridge: a case study of analogy and metaphor in the social construction of home-ownership'. *Urban Studies* 36 (10) pp. 1705–1722.
Harvey, D. 1976 'Labor, capital and class struggle around the built environment in advanced capitalist societies'. *Politics and Society* 6 pp. 265–295.
Hirayama, Y. and Hayakawa, K. 1995 'Home ownership and family wealth in Japan.' In Forrest R, and Murie, A. (Eds) *Housing and Family Wealth: Comparative International Perspectives*. London: Routledge.
Huang, Y. 2001 'Housing choice in transitional urban China.' PhD. University of California: Los Angeles.
Huang, Y. 2003 'A room of one's own: housing consumption and residential crowding in transitional urban China'. *Environment and Planning A* 35 pp. 591–614.
Huang, Y. 2004 'The road to homeownership: a longitudinal analysis of tenure transition in urban China (1949–94).' *International Journal of Urban and Regional Research* 28 (4) pp. 774–795.
Huang, Y. and Clark, W. 2002 'Housing tenure choice in transitional urban China: a multilevel analysis'. *Urban Studies* 39 (1) pp. 7–32.
Huang, Y. and Jiang, L. 2009 'Housing inequality in transitional Beijing'. *International Journal of Urban and Regional Research* 33 (4) pp. 936–956.
Jacobs, K., Kemeny, J. and Manzi, T. 2004 'Introduction'. In *Social Constructionism in Housing Research*. Jacobs, K., Kemeny, J. and Manzi, T. (Eds). Hampshire: Ashgate.
Kang, J.J., Wang, W. and Wang, B.C. 2009 'The orientation of housing purchasing of post 80's generation in China: the empirical research on the relationship between behaviors of housing purchase and loan for consumption' (*Woguo balinghou goufang xingwei qingxiang yanjiu: zhendui goufang xingwei yu xiaofei xindai guanxi jinxing shizheng fenxi*). *Modern Business* 2009 (24) pp. 36–37.
Kemeny, J. 1992 *Housing and Social Theory*. London: Routledge.
Kemeny, J. 1995 *From Public Housing to the Social Market: Rental Policy Strategies in Comparative Perspective*. London: Routledge.
Kemeny, J. 2001 'Comparative housing and welfare: theorizing the relationship'. *Journal of Housing and the Built Environment* 16 pp. 53–67.

Kemeny, J. 2004 'Extending contructionist social problems to the study of housing problem'. In Jacobs, K., Kemeny, J. and Manzi, T. (Eds) *Social Constructionism in Housing Research.* Hampshire: Ashgate.

Kemeny, J. 2005 '"The really big trade-off" between home ownership and welfare: Castles' evaluation of the 1980 thesis, and a reformulation'. *Housing, Theories and Society* 22 (2) pp. 59–75.

Kemeny, J. 2006 'Corporatism and housing regimes'. *Housing, Theories and Society* 23 (1) pp. 1–18.

King, P. 2010 *Housing Policy Transformed: The Right to Buy and the Desire to Own.* Bristol: The Polity Press.

Kirkby, R. 1985 *Urbanization in China: Town and Country in a Developing Economy 1949–2000 A.D.* New York: Columbia University Press.

Kirkby, R. 1990 'China'. In Mathey, K. (Ed.) *Housing Policies in the Socialist Third World.* New York: Mansell Publishing Limited.

Lambert, J., Paris, C. and Blackaby, B. 1978 *Housing Policy and the State: Allocation Access and Control.* London: Macmillan.

Lee, J. 1999 *Housing, Home Ownership and Social Change in Hong Kong.* Hampshire: Ashgate.

Lee, J. 2000 'From welfare housing policy to home ownership: the dilemma of China's housing reform'. *Housing Studies* 15 (1) pp. 61–76.

Lee, J. and Zhu, Y. 2006 'Urban governance, neoliberalism and housing reform in China'. *The Pacific Reviews* 19 (1) pp. 39–61.

Lewis, M. 2009 *China's Cosmopolitan Empire: the Tang Dynasty.* Cambridge: Harvard University Press.

Li, P. 2003 'Housing reforms in China: a paradigm shift to market economy'. *Pacific Rim Property Research Journal* 9 (2) pp. 180–196.

Li, S.M. and Huang, Y. 2006 'Urban Housing in China: market transition, housing mobility and neighborhood'. *Housing Studies* 21 (5) pp. 613–623.

Liang, S.M. 2005 *The Essential Meaning of Chinese Culture (Zhongguo wenhua yaoyi).* Shanghai: Shanghai Renmin Press.

Lim, G. and Lee, M. 1990 'Political ideology and housing policy in modern China'. *Environmental and Planning C: Government and Policy* 8 pp. 477–487.

Lin, H. 1989 'Better housing construction and improve the living conditions for urban residents'. *Urban and Rural Construction* 10 pp. 4–5.

Logan, J., Fang, Y. and Zhang, Z. 2009 'Access to housing in urban China.' *International Journal of Urban and Regional Research* 33 (4) pp. 914–935.

Lowe, S. 2011 *The Housing Debate.* Bristol: The Polity Press.

Lundqvist, L.J. 1998. 'Property owning and democracy – Do the twain ever meet?' *Housing Studies* 13 (2) pp. 217–231.

Marcuse, P. 1987 'The other side of housing: oppression and liberation.' In Turner, B., Kemeny, J. and Lundqvist, L. (Eds) *Between State and Market: Housing in the Post Industrial Era.* Stockholm: Almqvist and Wiksell International.

Marketplace. 2011 'Why China's real estate market is booming.' Accessed at www.marketplace.org/topics/world/china-5-year-plan/why-chinas-real-estate-market-booming on 17 March 2015.

McNamara, Carter. 1999 *General Guidelines for Conducting Interviews,* Available at http://208.42.83.77/evaluatn/intrview.htm .

Megbolugbe, I. and Linneman, P. 1993 'Home ownership'. *Urban Studies* 30 (4/5) pp. 659–682.

Mulder, C. 2006 'Home-ownership and family formation'. *Journal of Housing and the Built Environment* 21 (3) pp. 281–298.

National Bureau of Statistics of China 2005 *Statistical Communiqué of the People's Republic of China on the 2004 National Economic and Social Development*. Beijing: NBS.

Nie, C. 2015 'China's housing policy: reforms and impact'. In Ngok, K.L and Chan, C.K (Eds) *China's Social Policy: Transformation and Challenges*. Oxon: Routledge.

Oppenheim, A.N. 1992 *Questionnaire Design, Interviewing and Attitude Measurement (new edition)*. London: Pinter.

Ren Min Wang 2008 'Dreams and reality of home ownership' (*Juze you qiwu de mengxiang he xianshi*). Accessed at http://house.people.com.cn/GB/132241/8196157.html on 10 October 2011.

Richards, L. 1990 *Nobody's Home: Dreams and Realities in a New Suburb*. Melbourne: Oxford University Press.

Rohe, W. and Stegman, M. 1994a 'The impact of home ownership on the social and political involvement of low-income people'. *Urban Affairs Quarterly* 30 pp. 152–172.

Ronald, R. 2008 *The Ideology of Home Ownership: Homeowner Societies and the Role of Housing*. New York: Palgrave Macmillan.

Rosen, K. and Ross, M. 2000 'Increasing home ownership in urban China: Notes on the problems of affordability'. *Housing Studies* 15 (1) pp. 77–88.

Rossi, P. and Webber, E. 1996 'The social benefits of homeownership: empirical evidence from national surveys'. *Housing Policy Debate* 7 (1) pp. 1–35.

Ruonavaara, H. 1996 'The home ideology and housing discourse in Finland 1900–1950', *Housing Studies* 11 (1) pp. 89–104.

Sato, H. 2006 'Housing inequality and housing poverty in urban China in the late 1990s.' *China Economic Review* 17 pp. 37–50.

Saunders, P. 1989 'The meaning of "home" in contemporary English culture'. *Housing Studies* 4 (3) pp. 177–192.

Saunders, P. 1990 *A Nation of Home Owners*. London: Unwin Hyman.

State Council 1983 Ordinance on managing urban private housing *(Chengshi siyou fangwu guanli tiaoli)*. Document No. 1983/194. Beijing: State Council.

State Council 1991 Continuation of urban housing reform in a stable manner *(Jixu jiji wentuo di jingxing chengzhen zhufang zhidu gaige de tongzhi)*. Beijing, State Council.

State Council 1994 Decisions on deepening the urban housing reform *(Shenhua chengzhen zhufang zhidu gaige de tongzhi)*. Document No. 1994/43. Beijing, State Council.

State Council 1998. A further step on deepening housing reform and accelerating housing construction in urban area *(Jinyibu shenhua chengzhen zhufang gaige jiakuai zhuafangjianshe de tongzhi)*. Document No. 1998/23. Beijing, State Council.

Tang, Y.M. and Tse, S. 2005 'Housing reform and marketing implications: Evidence from Residential Property Development Companies in Guangzhou.' ANZMAC 2005 Conference: Marketing in International and Cross-Cultural Environments. Perth, Australia 5–7 December 2005.

The Economist Intelligence Unit. 2011 Building Rome in a day: The sustainability of China's housing boom. A report from the Economist Intelligence Unit's Access China service. Accessed at www.excellentfuture.ca/sites/default/files/Building%20Rome%20in%20a%20Day_0.pdf on 20 March 2015.

Van Dijk, T.A. 1998 *Ideology: A Multidisciplinary Approach*. London: Sage.

Wang, Y.P. 2000 'Housing Reform and its Impacts on the Urban Poor in China'. *Housing Studies* 15 (6) pp. 845–864.

Wang, Y.P. and Murie, A. 1996 'The process of commercialisation of urban housing in China'. *Urban Studies* 33 (6) pp. 971–989.

Wang, Y.P. and Murie, A. 1999 'Commercial housing development in urban China'. *Urban Studies* 36 pp. 1475–1495.

Wang, Y.P. and Murie, A. 2011 'The new affordable and social housing provision system in China: implications for comparative housing system'. *International Journal of Housing Policy* 11 (3) pp. 237–254.

Wang, Y.P., Shao, L., Murie, A. and Cheng, J.H. 2012 'The maturation of the Neo-liberal housing market in urban China'. *Housing Studies* 27 (3) pp. 343–359.

Wang, Y.P., Wang, Y.L. and Bramley, G. 2005 'Chinese housing reform in state-owned enterprises and its impacts on different social groups'. *Urban Studies* 42 (10) pp. 1859–1878.

Wang, Y.P., Wang, Y.L. and Wu, J.S. 2010 'Private rental housing in "urban villages" in Shenzhen: problems or solutions?'. In Wu, F.L. and Webster, C. (Eds) *Marginalization in Urban China: Comparative Perspectives*. Hampshire: Palgrave Macmillan.

Whyte, M. 1983 'Town and country in contemporary China'. *Comparative Urban Research* 10 (1) pp. 9–20.

Whyte, L. and Parish, W. (1985) *Urban Life in Contemporary China*. Chicago: University of Chicago Press.

Xu, X.Y. 1993 'Policy Evaluation in China's Housing Reform'. *Evaluation and Program Planning* 16 39–47.

Yao, S.J., Luo, D. and Loh, L.X. 2011 'China's monetary policy and asset prices'. *China Policy Institute*. Discussion paper No. 71.

Ye, J.P., Wu, D.Y. and Wu, J. 2006 'A Study on the Chinese housing policy during social transition: practice and development'. *Housing Finance International* 20 (3) pp. 50–58.

Ye, J.P., Wu, D.Y. and Wu, J. 2008 'Urban housing policy in China in the Macro-regulation period 2004–2007'. *Urban Policy and Research* 26 (3) pp. 283–295.

Zax, J. 1997 'Latent demand for urban housing in the people's republic of China'. *Journal of Urban Economics* 42 pp. 377–401.

Zhang, X.Q. 1997 'Chinese Housing Policy 1949–1978: the Development of a Welfare System', *Planning Perspectives* 12 pp. 433–455.

Zhang, X.Q. 1998 *A Study of Housing Policy in Urban China*, New York: Nova Science.

Zhao, B.J. (2007) 'Analysis and forecast on leases market of real estate'. In Niu, F.R. (Ed.) *Annual Report on the Development of China's Real Estate (NO.4)*. Beijing: Social Sciences Academic Press (China).

Zhao, Y. and Bourassa, S. 2003 'China's Urban Housing Reform: Recent Achievements and New Inequities'. *Housing Studies* 18 (5) pp. 721–744.

Zheng, S. 2007 'Discussion about the impacts of tradition culture on current house price in China (*Shilun chuantong wenhua dui zhongguo dangjin fangjia de yingxiang*)'. *Economic Manager (Jingjishi)* 2007 (2) pp. 74–75.

Zhu, J.M. 2000 'The changing model of housing provision in transitional China'. *Urban Affairs Review* 35 (4) pp. 502–519.

5 Beliefs and behaviours

Accessing higher education in contemporary China

Yu Chen

Introduction

In this chapter I explore the feelings, beliefs and behaviours of high school students as they face the transfer from their senior high school to university. I investigate these university applicants' experiences and understandings of the choices of higher education access. Through a close examination of students' voices, I will demonstrate the positive attitudes to attendance at university and the belief that higher education in China can act as the gateway to a comfortable life. I also engage with policymakers, and report on a contradictory set of attitudes from their perspective. What emerges through the contact with both sets of voices are the resonances with past attitudes to education, and also the deep structural divisions within contemporary society. What also emerges are the sociological issues of how students' trajectories through the Chinese higher education (HE) system are shaped by the nature of education policy, on the one hand, and their social backgrounds, on the other.

In order to set the scene for the discussion of the attitudes of high school students, I set out a number of contexts. In order for the reader to understand the beliefs and behaviours of the students who are the respondents in this chapter, I briefly discuss the aspects of the education system which are relevant here. I then comment upon China's economic growth and the development of HE and outline the contribution which theory has made to our understanding of the role of HE, particularly as an instrument which might create a greater measure of equality within the society in question. There are echoes here of Wei Fang's Chapter 2, earlier in this book, where a utopian view of the democratising effect of the digital revolution is discussed.

The progression from senior school to university

Most of the voices we hear in this chapter are those of students at senior high schools who are in the final year of their studies and who are possibly preparing for university. How do they arrive at this point? As Postiglione (2006) points out, the nine-year compulsory education system and the rapid expansion of post-secondary educational opportunities in China have increased faster than any other nation. For the first time in Chinese history, all children can freely attend a nine-year compulsory education programme (grade 1–6 primary school, and, grade 7–9 junior secondary school) following the compulsory education law launched in 1995.

Senior secondary schools in China enroll students from grade 9 on the basis of their academic results in junior secondary school graduation examinations, which is a provincial level examination. Key senior secondary schools select their students according to the principle of 'choosing the best' rather than from receiving students from the catchment area.

In the Chinese national education system, after the nine-year compulsory education programme, students will be divided into two groups: senior secondary school, and secondary vocation school. Senior secondary school, therefore, becomes the pathway towards HE in China. Senior secondary schools have been essentially designed to lead to university, not for professional or vocational skills training. As Giddens (1995) suggests, 'choice' can be a medium of both power and stratification. All my participants applied to senior secondary schools after their nine-year compulsory education, which demonstrates their ambition to achieve more, and perhaps to advance on to HE.

Some public senior secondary schools (non-key schools) in China have been characterised by poor teaching quality, poor facilities and equipment, large class size and low transfer rate to universities, compared to numbers of good public senior secondary schools (key schools or model schools). Thus the non-key school has been seen as a starting point for failure to achieve, and the latter has been characterised as the starting point for university education and for as a platform for social success. Key senior secondary schools are well supported by city, province or state and seize their advantages with highly qualified teachers and much better facilities and equipment; only about 4 per cent of public secondary schools are key or model schools in China. Therefore, getting an opportunity to attend a key secondary school is fiercely competitive. The National Higher Education Entrance Examination (NHEEE) is the instrument which senior high school students have to face in order to progress to university. This is a highly respected public examination which allocates senior high school students a number of points which in turn allows them entry into university. It is important for the reader to understand that the university system itself is highly stratified, as with many such systems in the West, and this helps to explain how the students use terms such as a 'good university'. I give more detail about the growth of the HE system in a later section.

A growing economy, a growing HE sector and the deep roots of learning

From 1978 onwards, China began to make major reforms to its economy. The Chinese leadership took a pragmatic view of many of its political and socio-economic problems, and sharply reduced the role of ideology in economic policy. Political and social stability, economic productivity, along with public and consumer welfare, were considered paramount and indivisible. In these years, the government emphasised raising personal income and consumption, and introducing new management systems to help increase productivity (Perry and Wang 1985). China's economy grew at an average rate of 10 per cent per year during the period 1990–2010, the highest growth rate in the world. China's GDP grew 10.0 per cent in 2003, 10.1 per cent in 2004, and even faster, 10.4 per cent, in 2005 despite attempts by the government to cool the economy, 13 per cent in 2007, 8 per cent in 2012 and 2013 (World Bank 2014).

In relation to higher education policy, from 1999 onwards there have been major changes which have provided new opportunities for higher education development in China. As a consequence, during the period from 1999–2014, the gross enrolment rate increased nearly six-fold. However, this expansion has been paralleled by other policies that allocate additional resources to the aforementioned model (formerly key) senior high schools as well as to a small group of already elite universities. Model or key senior high schools are those high quality institutions, competitively entered, which are designed to feed high status universities. Before we look at the detail of the major changes to HE at the turn of the twentieth century, it is important to dwell on the reasons why the Chinese have such positive attitudes towards education in general. There are deep roots to this positive attitude.

Some have argued that the roots of higher education in China are shallower than they are in the West, but that is a view that focuses only on the university as an institution, and ignores other leaning organisations. Nevertheless, it is generally held that though traditional Confucianism extolled the virtues of education, it was education for a particular set of values. 'Broadly the object of education was two-fold: to imbue the pupil with a sense of right and wrong and to awaken in him a sense of mission towards the masses' (Wang 1997: 9). There was an emphasis on the acceptance of moral values, on a cohesive, stable society, with an 'excessive concern for human relations (Wang 1997: 7); personal self-examination and self-criticism were encouraged. Deprecated in this pedagogy were law, compulsion, technology and commerce; the aversion to these areas of knowledge is imbued with particular importance regarding later approaches to higher education.

Importantly, Wang cites a number of writers whose work suggests that the scholar-administrator system enjoyed broad-based social and geographical appeal; not only was entry into the hierarchy allowed from all classes, but there was a quota system which involved all parts of the nation. He also makes the point that an individual village would often sponsor a local scholar in the hope of accruing benefits from a successful candidate (Wang 1966: 3–37). This is highly significant to this chapter, as the evidence points toward the imperial civil service examination, detailed below, as an instrument of social mobility.

Traditionally, a system of state-run schools was geared exclusively toward the imperial civil service examination. This examination, based on the tenets of Confucianism, was one of the routes allowing entry into the civil service, an examination which is judged to have required perseverance and prolonged study of the classics, and resulting in the scholar-administrators who shaped policy and practice in China for centuries. It was this position of the 'literati' which welded learning and governing together, within the same elite class.

Recent research (for example, by Wu) has focused attention on the role of the ancient Chinese academies (*shu yuan*), a parallel system of higher learning which operated independently of the establishment since the late Tang Dynasty (619–907 AD). These academies were private, local, educational institutes, which are said to have attracted scholars from the entire Chinese Diaspora. They developed into a new educational system from the Song Dynasty (960–1279 AD), when their numbers and influence grew. In contrast to state-run schools, academies took the pursuit of true knowledge as the goal of education. Independence was also a feature of early Western universities, but the approach to knowledge was not a shared feature of East and West. Scholars suggest that it was (and perhaps still is) the view of knowledge as a totality, always referenced to nature, which characterised traditional Chinese learning (Wu 2008), rather than the exhaustive examination of a particular aspect of reality, the approach which has since been adopted globally.

However we view the traditional Chinese approach to learning, the formal system as a whole was regarded as being highly resistant to change, and though there are many individual instances of scientific enquiry in China, new knowledge did not prosper in the way which it did in the West (Wang 1997: 3–37). Thus, constrained by feudalism, Chinese higher education in its present form evolved only after the traumas of the nineteenth and twentieth centuries. I omit that evolution and take the reader directly to the new policy developments of the 1990s.

'The Ninth Five-Year Plan for Education and Layout for the year 2010' was promulgated in 1996 with the aim of achieving an enrolment rate of 15 per cent in the year 2010 (MoE 1996). This was breathtakingly ambitious. On 24 February 1999, the MoE formally circulated the 'Action Scheme for Invigorating Education Towards the 21st Century', which made clear the objectives for the development of HE in China from 2000 to 2010. It included four key reform fields: structural reform, institutional autonomy, the 211 and the 985 Projects (see below), and HE expansion (MoE 1999). The Action set the following two goals to be achieved: First, by the year 2000, 11 per cent of those aged 18–22 years will get into HE; second, by the year 2010, the gross enrolment rate (GER) should approach 15 per cent. Actually, in 1999, the MoE proposed a 20 per cent increase in enrolment in that year, and the Ninth Five-year Plan of 15 per cent GER was actually achieved in 2003, seven years ahead of the original plan. According to MoE statistical data, the gross enrolment rate was lower than 7 per cent in 1998, and increased to 9.8 per cent in 1999. The gross enrolment number has increased nearly four times from one million in 1997 to 3.8 million in 2003. In 2010, the GER in China reached 29 per cent, with the number of students reaching 6.6 million. This speedy expansion of HE in China has fundamentally transformed the HE system from an elite to a mass system.

Bearing in mind the increasing global integration of the Chinese economy, the Chinese leadership formally associated the nation's future with the growth of a high technology knowledge economy (Ngok and Guo 2007: 22); in an anthem repeated across so many nations, international competitiveness is linked to educational development, technology and the degree of knowledge innovation (MoE 1998). Amongst the range of declarations in the early 1990s, of particular significance is the announcement of the '211 project', which sparked intensified investment 'in (95) key universities and a batch of academic disciplines and specialisms ... to enable them to reach the higher level in terms of educational quality, research, and management' (Ngok and Guo 2007: 23). These scholars claim that this is the most ambitious project for the development of higher education in which the Chinese government has been involved. Huge sums have been invested and significant improvements have been achieved: 'the overall situation (in higher education) has been improved' (ibid.: 25). The second phase of the project commenced in 2001 with the aim of continuing the development of key institutions and developing a number of key projects 'to international standards' (ibid.: 25). This notion of reaching international standards is also reflected in a further strategy, henceforth referred to as the '985 Scheme'.

The '985 Scheme' was first referred to by the then President and Vice-Chairman on separate occasions in May of 1998, hence its title. Its significance is that it was the first time that a national project to upgrade a number of universities to the level of the top flight of higher education institutions had been announced. The '211 Project' is so called because it was introduced as a scheme which was aimed at transforming about 100 universities in the twenty-first century. The specific aim of the project is to assist the selected institutions 'approach and reach the advanced international standards for the overall quality of teaching, scientific research, and the training of professional manpower, so as to establish their international prestige and position among universities in the world' (ibid.: 27).

Inherent in this project is the acceptance of stratification within the PRC higher education system, a feature which has emerged, either as an issue or a present reality, in the literature relating to other higher education systems in this study. The notion of a top rank of universities known as '2 plus 7' (Beijing University, Tsinghua University, plus seven other regional universities) is now often used. Other ideas, which one could argue are linked to stratification, will also be present in the discussions around those systems: international competitiveness, the link between technology and nation building, and the 'world-class' university.

Theoretical perspectives

HE in China has expanded rapidly since 1999 in order to face the challenges of a rapidly developing economy, adapting to the needs of a market economy and to enhance opportunities for HE access. However, this has aroused debates about the relationship between access and equity. Educational expansion has been analysed and interpreted from a variety of disciplinary and ideological perspectives, including human capital theory, consumption theory, sociologist perspective and political integration theory (Archer 1995). Consumption theory claims education as a normal good, which should rise with real income, and turn results in educational expansion (Fishlow 1966). Human capital theorists argue that education expands as a result of the demand for the increasing need for high skilled workers; they also suggest that education expansion can both enhance wages and promote greater equity (Wan 2006). According to education economists, human capital theory and the issues of cost and financing of education are at the heart of the economics of education (Blaug 1970). More critical social theorists, however, point out that educational expansion can be explained through the need to create a particular kind of worker for the economy (see Bowles and Gintis 1976) and to secure and maintain a ruling class hegemony (see Bourdieu and Passeron 1977); political integration theory suggests that expanding education helps political elites to integrate within national political cultures using a common world script that is taken up in different parts of the world (Benavot 1996; Meyer 1977).

Although many of these different theories have tried to explain educational expansion (its causes, process and outcomes), they tend to be somewhat limited in their capacity to understand the dynamics of social equality and mobility. Indeed it is the more critical sociological perspectives that have contributed more to debates on social equality and mobility in HE, largely around how questions of class, gender and race dynamics play out, and the role of education in mediating or conditioning opportunities and thus outcomes.

The issue of access to HE is a central debate in the field of sociology of education, as a human right is stated either in international agreements (for example, United Nations 1966) or in national policies. Yet clearly access to and the outcomes from HE reflect the prevailing ideologies and power relations in any society in terms of social mobility and equity and which are in turn constitutive of that society. Neubarer (2007: 51) states: '... in the modern period education has been viewed as the great leveler with respect to social disparities'. Education, especially HE, plays the role of guiding people with the hope that if one has a good educational background, one's future is secured in a wealthy and high social status situation. In China, understanding HE has been dominated by traditional cultural values. As a well known Chinese saying goes, all others are disgraced, except education. HE leads to long-term financial, social and political benefits; indeed Lin (2006) suggests that education is becoming the gatekeeper for social and economic mobility, and as a platform for the political arena as well.

In Chinese society, HE is perceived as a route to social mobility because of the social prestige that can be acquired, and as a result of differential capacities to mobilise forms of social and cultural 'capital' to enhance the 'bright' future. Many researchers have investigated the influence of home background and family socio-economic circumstances on an individual's capability to achieve access to different levels of education. Family backgrounds, including parents' educational attainments, occupation and family income have been factors which show a strong and positive influence in students' deciding to, and eventually attending HE (Stafford *et al.* 1984; Carpenter and Hayden 1993; Kuo and Hauser

1995). There are other factors at play which also have a significant role in the impact on an individual's chances of HE; for instance, differential access to educational facilities according to socio-economic status, religion, race and ethnicity (Sewell *et al.* 1957; Sewell and Shah 1967; Cabrera and La Nasa 2001). Following those views, some researchers take the position that our social and economic backgrounds mediate both our educational chances and our future occupational achievements (Erikson 1987; Husen 1989; Erikson and Jonsson 1998). Other research indicates the highly complex process of social and economic selectivity in individuals' academic performance. For instance, social and economic selectivity operates powerfully in the context of HE entrance, which maintains strongly the outcome for certain groups of people regarding entry to only a certain stage of education and not others (Collins 1979; Alexander *et al.* 1987; Cabrera and La Nasa 2000).

It is therefore not surprising that the expansion of HE in China has attracted wide attention from the media and the research. The studies on this topic, however, seem to be inadequate. That is, discussion about the impact of social and economic factors, and the analysis of its causes and outcomes, tends to be too general and often lacks empirical evidence. Individuals' biological factors (intelligence, sex, race) seem to be discussed rather than the power of wealth and social prestige. There is a real shortage of studies which assess, with empirical data and analysis, the issue of access to higher education regarding individuals' different social and economic strata, in the context of China. I argue that measuring university students' social and economic backgrounds tells only part of the story; educational competition begins *before* the student enters HE. This is critically important, largely because the different types of secondary schools in China *are not* equally valued in HE access and thus mediate opportunities for ongoing access to HE. There is an extremely limited literature on how these factors (social prestige, political power and economic class) influence an individual's educational position at secondary education level, how these factors shape an individual's belief, behaviours and expectations, and how an individual's educational position in secondary education level operates their positions in HE access.

Higher education, and the question of class

From a historical perspective, with the powerful influence of Confucian doctrine, education – and especially HE – has played a significant role since Chinese imperial times in terms of social stratification. Watson (1984) suggests the understandings of 'social class' in Chinese society do not compare with those from the West. He also explains that the Marxist notion of class, as a set of relationships based ultimately on the ownership of the means of production, is not applicable in China. Lin *et al.* (1994) argue that after 30 years of desertification campaigns (1949–1979), China was slightly more equal (with respect to income) than the average socialist state. But Lin *et al.* also consider education, housing and the distribution of consumer items, all of which were in short supply during that period. In the early 1980s, China's society had only 'two classes and one stratum', i.e. the working class, the farmer class and the intellectual stratum. Economic reforms have broken down the restriction of the Chinese people's social and occupational mobility in the old system and new social, professional categories have emerged (Kane 1994; Unger 1994; Wong 1994; Goodman 1996; Gu 1997) which have fundamentally transformed the social structure.

Regarding the dramatic economic growth since the 1980s, a 're-stratification and social class formation' has been underway in China's society (Mok 2000); the understanding of social class and structure has changed as the economy itself has also changed. For instance, the idea of 'social class' has more recently been referred to as relating to people's social, economic, cultural and educational background. For example, the National Bureau of Statistics released a survey result in 2005 stating that the urban middle class should have a yearly income between 60,000 yuan and 500,000 yuan. This is the first time in China that the 'middle class' was defined clearly with a number (National Statistics Report 2005). The debate about the existence of a middle class in China began in the late 1990s. In 2001 the Chinese Academy of Social Science surveyed 6,000 participants in 12 provinces and indicated that 7 per cent of the Chinese population, 60 million people, met the criteria of a middle class (in occupation, income, lifestyle and personal identification).

A McKinsey study (2006) shows the changing social structure since 1985: it reveals that 1 and 99 per cent of the population are counted as lower middle class and working class in 1985 respectively, whilst 12.6 and 78 per cent are lower middle and working class in 2005. And, as Reusswig and Isensee remark: 'Cultural values need social actors to become reality' (2010: 129). The growth and structural change of China's middle class is a significant context for debating the social inequality in HE access in this global era. The emergence of the Chinese middle class with traditional values could be seen here in terms of HE, as more and more university applicants from the middle class have been strongly encouraged by their parents to enter either elite universities or semi-elite universities. HE has been fully self-paying since 1999, whilst Project 985 created a layer of research-intensive universities. Marginson (2010) argues that a feature of Chinese Confucian society is the willingness of most families, and in particular the middle class, to invest privately in secondary and tertiary education and tutoring in order to position their children for the one-off contest for university entry which determines their life chances. Therefore, have any social inequalities in terms of HE access substantially grown during this period?

HE has long been recognised as a mechanism for equalising opportunities for social mobility in China. Students' academic capability has been more heavily emphasised than anything else; and students' family backgrounds have been neglected in HE access. In the West, many studies have made a powerful statement that access to HE is heavily influenced by an individual's socio-economic background. Students have been stratified based on their socio-economic background, whilst the schooling system systematically reproduces students by their social group.

School does not serve a role in terms of increasing social equity and justice, but trains students to adopt the required attitudes and attributes for serving the needs of a hierarchical capitalist economy (Bowles and Gintis 1976; Rist 2003; Bourdieu and Passeron 1979; Oakes 1985; DeMarrais and LeCompte 1995). However, in China, people believe the education system stratifies students based on their academic performance rather than their family socio-economic background. Personal aspiration seems to play a more important role than personal socio-economic background. There has always been a deep conflict between encouragement to achieve personal success and the realities of limited opportunities in China's HE. Chinese values demand that individuals work as hard as possible in their daily social life because Chinese people believe social mobility is universally possible in terms of the degree of hard work in the education system. Social status will definitely be won by individual effort, and rewards are to accrue to those who try their best. But HE is a selective process which allows the number of people who succeed to be much fewer than the people who fail. This social agreement has caused fierce competition in terms of HE access. Does HE automatically provide upward mobility for all? Or have some social groups been disadvantaged in terms of educational opportunities?

The old social class categories have been replaced and diversified with China's rapid economic growth since the late 1980s. A new market-oriented socialist economy has directed a redistribution of resources and wealth, which in turn is affected by the rise of the middle class. A newly formed 'middle class' is exercising their impact on HE to sustain an advantageous position in the competitive economy. However, inequality of HE opportunities may disadvantage both the urban working class and rural peasants who are lacking in social, economic and cultural assets (Lin 2006). According to Zhu Guanglei (1998), economic reforms brought a tremendous wave of industrialisation which significantly changed both Eastern and Western China, and brought about a huge number of rural migrations to urban areas. Associated with this social change, the classification for social stratification has been gradually changing from a politically-based criteria to a new combination; it includes income, educational level, occupation and political background (Lin 1999).

However, with the changing of social class structure, HE credentials are still officially promoted by the government. For example, university graduates usually have more opportunities in finding high-paying positions in the job market (white-collar jobs) than who are without a university degree. Most low-paying manufacturing jobs have been taken by millions of rural migrant youth workers without university degrees, who have barely any chance for upward social mobility. The rise of the middle class can also be seen as a sign that the gap between rich and poor has dramatically enlarged since then.

Li Qiang argues that occupation has become the main demarcation of an individual's social status, which has been determined by an individual's education level:

> One's social status, whether high or low, is quite precisely reflected in one's occupation. A person's occupation reflects not only economic, social,

cultural status, but also reflects a person's position in the power structure and prestige categories. Hence there is a great match of one's social class status with one's occupation. Furthermore, most people rely on their education level to gain access into the occupational structure; hence education in modern society has become the main screening mechanism for social stratification.

(Li 2003: 3)

Although after China's economic reform, an individual's wealth has become more and more important in social stratification, a new middle class is still identified as heavily based on educational background. Lin (2006) identifies the new middle class in China as consisting of six groups of people: private entrepreneurs and business owners; white-collar workers; intellectuals who consult or own their own high-tech companies; university teaching members and good primary and secondary school teachers in major cities; government officials or civil servants; senior management team members who work as estate agents, stockbrokers or entertainers. Apart from private entrepreneurs and business owners, the other five groups all have a really close link with the individual's educational background; anyone without a university degree cannot be in any of these groups.

The middle class has traditionally maintained their social advantages through HE. For example, in the United States, schools usually favour children from middle-class family backgrounds and value middle-class culture rather than working class (DeMarrais and LeCompte 1995). In the U.K., elite private schools open their doors to the middle and upper-middle class families who can afford the tuition fees. In China, accessing HE is closely related to what type of senior secondary school students have attended.

There is little literature to explore the distribution of students in senior secondary school based on their family social status; once again, students with better academic performance certainly will take all the positions in these schools. The issue of social class in HE access has not been given much attention and only a few researchers have carried out studies in terms of access to HE in China. Universities are again filled overwhelmingly with students from families who are either politically advantaged, intellectuals, or urban, despite the efforts and painful price paid by the nation and the people during the three decades after 1949 (Pepper 1984). It seems there is a similar pattern at the senior secondary school level, as with students in HE. Social factors seem to influence the selection before and after senior secondary school and universities, which disadvantages students from working class and rural families (Thogersen 1987).

There is still a shortage of statistical data about students in HE as a whole; indeed official statistics have been silent about the issue of the social structure of the student body in HE since 1977. However, there is information about rural–urban students at all levels of the education system, except post-secondary. The well-known National Higher Education Entrance Examination (NHEEE) gives the clear impression that HE access is based solely on the academic performance of students whose social origins have not been taken into account. In the early 1980s, parental educational background and fathers' occupation as civil servants were the decisive factors for students enrolled at senior secondary schools, while family income played no role (Unger 1982; Thogersen 1987; Broaded and Liu 1996). By the late 1990s, it was shown that the probability of the number of students in HE increased with the increase of their parental education background and family income (Li and Min 2003). HE used to be free for all in China until 1997; since then, graduates are no longer assigned jobs by government organisations. It brought a social problem to the fore; students from poor family backgrounds were struggling with rising tuition fees. In 2002, universities started establishing so-called independent or third-tier colleges, which take advantage of the resources, reputation and facilities from those universities, and continue to charge tuition fees that are much more expensive than the usual university tuition fees. Their admission criteria are significantly lower than the university entrance requirements from NHEEE. Thus, the number of students from the middle class who are experiencing HE provided by public universities has been growing. Again, there is little literature in the field investigating the proportion of students in universities based on their family social background. However, it is clear that students from richer families have more opportunities to access HE by attending independent colleges, where much lower NHEEE results are required, but more expensive tuition fees are demanded. Family financial resources have been taken into consideration at this stage.

Voices from the policymakers

Before I move on to presenting the voices of the consumers of HE, the aforementioned senior high school students who are making the transition to HE, it is pertinent here to examine the perspectives of the policymakers. I include some relevant extracts from policymakers and officials from the Ministry of Education (MoE) in Beijing. Both sets of voices, that is, the officials and the senior high school students, offer an insight into attitudes about education generally and HE in particular, and the insights may be allow us to observe a certain complexity that may previously have been obscured. In the context of the economic reforms in China since the early 1980s, there has been broad consent among economic scholars and policymakers from state councils that HE should be expanded in China to meet the needs of national economy development, and economic growth has been the central task on the political agenda since the 1990s. The policymakers in this section reveal that educational policies have served this central, national political strategy. We should bear in mind that HE expansion in China has always been accompanied by rising college tuition fees and multiple funding resources; this is also reflected in the change of the national HE strategy from an elite HE system to a mass HE system.

In their rather utopian view, Hannum and Buchman (2003) suggest that there may be three outcomes of educational expansion for economic and social development: first, educational expansion is essential to national economic development, as better-educated citizens are more productive; second, it narrows social inequalities within nations by promoting social mobility; and third, it contributes to the development of a more democratic society, as more educated people are able to make more informed political decisions. In China, were the reasons for HE expansion also based on those assumptions about its outcomes?

Former vice prime minister in charge of the education sector at the time of the expansion policy, Li Lanqing, explains the four key reasons for the expansion from his perspective:

1 The need for more talented personnel to sustain the rapid development of the Chinese economy;
2 The increasing public demand for HE and the consequent government obligation to meet that demand;
3 Enrolment expansion has the potential to postpone the employment of senior secondary school graduates and increase educational consumption, which is an important means to stimulate domestic consumption and promote growth in related industries;
4 Enrolment expansion will reduce the pressure on senior secondary schools, discouraging an examinations-driven education system and promoting 'all-round education' (*suzhi jiaoyu*) in primary and secondary schools.

(Li 2005)

His statement could be seen as an authoritative voice explaining the reasons and outcomes of the HE expansion; this is a clear functionalism perspective in economic and social development permeating the statement. Only reason four directly presents how the expansion will have an impact on the education system to reduce the pressure on senior secondary schools. Reason one, two and three show functionalist assumptions regarding both economic and social development on expansion. HE development has always been one of the most significant parts of the development-underpinned agenda of the government. The reasons reflect the degree of power the state council has in HE policy sector; they also demonstrate a close connection between economic development and HE expansion in China.

Li's statement presents a strongly-expressed belief that education policy therefore matters to economic reasoning (Wan 2006). It has become clear that the Chinese government were trying hard to meet the growing and diversifying demand for HE. The expansion was essentially a result of state planning and was controlled by the central government, which was a typical case of Chinese central government intervention in HE. The process of HE expansion reflected the central government's social and economic development strategy (Wan 2006).

Li's reasoning relating to the postponement of the employment of senior secondary school graduates, increasing increase educational consumption and the stimulation of domestic consumption, resonated with the perspectives of a policymaker from the MoE in Beijing, with whom I conversed in 2011:

At the very beginning, some economists suggested the expansion of HE as a solution to economic difficulties following the Asian Economic Crisis in 1997, to our Prime Minister Zhu Rongji; we did not think about the opportunity for social equity and mobility. Simply letting more young people go to university would not be a bad idea; it could stimulate householders' investment in HE, and also reduce the pressure of the increasing unemployment rate. Our nation should benefit from expanded HE, as should the economic development...

(Policymaker 1 from the MoE in Beijing 2011)

Kindleberger (1964) suggests that both Germany and Japan have experienced fast economic growth and increased wealth to consequently be able to invest more in education. China's case may demonstrate that HE expansion precedes economic development. China's central government had faced the pressure of a higher unemployment rate since 1993, especially after 1998. In 1998 there was 'a surplus labour force of 28.6 million competing for a shrinking number of job vacancies' (Zhang 2000: 46). In 1999, there were over 3,000,000 university applicants around the age of 18; if most of them could not enter universities, the government had to deal with a huge pressure on the national unemployment rate. Tang Min, chief economist of the Asian Development Bank Mission in China, proposed 'some thoughts on revitalizing the Chinese economy: double enrolment in HE', which presents an idea of expansion of HE to stimulate domestic consumption and decrease the unemployment rate in China. The cost of tuition fees in China (for undergraduate study) is almost always covered from family resources; private resources are the traditional solution for the cost of HE.

Expansion, therefore, was suggested based on the Chinese traditional ideology, that HE is the primary motive for Chinese families' investment. Chinese policymakers and economists believed Chinese families were and are willing to pay for HE. Their other important concern was postponing the employment pressure until after the 1998 Asian economic crisis by letting more and more young people have access to universities. Since then, China has experienced a significant HE transformation with an unprecedented speed until 2010. The expansion illustrates that the state council has identified HE as a promising economic activity and an important source of additional income to meet the increasing demands of HE for both individual families and national economic development. It is important to note that the Chinese state council's shift to expand HE a year after the 1998 Asian Financial Crisis is underpinned by human capital theory. During the interview with the policymaker earlier, the change of national HE strategy in 2010 was also mentioned. Expansion was no longer the prime national strategy in HE. The emphasis had shifted:

The policy should always focus on current issues. The expansion is designed to let more young people into universities, but after a dramatic development, we started to make modifications after 2010. In other words, we have controlled the rate of increase; we have lowered increases down to 5% since 2010, as there was an annual increase of more than 15% during 1999 to 2009…

(Policymaker 1 from the MoE in Beijing 2011)

In the context of this chapter, my interpretation is that the MoE officials were implicitly recognising a widely-held value in Chinese society that education in general and HE in particular are held in high regard. We have seen earlier in this chapter how deep are the roots of this high regard, and how there is a belief that education can be an instrument for social mobility. Perhaps one might argue that the officials are subverting this belief in the interests of economic development. It is generally held that Chinese parents have always been willing to invest a large amount of their family savings into their children's education. Set against the national 'one child' policy, families set great store on saving for their children's education. They would probably not see the link between HE expansion and economic development, but can only see hope for their children to achieve a better life through HE.

Other MoE officials reveal how the expansion of HE after the Asian economic crisis was not universally welcomed; most education experts at the MoE thought the sudden expansion would be harmful in terms of the quality of HE.

> The expansion policy had been suggested by the group economist, and decided on by the state council; it was macro-level national policy. The HE expansion policy, therefore, was mainly for national and economic development, not simply an education policy. The truth is that all the highly placed people in the HE field disagreed with the expansion idea, including the Minister for Education. The education experts thought the sudden expansion would be harmful in terms of the quality of HE. But, as we can all see, there has quickly been a large development since then; the development of HE has been stimulated since the policy was launched. We cannot say that we have the best universities in the world, but we do have first-class campuses in China.
>
> (Policymaker 1 from MoE Beijing 2011)

Another confirmed that economic needs were in the driving seat, and that it was a calculated political gamble that the traditional attitudes to education and the belief in the value of education could be used pragmatically as an instrument of national financial stimulation:

> At the very beginning, some economists suggested this as a solution to the economic difficulties following the Asian Economic Crisis; we did not think about equal opportunity or social equity and mobility. Simply letting more young people go to university would not be a bad idea; our nation should benefit from expanded HE, as should the economy. Our tradition is that all families will invest in education; we can live without a big house and car,

but not without HE. For example, if there is a university in a city with 20,000 students, it will definitely help economic development in this city. Furthermore, if more and more young people go to university, there will not be such pressure on the rate of unemployment following the Asian Economic Crisis.

(Policymaker 2 from the MoE in Beijing 2011)

A third official opined that this was an opportunity to limit the institutional power of the NHEEE, to loosen the curriculum from its grips and to allow that curriculum to evolve:

It is more appropriate here to talk about the group that is most influenced by HE expansion. We cannot view HE policy as only being for a certain group of people, because there are different fields and groups of people involved in HE policy. We should not be talking about 'benefit', but influence. The key point in our HE reform from our political perspective is the transformation from the examination-driven education system to an all-round education (*suizhi jiaoyu*) system. The national HE entrance examination is still in the core part of our HE policy, it means university cannot be for all, only for some who meet the requirement to get into university.

(Policymaker 3 from the MoE in Beijing, 2011)

Attempting to judge HE expansion policy as either successful or failed is a difficult and complex task. I am not trying to problematise this policy in terms of development, but I am trying to explore the issue in terms of beliefs and behaviours. Policymakers, for example, have presented their understandings of HE expansion as having links with economic development, where theorists such as Hannum and Buchman's idea of HE expansion is in terms of social mobility and equity. Policymakers do not understand HE expansion as an academic discussion; they understand the power of HE as being a core social activity with social purposes, and have used people's social beliefs and their willingness to invest their savings in their children's education. It seems HE expansion has been driven by an idea of economic development rather than an idea of public good. From my evidence, it seems that policymakers held the belief that HE expansion would reduce the tension connected with the unemployment rate and contribute to economic development; they are also proud of the changes in HE since the policy was introduced. As we move on to the voices of senior high school students as they progress to the next stage of their learning, we will meet with a different set of attitudes.

The voice of university applicants

In this section, I aim to focus on students' beliefs and behaviours regarding HE; this requires a focus both on their families' social, cultural, economic and political background, and their personal understanding of their choices and experiences. As I argued earlier, the higher education system in China has been transformed as a result of the introduction of market forces in China, and as the result of expansion post '99. We have already seen that as a result of the expansion, the HE system has become highly stratified, with the 985 and 211 projects aiming to create a select group of high status, research based universities. This is an important point here, because many of the respondents below refer to this group of universities, which they generally describe as 'good universities'. It is also important for the reader to remember that these students were facing the NHEEE, the entrance examination for HE admission, which some refer to colloquially as *Gaokao*.

The voices presented below are from 20 interviews with key schools students, and six interviews plus two focus groups with non-key school students. The research here uses fictitious names. None of the participants had a clear idea about the concept of social class; they all thought that they were from the working-class, but they were very different in their families' social, cultural, economic and political status. They were all very likely to be applying to university, although their narratives are not typical of the entire university applicants' group. The non-key school students were all keen to go to university. However, not only did the key school students have an ambition to attend university, they were also clear about *what kind of university* they wanted to go to, and not a university in general. They therefore were an interesting comparison in my study. In short, my participants from both key schools and non-key schools shared similar understandings about their secondary school life and the importance of HE in their future life, but were different in their perspective of how their life could be shaped.

The idea of progression to university

In relation to my question about the reason they had been preparing for the NHEEE, all of the participants said the same thing. Mimi is a typical example of a non-key school student from a working-class family; most working-class non-key school students felt they had no option but to prepare for the national exam:

> I went to the senior high school after the junior high school rather than be a secondary vocation school student to be trained as a professional. Compared with the majority of my classmates in the junior high school, I paid much more for the university than them, because most of them did not go to the senior high school, so they have been earning already. If I am not going to the university, the three years in the senior high school are totally useless, wasted!!!
>
> (Mim, senior high school)

Kai is from a local non-key school. He has been recognised as one of the best students among his classmates and teachers. In this example, Kai says he does not want to miss HE which should be the most important part of mainstream education:

Beliefs and behaviours 169

I did not miss any part of the mainstream education system, namely, kindergarten, primary school, junior and senior secondary school, so why would I miss the experience of the university? It is the most important part of this mainstream system.

(Kai, senior high school)

Rong is from same school as Kai. Similar to her classmates, she does not want to miss HE, which she says means too much to her life and to her future:

On the one hand, I think the majority of students expect to go to university, because we have been through the primary, junior secondary and senior secondary schools, so why not the university? If I am not going, it would be a big loss in my life.

(Rong, senior high school)

This claim could partly be attributed to the belief that HE is a mechanism of social acceptance in China's society, which shows how non-key school students are keen to get into university as much as the students at key schools. They are not aware of the big gap between themselves and other key school students regarding access to HE in China, particularly with regard to the choices they could make.

However, choice of HE is also certainly hindered by the prediction of their academic performance and the actual national examination grades achieved by them. Clearly, the academic results of the national examination are affected by a range of factors. One of the most important factors is the 'school type' they have been studying in during the last three years. Students from both key schools and non-key schools spend similar amounts of time devoted to study at school and at home. However, they are completely different in terms of the resources allocated, the quality of the teaching staff and what seems to be their 'academic ability'.

One of the key school students spoke how about they would like to be at a good university because they had studied for 12 years to prepare for this. The idea of progression on to university clearly plays a major role in their minds. But key school students may want something more than what the non-key school students wish for. The academic difference between these two cohorts makes key school students pay little attention to going to just 'a university', and more attention to going to 'a good university'. The data sheds light on this. Xuan, who was one of best students in her class at a key school, had been hoping to go to Tsinghua University in Beijing, one of best universities in China. She demonstrated that she cared a great deal about what a kind of university she could and go, and what kind of classmates would be around her at the university:

If I do not go to a good university, I would waste all my previous 12-year study. Also, it will be hard to meet people with a similar IQ or background, if I do not go. It means it will be far away from the best way.

(Xuan, key senior high school)

Another key school student felt that getting into a high status university offered the hope of a different style of learning, in contrast to the diet of memorising and rote learning which she had endured!

> The reason we went to the senior secondary school was because we went to the primary school and junior secondary school before. Therefore, as I am about to finish my senior secondary school, if I am not going to the good university, I do not need to spend 12 years to do my primary school and secondary school. In 12 years from my primary to my secondary school, we always have the same learning style. It is as if we are audiences to sit and listen to what the teachers say at the school, and do homework every day. My past 12 years study experience sounds more like being a 'study or exam machine'. But, I believe the good university will be different. We are not 'exam machines' anymore and I will meet people who are smart and nice.

Yang's description was similar to non-key school students, but not his classmates from a key school. He is from a really high-ranking military family, but lacked confidence in his academic ability, especially compared with his excellent classmates. It is true that being in a key school as opposed to a non-key school is an important variable in predicting results in the national examination. But not all students are academically excellent at key schools:

> For me, there are two purposes for going to university, one is for my future life; the other is not wasting my 12-year hard study since my primary school. If I cannot get into a good university, it feels like I am a loser forever.
>
> (Yang, key senior high school)

Yang used the term 'loser' to define how he would feel if he failed to enter a good university, which is different from a non-key school participant, Jinjin, who used the term 'loser' with regard to not going to university. Yang was the only participant from a key school in my sample who, under parental pressure, took one extra year to prepare for the national examination, rather than go to a less good university; he had received an offer from a university, but not a 'good university' (985 or 211). This will not be the only reference to parental pressure in this section!

Xin's case highlights the ambition among students to pursue access to a good university. He is the only one of the key school participants from a working-class background. And, as he notes:

> I have been working hard for 12 years in order to go to a good university. Compared with most of my classmates, I am the one who did the most. I had to wake up at 6 o'clock every morning since I was 10 and take a one-hour bus journey to the school.
>
> (Xin, key senior high school)

In Xin's, Yang's, Kewei's and Xuan's accounts we can see how they have been influenced by the structuring of the key-school students' range of choice. They only focus on achieving entry to a high status university. Without exception, they all mention 'good university' during the interview, and aim to maintain their advantage in studying with this end goal in mind. But in the conversations with Mimi, Kai and Rong, they did not mention 'good university' at all. For them, university is the best thing they could imagine; but for my key school participants, only a 'good university' counts in their strategising of access to HE.

Parental pressure

The schooling system plays only a part in the process of individual choice of HE. The family is the other significant part able to influence a student's daily life. In Chinese society, there is a social agreement that people highly value HE as the mechanism of social stratification, on the one hand, and social mobility that might alter their living status and life style, on the other. Or, to put it another way, the reason that HE has been highly valued in China's society is because of its function in social mobility. Jun (from a local non-key school) described himself as a 'loser', according to his parent's idea of HE, when he asserted:

> The reason I am preparing for the national examination is because of my family. My family makes me think that going to university is the best thing I can do in my life, or that only by going to university I can have a better life. They never tell me directly that I would be 'a loser' if I do not go to university. But they make me feel exactly like I will be a loser if I do not go.
> (Jun, senior high school)

For Jun, going to university is important because his target is to go to university where it could help him, and his family, to have a better life. Many of the working-class non-key school students echo not only similar sentiments but also mention pressure from people around them:

> I do not have a clear idea how much I want to go, but my parents always want me to get in ... they said it will be my best and only chance to have a better life than them ...
> (Ni, senior high school)

> The most frequent sentence my parents spoke to me since my first day at the senior secondary school is that I will be nothing if I do not go to the university ...
> (Jian, senior high school)

> There is a huge pressure from my parents. They always say how important the university could be, if I cannot get in, my whole life will be a failure bla bla bla ...
> (Mimi, senior high school)

> I hear my parents say every day, if you are not going, what else you can do, nothing...
>
> (Wan, senior high school)
>
> We all are same; most of the pressure is from our parents...
>
> (Jinjin, senior high school)
>
> My parents desperately want me to go to university; there is no other option I could have in my life...
>
> (Xiang, senior high school)

They also mentioned pressure from others, such as relatives, or other people around them. Going to a university is not only an issue inside the family, but is also the benchmark for wider society. The student respondents appeared to believe that whether you go to university or not was the crucial step for judging whether you are successful at this stage in your life.

Here my key-school participants described similar pressures they faced from their parents and other people, especially through the ways in which they are compared with others. This places deep emotional obligations on the student (Reay *et al.* 2001). In terms of the influence from their family, such discourses make possible an understanding of how important HE could be in an individual's life. The responses highlight awareness of the importance of HE among people from different social, cultural, economic and political backgrounds:

> I have been told by them since childhood how important and good attending university could be. They always say that people with a university degree definitely have a better life than those without a university degree, and the social status they could have is much greater than people without...
>
> (Haiyun, key senior high school)
>
> They always set high standards for me, must be the No. 1. They tell me very often how important going to a good university will be. My dad passed away when I was 13, mum still keeps doing the same thing; just tells me every day how important a good university is. They never say it must be Tsinghua University or Beijing University, but I know, it should be a top university...
>
> (Xin, key senior high school)

Here, non-key school students and key school students have similar conversations. Discussion of class issues within research into HE access in China has been largely neglected in China's literature; one of the most important reasons is people from different family backgrounds hold similar expectations towards HE. Of the students in this study, few did not want to go to university, viewed from both their parents' and their own perspective. There is a widely held attitude that HE is open to everyone who is capable of achieving high enough scores in the

NHEEE. I did not come across any ideas of a class issue. However, in the conversations with key school students, the most frequent words they mentioned were 'good university', whilst none of non-key school students did. Moreover, most of the key school students in my interviews mentioned pressure from teachers and classmates, but it had not been talked about at all in the interviews with non-key school students. The participants from key schools and non-key schools share the same fundamental value orientation: HE is very important in life. But key-school students' parents seemed to have more structured behaviours than non-key school students' parents; they did not just put pressure on their children's shoulders but they had their plans to contribute to their children's life to help them to be good:

> I could go to the one of the best senior secondary schools, because my parents gave me a good family education plan since the kindergarten. They decided to send me to the one of the best kindergartens when I was only three. They tried really hard to find a proper person to help them, and also paid a huge amount of money to the supportive funds for the kindergarten.
> (Xuanyi, key senior high school)

> When I was in the Fourth Grade at the primary school, my mum sent me to take the entrance examination for a key primary school which was far away from home. I did not understand why they wanted me at the primary school far away from home, but I did take the exam and got in as well, because my parents wanted me to. After that, I went to the key junior secondary school and key senior secondary school, they are all far from home, but they are both some of the best secondary schools in the city. I think some of my understandings are from my parents' influence. I am different from most children in my living place, because I am really good at studying. I became my parents pride and joy since I was just 6 or 7. They tried their best to let me study at the key primary school and secondary school; I really thank them for what they did for me. Their expectations became my self-motivation, I just want to prove that I am a good kid, I am different from others who live around here. My parents did not push me to go to a 'good university' only, but I want myself to go to a 'good university'.
> (Xin, key senior high school)

Xin is the only working class student respondent from one of the key senior high schools; his description is different from his schoolmates. He emphasised again and again how hard he worked; indeed more than anybody else he knew from his school. But probably Xin's parents planned carefully ever since he was really young (age 6 or 7), which most key-school parents did for their children since their early age at primary schools. What we see is a pattern of belief and behaviours on the part of parents, who are prepared to plan carefully and send children away on a boarding arrangement in order to attend the school which they believe will be best for their children.

Societal pressure

As Sayer (2005) points out, people from disadvantaged backgrounds are not disadvantaged primarily because they lack the means to live in ways which they, as well as those with better backgrounds, value. He claims that sentiments such as pride and shame are evaluative judgements of how people are being treated as regards what they value in society.

Those sentiments are shaped by HE as a moral value in Chinese society. HE has been recognised as a social moral value in the whole society, which makes going to university an ideal and a goal for all students from poor and rich families. Mimi describes herself as a working class girl from a non-key school academic background who was willing to go to university to have the best life she could have. For Mimi, her priority was to go to a lower status university, where she passed a particular subject interview only for students who are going to learn arts subjects. She still needed to get enough points from the NHEEE which was required for entrance. She seemed to be aware of the degree of difficulty she was going to confront, and had doubts about her academic performance, but she showed a passion and a determination to go to university. Many of the non-key school students echoed similar sentiments:

> We all say there is not only one way to Rome, but going to university is the mainstream awareness of being any good. If you do not go to university, and just do some low-paid simple job (cleaner, waitress, etc.), the people will see you differently, compared with the students who go to university. Others always think only good students go to university; only students who deserve a better life go to university.
>
> (Ni, senior high school)

> All students who are at senior high school want to go to university for sure; because this is the social value that has been agreed with people in this society; because this is the only social value of real worth that has been agreed in this society.
>
> (Kai, senior high school)

> I think going to university is a 'must-be' in our life, no matter whether your future could benefit from a university degree or not. If I am not going, I will regret it for the rest of my life...
>
> (Xiaoxiao, senior high school)

> What else could we do, if we are not going to university?
>
> (Jian, senior high school)

Here, Ni, Kai and Xiaoxiao exhibit a different view from the Bourdieurian sense in relation to access to HE, where choices are governed by what it is 'reasonable to expect'; and all of them have developed expectations, which is a clear consequence of the idea of HE's value in China's society. Their attitudes are constructed from the social and moral contours in China's society rather than what it is 'reasonable to expect'. The importance of being at university, where they can prove they are of value, being respected by the whole of society, making their parents satisfied and proud. They frequently used the words 'having a good life' and 'being a good student' to highlight the importance of university in their life:

> We cannot talk about higher education out of China's context, as an individual, I cannot expect anything, but a degree...
>
> (Jang, senior high school)

> It is not only because of parents, but the whole society. Parents keep telling me the only way I could be better and have a good job is by going to university. Although they keep silent, I still know, the whole of society values the university degree at such a high level, you are in the society, and do you have any chance of being different? I do not think so...
>
> (Xiang, senior high school)

Jang and Xiang expressed their emotional constraint that simply being in society allows one no option but to follow what has been highly valued by others and the society. As Smith (1759) argues, we are vulnerable, deeply social beings psychologically dependent on society and others, and in need of their recognition. Being respected and recognised through HE is a cognitive view of emotion, rather than affection, which is believed to affect well-being in the future. Most key school participants present a similar understanding:

> To be honest, within Chinese society, going to university is the only way I can expect. This is the reality, the reality forces you to believe that going to university is the only good way instead of the belief from your deep heart. The reality in China is that you cannot find a good job unless you have a university degree. Going to university, therefore, is not my dream but the reality I have to face. Going to university is the ideal, dominating the mainstream understanding of all young people. Otherwise I am a loser forever. In China, I have no idea what else we could expect, this is the only way. I cannot go abroad, because my dad is a very high-ranking officer in the military, our relatives are not allowed to go abroad. For me, going to university is my 'must' part of life; I must have the piece of degree paper, because it will decide my future.
>
> (Yang, key senior high school)

> What a pity, if I cannot get into university after my secondary school. I always have been taught how important the university is since my childhood. Therefore, since then, I think only the people who are not good enough cannot go to university. I have had this clear idea of going to university since my kindergarten; because my mum is a secondary school teacher, most people I know

since my childhood are teachers. I think going to university is a 'must' part in everybody's life, unless you are too bad to get in....

(Meng, key senior high school)

Because of society, we all know the best way to grow up in China is to go to university. I guess there are some people who may think differently, but from my point of view, there are is no way that could be better than HE...

(Wei, key senior high school)

My family is a typical upper-middle class family, which is better than the middle class, but worse than the upper class. My dad's business is going better and better since my secondary school. But I was lost during the second year at the senior secondary school, I thought I did not need to work hard; my parents can support me to study abroad. Finally I recognized you will not be respected in China's society no matter how rich you are. The only way in China's society for young people is to get a degree from a good university. Although you go abroad for your study, you will still be seen as 'a loser' unless you go to a university like Harvard and Yale, or Cambridge and Oxford. My family could help me to have a good life, but not being respected is something that I do not want...

(Yi, key senior high school)

My key-school students showed more confidence than those from non-key schools, and they talked much more than non-key school students. But interestingly, none of them considered the 'fit in' issue, which was explored by Reay *et al.* (2001: 865), where she states: '...the importance of choosing somewhere where one feels safe and/or happy raises the issue in relation to university choice'. This is a concept that appears to be absent in the Chinese context. In my interviews, the same awareness is largely absent among the participants from both key schools and non-key schools who tended to only emphasis the social moral value and belief of being a good one (being a good student at a good university). They have never considered whether they could fit in at university, they only considered they must go to university. The rare occasions when 'reasonable expectation' is considered to be an issue, more 'social mobility' attitudes emerge from participants with less good family backgrounds. The following three respondents are all from working class families:

If you cannot go to university, you can never ever live with a good social status. I spent 12 years preparing for the two-day national examination, the national examination; it sounds horrific, but it is my life. Because it is the only way to prove I am of value...

(Xin, key senior high school)

The university is the place to make you become a better person, and you could have a better life after graduation...

(Xinyi, senior high school)

> I do not think I can go to university, because my academic results are bad. But I still believe the people who go to university will achieve respect from others and a good life more than the people who do not, especially from poor family backgrounds...
>
> (Jie, senior high school)

An equality of belief, an inequality of opportunity

The national HE entrance examination has been designed by the MoE as a national test and all students across the country take exactly the same examination. The character of the exam has been cited as the most powerful evidence to show absolute equality for all university applicants across the nation; also it supports the idea of HE as an academic good. Social class inequality has not been an issue in the HE debates in China, especially after HE expansion. The situation throughout the HE expansion in China since 1999 has been one of a strong achievement; more and more young people have an opportunity to go to university, which has been promoted as the big contribution to class equality, but the effects on social class have been neglected by the academic world. As Lesley Pugsley (1998:85) points out: 'there are class inequalities involved in making decisions about higher education which have persisted for the 40 years since Jackson and Marsden's 1962 study'. Class differences with regard to HE access have not been taken into account in China. However, data from my interviews with university applicants illustrated a significant difference between the two cohorts (key school and non-key school applicants) and their understanding of the national examination, HE access and the HE system. All students shared the belief in HE, and a positive attitude to attending university, but non key-school students were unsure of their direction:

> ...the life I have at the secondary school so far is so boring, I cannot do anything I want or am interested in, even play football or instruments, I cannot do anything but study for the national examination every day. I think I will be happier at university...
>
> (Kai, senior high school)

> The reason I want to go to university is not for a good job. Rich families may be able to give you a good job, but not the life you could be pleased by. I am so curious to know what the university looks like. I heard from others ... they said studying there is such a fun experience; you can do whatever you want to do. I know some will say you cannot know anything about the university till you are there. Therefore I would like to be the one at university.... There is nothing about my academic performance; I do not want to lose the chance.... If I do not try, I will definitely regret it for the rest of my life...
>
> (Rong, senior high school)

> My self-motivation for going university is to achieve a good job, and also study at the university does not look like study at my secondary or primary school; we will have lots of free time to do things we are really interested in. But now, the only thing we should and could do is preparing for the national examination. I think I will have more autonomy in my learning and daily life when I am in the university...
>
> (Mimi, senior high school)

Most non-key school students are curious about university life; they believe they could be more independent there. Some of them mention good jobs, but they were unable to give me a clear definition of a good job. They are full of passion and personal aspirations when they are talking about university. However, they have no idea of what university is like and should be like. Few of their family members had attended university before; only two of the non-key school students had relatives who had been to university. They believe that university is good for them, although none of them can explain why and how:

> I am curious about the university; none of the people in my family or my parents' friends went to the university before, none of them experienced this before...
>
> (Jinjin, senior high school)

> ...the students like us from a poor family background, none of our family members went to university before, even the people we know closely, hardly any went to university. You will be the proud one of your whole family after going to university. We know that not all students go to the university, but for myself, I definitely want to be a university student. Also I think you can find a good job with your degree, so going to university is for a better job and a better life.
>
> (Liu, senior high school)

Rong is a typical example among my non-key school participants, who have not benefitted from a less educated family background; they still believe that university is a good route to go down but are unable to articulate why:

> My parents are not well-educated; they were unable to help my study in my later primary school. They could not supply me with a good family education, therefore, going to university is my choice and my life. My parents cannot give me any advice about which university to go to, or the subject I may study. One of the most important reasons I want to go the university is, that I think I will be able to give my parents a better life after my graduation...
>
> (Rong, senior high school)

Some express a lack of confidence with their academic performance:

> Although more and more students can go to university due to the expansion of higher education, the university is still for the good students from good schools...
>
> (Mimi, senior high school)

> My dad thinks international trade is a good area for me to look for a job. I do not have a clear idea about what I am going to do. I did have lots of discussion with my dad, about what I am going to do after university. But my uncle, who is the only one of our family who went to a really good university, does not want to talk with me; he said I am at such a poor senior high school, he could not expect anything...
>
> (Kai, senior high school)

Thus this data suggests that university applicants have very different experiences depending on their family background and school type. These students (from non-key schools) have been limited in HE access in terms of their family and the non-key schools they have attended. They position themselves very differently from key school students; they have a lack of social, cultural, economic and political capital as a result of their family background; also they have less confidence and do not know university well, and this is related to the school they come from: a 'non-key school'. My quantitative data shows that there is this disadvantage of non-key schools in developing social, cultural, economic, political and academic capital. With regard to the political connections, for example, it may be interesting to note that during the course of this research I discovered that parents' political status, by which I mean membership of the Chinese Communist Party, has a statistically significant impact on their children's entry into a key senior secondary school. The route to a high status university is often a progression from the key senior secondary school. My qualitative data demonstrates this phenomenon again, and shows an even deeper level from individuals' understandings and experiences.

The dialogue with key school students is demonstrably different:

> I think going to university is the bridge to help me to achieve my goal. I did not have actually any goal when I was a kid, because there is the whole system you must go through, I mean the education system. After I went to the senior high school, I started to think what I want to do in my future. Since then I recognised going to university is the must-be part in my life. The best way is to go abroad. Going to university is the best way I can imagine; this is the ideal way for all of us. HE is the platform; you meet teachers, professors, scholars, and your classmates, who will be more like you and understand you easily. I need to study the subject I am good at. All Chinese young people know, only a good university means a good job, a good future, a good life. There are so many universities in China, but they

are so different. I need to find ones which are really good and which suit me as well.

(Yi, key senior high school)

Yi clearly expresses his understanding of HE in China, and he is a distinctive example of key school students, who know HE or university well. They seem to have a clear strategy and a personal plan to construct their future life, and are fully confident rather than just having only personal aspirations and passion. They are totally different from the non-key school participants; they are more confident and knowledgeable; they seem to have benefitted from their family and their key school backgrounds; they also show they are the group with an advantageous position:

My family is different from most of my classmates; both my parents are officers in the military. I grew up in the military residential area; I went to the primary school in the same area. Back in my primary school time, I already knew I wanted to go to a really good key secondary school; otherwise I cannot get into a good university. I think most of my friends back in my primary school thought the same. My parents definitely were happy about my idea; they sent me to this secondary school, one of the best in this city, and then after this I will go to university, but only a good university. Because both my parents went to university, going to university is a must for me...

(Yang, key senior high school)

A good university is able to supply a better platform to help you be better. HE is the shortcut to position ourselves in a good place. We are similar when we go to university, but we will be different after graduation. It is impossible for graduates from non-985 universities to be as good as the graduates from 985 universities. If I did not go to a good secondary school, I would not be as good as now. The average maths scores in *Gaokao* at my school last year was 140 out of 150, it is almost impossible for me to get bad scores, because of my school. I believe HE is so important, but I do not think everyone should go. The students who are suited for HE in China should go, but it's not for all. If your academic performance is not good enough, university will not be a good place for you. I also do not think only good students go to university, but I am going, because I am good at it. The people you will meet, and the university you will go to, will do something to make you different. Although I do not think either Tsinghua or Beijing university will suit me, I still would like others in the 2 plus 7 group (high status); it is crucial for me to go to a good university...

(Meng, key senior high school)

Yang above highlights the importance of family; Meng highlights the importance of the key school he was attending. Both demonstrated their psychological and academic preparedness for HE. For some students, a high status university is very definitely where they want to be:

> For me, to be honest, it is not the most important part of my life, and not the only road to pursue a better life, in my case at least. I am preparing SATs now as well, I will make the decision to stay here in China for university, or go abroad....
>
> (Qi, key senior high school)

> I must go to a good university, what I mean is good universities such as Tsinghua University or Beijing University, or at least a 2 plus 7 university. I never think I could not agree with the education system or the moral values in this society, I mean the way people evaluate the universities ranking system...
>
> (Kewei, key senior high school)

> Going to a good university is my goal. I will primarily consider the university's ranking, not only a university, but a good university. It must be a good university; I mean 2 plus 7 or the 985 universities at least. Not only because I will be respected by my parents, but by others as well. Also I am keen to meet people like me from good senior secondary schools and from a good family as well. Most of my classmates are from local families, but at university you will meet people from all of China...
>
> (Keyi, key senior high school)

The importance of knowing their position in HE access raises the issue of inequality in relation to university choice. Most key school students in my interviews were ready to go to a high status university; they know why those universities are of high repute and how to get into them. They seemed privileged in HE access, and they wanted to be in the place where they will find intellectual and social peers. The issue is not simply 'fitting in', but they wanted to maintain or sustain their future strategy for their social and academic good. It appeared to be different for the non-key school student: even when non-key school students said they wanted to be successful and go to university, they still demonstrated less awareness of the system as a whole. They were different from key school students; though they had the passion and aspiration, they have less knowledge about university; they lacked the support from their families' social, cultural, economic and political capital.

Conclusion

I have attempted to demonstrate that there are a number of certainties and a number of complexities within attitudes to education in China, and in particular to the progression to HE. Bearing in mind that we use the tripartite model of attitudes in this book, where we view an attitude as being composed of beliefs, feelings and behaviours, it might be argued that there are no internal contradictions regarding the beliefs about education as exhibited by the respondents in this study. Feelings and beliefs about education in general and about progression to university are overwhelming positive. There is positivity about the instrumentality of education, about its transformative powers, about its ability to bestow prestige and comfort upon the recipient. There is positivity about the role of university in these functions. The respondents have noted how these positive attitudes are widely held by Chinese society. And respondents have opined that there are positives for the parents and families of those who are educated, such as pride in those children who attend university and once again, the possibility of prestige and comfort.

However, there is also nuance and contradiction, and if we consider behaviours rather than beliefs, there is more complexity. I have presented evidence to show how political leaders and policymakers may share the same belief as that held by wider society, but they appear to have behaved in a more complex way, harnessing the widespread belief for shorter term economic ends. From the political point of view, the strategic expansion of HE in the 1990s helped economic growth, and lower unemployment rates, through letting more young people get into universities. If the result is greater graduate unemployment, then this could result in changes of attitude: there may well develop a greater scepticism about the value of HE. And whilst HE expansion increases HE access for secondary school graduates, and while Chinese families believe millions of young people have the opportunity to attend institutes of HE as a result of expansion, they may not benefit from the economic and social returns as much as they believe.

There is further complexity in the behaviours around education, and it seems clear that one social group is behaving very effectively in such a way as to accrue benefits for their offspring; in this sense we can observe an asymmetry of behaviours. We have seen that the middle class have acted on their belief about the benefits of HE and have tried to ensure that their children are the beneficiaries. And as the expansion of HE has inevitably occurred alongside a stratification of HE, it seems from the data that it is the children of the middle class who have understood the implications of that stratification and have sought to take advantage of it. My interview and focus group data, collected from students of different family backgrounds, revealed that the concept of a high status university was only mentioned by key school students, and not at all by non-key school students; as a result, the key school students' knowledge of the university system, their academic achievement and material circumstances provide them with wider choices in HE access. At the same time, non-key school students appear to be disadvantaged as a result of both their family background and school. It is through the national HE examination system that the HE system in China appears to be producing an unequal distribution of social, cultural, economic, political and academic resources and securing privileges for certain groups of people. Perhaps the issue of social equity and mobility will be the most important challenge that HE expansion has brought.

References

Alexander, K.L., Pallas, A.M. and Holupka, S. 1987 'Social Background and Academic Determinants of Two-Year versus Four-Year College Attendance: Evidence from Two Cohorts a Decade Apart'. *American Journal of Education* 96 (1) pp. 56–80.

Archer, M. 1995 *Realist Social Theory: the Morphogenetic Approach*. Cambridge: Cambridge University Press.

Benavot, A. 1996 'Education and Political Democratization: Cross-National and Longitudinal Findings.' *Comparative Education Review*.

Bourdieu, P. and Passeron, J. 1979 *The Inheritors, French Students and their Relation to Culture*. Chicago: University of Chicago Press.

Bowles, S. and Gintis, H. 1976 *Schooling in Capitalist America: Educational Reform and the Contradictions of Economic Life*. Chicago: Haymarket Books.

Broaded, M. and Liu, C.S. 1996 'Family background, gender and educational attainment in urban China.' *China Quarterly* 145 pp. 53–86.

Carpenter, Peter G. and Hayden, M. 1993 'Improvements in equity in the participation of young people in higher education in Australia during the 1980s'. *Higher Education* 26 pp. 199–216.

Cabrera, A.F. and La Nasa, S.M. 2000 *Understanding the College Choice of Disadvantaged Students: New Directions for Institutional Research*. San Francisco: Jossey-Bass.

Collins, R. 1979 'Functional and Conflict Theories of Educational Stratification.' *American Sociological Review* 36 (6) pp. 1002–1019.

DeMarrais, K.B. and LeCompte, M.D. 1995 *The Way Schools Work: A Sociological Analysis of Education*. New York: Longman.

Erikson, R. and Jonsson, J. 1998 'Social Origin as an Interest-bearing Asset: Family Background and Labour Market Rewards among Employees in Sweden.' *Acta Sociologica* 41 (1) pp. 19–36.

Fishlow, A. 1966 'The common school revival: fact or fancy.' In Rosovsky, H. (Ed.) *Industrialization in Two Systems*. New York: Wiley.

Giddens, A. 1995 'Living in a post-traditional society' in *Reflexive Modernisation: Politics, Tradition and Aesthetics in the Modern Social Order*. Cambridge: Polity Press.

Goodman, D. 1996 'The People's Republic of China: The party-state, capitalist revolution and new entrepreneurs.' In Robinson, R. and Goodman, D. (Eds), *The New Rich in Asia*. London: Routledge.

Gu, X. 1997 'Elitist democracy and China's democratisation: A gradualist approach towards democratic transition by a group of Chinese intellectuals.' *Democratization* 4 (2) pp. 84–112.

Hannum, E. and Buchmann, C. 2003 *The Consequences of Global Educational Expansion: Social Science Perspectives*. Cambridge, MA: The American Academy of Arts and Sciences.

Kane, D. 1994 'The social and intellectual elite.' In Goodman, D.S.G. and Hooper, B. (Eds) *China's quiet revolution*. Murdoch: Longman Cheshire.

Kuo, H.H.D. and Hauser, R.M. 1995 'Trends in Family Effects on the Education of Black and White Brothers.' *Sociology of Education* 68 pp. 136–160.

Li, H., Zhang, J., Sin, L.T. and Zhao, Y. 2006 'Relative earnings of husbands and wives in urban China.' *China Economic Review* 17 pp. 412–431.

Li, L. 2005 *Education for 1.3 Billion: Former Chinese Vice Premier Li Lanqing on 10 years of Education Reform and Development*. Beijing: Foreign Language Teaching and Research Press and Pearson Education Asia.

Li, P. 2004 'New Change of Chinese Social Stratification Structure.' In Li, P. (Ed.) *Social Stratification in China's Today.* Beijing: Chinese Academy of the Social Sciences.

Li, Q. 2003 *Constitutional Liberalism and State Construction.* Beijing: SDX Joint Publishing Company.

Li, W. and Min, W. 2003 *Tuition, Private Demand and Higher Education Expansion in China.* Beijing: People's Educational Press.

Liang, H. 1998 '985 Universities, World-Class universities.' *Daxue ershiyi shiji de shijieji daxue. People's Daily.* Beijing: People's Daily Publisher.

Lin, N., Nee, V., Parish, W. and Yu, E. 1994 'The Development of Sociology in China: A Delegation Report'. *The China Quarterly* 137 pp. 268–270.

Liu,Y. 2013 'Meritocracy and the Gaokao: a survey study of higher education selection and socio-economic participation in East China.' *British Journal of Sociology of Education* 34 (5–6) pp. 868–887.

Marginson, S. 2010 *Higher Education in East Asia and Singapore: Rise of the Confucian Model.* The International Conference of the Higher Education Evaluation and Assessment Council of Taiwan. Taipei: Springer.

Meyer, J.W. 1977 'The effects of education as an institution.' *American Journal of Sociology* 63 (1) pp. 55–77.

MGI (McKinsey Global Institute) 2006 *From 'Made in China' to 'Sold in China': The rise of the Chinese Urban Consumer.* Los Angeles: McKinsey & Co.

Ministry of Education PRC. 1996 *The Ninth Five-Year Plan for Education and Layout for the year 2010.* Beijing: People's Educational Press.

Ministry of Education PRC. 1998 *The Action Plan to Visualise Education Towards the 21st Century.* Beijing: People's Educational Press.

Mok, K.H. 2000 'Marketizing Higher Education in Post-Mao China.' *International Journal of Educational Development* 20 pp. 109–126.

Neubauer, D. 2007 'Globalization and Education: Characteristics, Dynamics, Implications.' In Hershcok, P.D., Mason, M. and Hawkins, J.N. (Eds) *Changing Education: Leadership, Innovation and Development in a Globalizing Asia Pacific* University of Hong Kong, Comparative Education Research Centre.

Ngok, K. and Guo, W. 2007 'The Quest for World Class Universities in China: Critical Reflections'. *The Journal of Comparative Asian Development* 6 (1) pp. 21–44.

Oakes, J. 1985 *Keeping Track: How Schools Structure Inequality.* New Haven: Yale University Press.

Pepper, S. 1984 *Chinese University post-Mao Enrolment Policies and their Impact on Structure of Secondary Education: A Research Report.* Ann Arbor: University of Michigan.

Perry, E.J. and Wong, C. (Eds) 1985 *Political Economy of Reform in Post-Mao China.* Cambridge: Harvard University Press.

Postiglione, G.A. (Ed.) 2006 *Education and Social Change in China: Inequality in a Market Economy.* New York: M.E. Sharpe Inc.

Reay, D., Davies, J., David, M. and Ball, S. 2001 'Choices of Degree or Degrees of Choice? Class, 'Race' and the Higher Education Choice Process.' *Sociology* 35 pp. 855–874.

Reay, D. and Luce, H. 2003 'The limit of "choice": Children and Inner City Schooling.' *The British Journal of Sociology* 37 (1) pp. 121–142.

Reusswig, F. and Isensee, A. 2007 'Rising Capitalism, Emerging Middle-Classes and Environmental Perspectives in China: A Weberian Apporach.' In Lange, H. and Meier,

L. (Eds) *The New Middle Classes: Globalising Lifestyles, Consumerism and Environmental Concern.* Netherlands: Springer.

Sayer, A. 2005 'Class, Moral Worth and Recognition.' *The British Journal of Sociology* 39 pp. 27–41.

Stafford, K.L., Lundstedt, S.B. and Lynn, Jr., A.D. 1984 'Social and economic factors affecting participation in higher education.' *The Journal of Higher Education* 55 (5) pp. 590–608.

Sewell, W., Haller, A. and Straus, M. 1957 'Social Status and Educational and Occupational Aspiration.' *American Sociological Review* 22 (1) pp. 67–73.

Sewell, W. and Shah, V. 1967 'Socioeconomic Status, Intelligence, and the Attainment of Higher Education.' *Sociology of Education* 40 (1) pp. 1–23.

Smith, A. 1759 *The Theory of Moral Sentiments.* Oxford: Oxford University Press.

Thogersen, S. 1987 'China's senior middle schools in a social perspective: A survey of Yantai District, Shandong province.' *China Quarterly* 109 pp. 72–100.

Unger, J. 1982 *Education under Mao: Class and Competition in Canton Schools, 1960–1980.* New York: Columbia University Press.

Unger, J. 1994 'Rich man, poor man: The making of new classes in the countryside.' In Goodman, D. and Hooper, B. (Eds) *China's Quiet Revolution.* Murdoch: Longman. Cheshire.

United Nations 1966 International Covenant on Economic, Social and Cultural Rights.

Wan, Y. 2006 'Expansion of Chinese Higher Education since 1998: Its Causes and Outcomes.' *Asia Pacific Education Review* 7 (1) pp. 19–31.

Wang, Y.C. 1966 *Chinese Intellectuals and the West 1872–1949.* Chapel Hill: The University of North Carolina Press.

Wong, L. 1994 'China's urban migrants – The public policy challenge.' *Pacific Affairs* 67 (3) pp. 335–356.

Wu, X. 2005 'Yuelu Academy: Landscape and gardens of neo-Confucian pedagogy.' *Studies in the History of Gardens & Designed Landscapes* 25 (3) pp. 37–72.

Zhu, G. 1998 *Social Classes Analysis in China.* Tianjing: Tianjing Renmin Publisher.

6 Conclusions

Paul Morrissey

As our writers have presented, in the preceding chapters, their fresh insights into attitudes in contemporary China, there are a number of areas where there is clear convergence between them. It is upon these areas of convergence that I will dwell for the next few paragraphs. Significantly, each writer is working in a context of change, which adds an extra dimension to the gathering of data on attitudes. Yu Chen is working in the context of Higher Education, a sector which has experienced extraordinary growth in the last three decades. Chen Nie's work is in the area of housing, where a quiet yet dramatic revolution has taken place during the same time frame. Liqing Li explores attitudes to nationalism in the context of an awakening regional and global dragon. Wei Fang looks into young people's beliefs and behaviours within the digital technologies which have taken China and the world by storm in such a short time span.

It is important here to reiterate that the writers of the case studies are all Chinese, another area of convergence; and because of their chosen research methodology, the interview conducted in Mandarin, they have each been able to capture the nuance of each interview response. Further, they, or their respondents, have been able to act as mediators in that they have been able to explain to the reader, who may well be from beyond the shores of greater China, areas of confusion or problematical meaning. Of course, the interview itself is an area of convergence in itself; each writer has used this method, though clearly there have been other research activities such as the survey and literature reviews. The interviews have allowed fresh data to be available for consideration. And as a result of the interview data, each writer has challenged existing research in their chosen area. Wei Fang has a different view to the notion that the digital revolution can be transformative with regard to interactions between people of different classes. Liqing Li challenges the over-simplification in reported responses of young people with regard to their attitudes to nationalism, and provides evidence to show these are much more complicated than some previous research has suggested. Chen Nie also questions previous work where the individual is seen as a passive agent of pressures which are outside of his or her control, and attempts to combine the processes of decision-making and negotiation among individuals with an understanding of macro, external forces. Yu Chen questions the perception of the growth of higher education as an opportunity for all in society, and points out that there is a lack of empirical evidence relating to access and individuals across different social and economic backgrounds.

The interview has also been the perfect tool to allow us to observe emergent attitudes and cultural, social or administrative structures which have arisen during attempts to explain responses from those interviewed. What do I mean by emergent attitudes or cultural, social or administrative structures? I am referring to ideas or explanations which were not specifically sought but which emerged during the course of an interview or lay behind a reported attitude; often the respondent needed to explain this emergent attitude to the interviewee, and at other times the writers felt the need to explain a response to the non-Chinese reader. Thus, through the interviewing activities of this study we can see broader facets of Chinese society. For example, in Wei Fang's discussion of the digital preferences and behaviours amongst Chinese youth, she cannot avoid explaining to her readers about an important social fracture – the rural–urban divide – which allows us to better understand the responses to the questions she asked. This social fracture would thus fit into the category of an emergent social or administrative structure. Thus the methodology has allowed insights into wider areas of society, and the data generated by the researchers, and reproduced here, allows a deeper understanding of the topics under discussion. Such emergent structures demonstrate that we do need to take seriously de Menthe's insistence in *The Chinese Mind* (as mentioned in Chapter 1) that certain historical concepts are vital for an understanding of contemporary Chinese attitudes and behaviours. Similarly, the notions of strong family ties and filial piety are two such historical cultural traditions which underpin some of the responses in Wei Fang's chapters.

And the respondents have all been young. Not all have been of the same age group; some were college or university students, some in their later 20s, and in the position of wanting or needing to purchase a house. Certainly, most have the same general background of academic success, though we must bear in mind some of Wei Fang's respondents who were from rural areas and perhaps in lower status positions. But what is fresh here is not the debates within which the ideas are framed, but what the writers bring to us in terms of the words of their young Chinese respondents. And we have underlined before how this group is regarded as significant, in that not only do the young and educated form a defined consumer base, but they are seen as a barometer of changing attitudes and values.

Another area of convergence is the fact that all the writers were faced with data that was highly nuanced and often contradictory in some way. For example, Liqing Li's respondents may have demonstrated great patriotism, in that they generally exhibited a genuine love of country, but they would not all extend this feeling into unconditional and active support of street demonstrations. Wei Fang brings us into contact with new technologies which offer the promise of greater democratisation, and yet through her analysis we stumble across a social order which shows a stubborn resistance to change. Yu Chen also comes across a social inertia within a context of an expanding university system, which seems to offer so much in terms of social equity and opportunities for those who have had fewer opportunities in the past. Chen Nie's examination of a very modern, inflation-fuelled housing bubble reveals attitudes which are deeply rooted in traditional beliefs and behaviours. So much for the convergence between the writers. Of course, there are many areas of divergence and difference between the writers, and I discuss these in the more general summary which follows here.

In Chapter 2, Wei Fang's focus has been upon Chinese young people's attitudes towards online communication and relationship formation, their beliefs in the extent of liberation and autonomy facilitated by the internet regarding communication and relationship formation, and their behaviours of building relationships online; and on the great social chasm that is the rural–urban divide in China, whether there are differences in these attitudes, beliefs and behaviours between rural and urban young people. Not only does Wei Fang write about the product details of particular digital services, and their importance in framing the responses of users of these products and services, but also the stubborn continuity of the established social order revealed by the adoption of new digital technology.

We learn, in Wei Fang's chapter, about the 'utopian' view of the internet as liberator from time, space and social class; in this new digital age, one has more opportunities to reach outside one's own community and build connections with people from geographically and socially different communities. There is the potential to open up the possibility of increasing the diversity of one's networks and contributing to social ties built between members of a different social status, and the potential to degrade rigid hierarchical orders, gender roles, ethnic designations, and class relationships.

As previously stated, one of the privileges of involvement in this project has been to observe how the writers or respondents have reflected upon the underlying causes of the attitudes expressed. Nowhere is this clearer than in where Wei Fang reflects upon the potential of digital services to unlock rigid structures in China, as the utopians would have us believe. And yet her data suggests that this potential is not realised, and thus she cannot escape from the duty of explaining to her reader about the *hukou* system. This system is a fundamental determinant of the life of each Chinese citizen through its identification of individuals within an administrative unit, through its control of an individual's movement, and through its allocation of resources. The *hukou* system has an enormous role to play in the distribution of opportunity. As Wei Fang tells us, the system has played a crucial role in shaping rural and urban residents' positions in the social stratification, as well as in distinguishing them socially and culturally. Perhaps what is surprising is that this established order which the *hukou* imposes is a relatively new construct, in operation for little more than half a century, a system which counters the long held values of a society where for generations the work of the countryside was always valued. But of course there are other long held value positions in play; the acceptance of this system mirrors the general acceptance, over generations, of a hierarchical central authority.

There are other emergent attitudes. A number of respondents revealed an interest in developing relationships with those of a high status, a reaction which, so Wei Fang tells us, is embedded in the Chinese *guanxi* culture, where personal

Conclusions 189

contacts may be as important as any other factor in determining one's life chances. The strength of family ties and filial piety are another emergent notions in the piece, strongly coming to the surface both in Wei and Chen's chapters on the digital divide and housing preferences respectively.

Later in her chapter, Wei Fang mentions 'social capital' in the context of young people's access to institutional resources and people who are well connected, and here a broad theme in the social sciences emerges. Since the 1980s, the literature on social capital has associated social norms and networks of cooperation with positive economic, social and political outcomes: improvements in economic development, social cohesion and democratic governance. However, Bourdieu and others, unlike these integrationist scholars, formulate the concept of social capital in relation to the process of continuing social inequality, particularly so in regard to class relations. She implies the concept of 'habitus', as does Liqing Li in Chapter 3. For Wei's respondents, the 'habitus' is in the sense of an individual's disposition towards the social group, a result of acculturation and educational background; for Liqing Li, 'national habitus' expresses the societal input of attitudes and beliefs which shapes the citizen's perceptions towards questions of nationalism.

Wei's respondents evoke the idea that dominant and dominated groups tend to have differential strategies and power in the acquisition and conversion of social capital, due to their unequal possession of resources in the field in which they find themselves. There are echoes of another of Bourdieu's concepts, that of social capital, seen as an investment made by members of the dominant class, and an engagement by that dominant class, in mutual recognition and acknowledgement, in order to maintain and reproduce group solidarity and preserve the group's dominant position. As we have seen, Yu Chen uses the same analytical tools, that is, Bourdieu's perception of social capital as an instrument of social inertia, in Chapter 5, in the context of higher education preference.

In summary then, we have seen how Wei Fang's respondents are enthusiastically engaged in online communication with peers and others, and also in building various forms of relationships online. The technical features of online communication, which allow the user to retain anonymity, promote positive attitudes towards interacting with and befriending strangers. This positivity is only enhanced by the perception that adults may attempt to intervene in young people's relationships in respondents' offline lives, and encourages young people towards online communication and relationship formation. They believe that through online communication they can have a greater degree of autonomy. Wei Fang's study also reveals inconsistency and ambivalence in attitudes towards with whom to communicate and with whom to form relationships online, in terms of the location of the individuals (rural vs. urban). Urban respondents revealed negative attitudes towards developing relationships with individuals from rural areas, and vice versa, showing that offline prejudices extended into the online space.

Continuing Wei Fang's interest in the here and now, Liqing Li dwells on attitudes to a very current theme in Chapter 3. Though there has been an erstwhile traditional patriotism in China, her investigation is into nationalistic beliefs and behaviours in a country which has never before been so active and engaged in global affairs. She informs us of the perceived importance of nationalism in the China that emerged from the shock of nineteenth century foreign intervention, a nationalism that survived the coming and going of various political movements and ideologies, a nationalism which was indeed deliberately reinvigorated following the Tiananmen demonstration in 1989, and which is now on the rise. We can detect a real change from the pre-Qing Confucian notion of China as a cultural identity towards the current position of China as a political entity. She reminds us of the view that the Chinese Communist Party should be seen as essentially a nationalist political movement which is motivated not by a purist, Marxist solidarity with others, but by a desire to see China as strong and autonomous in a context of competing nations, which we might see as a very modern Western position. The current rise in nationalism can be observed perhaps most importantly in the state apparatus, but also in intellectual discourse, and within popular society. For example, we might interpret the recent (2015) pronouncement from Yuan Guiren, the minister of Education, regarding the rejection of Western values, as part of the state involvement in the nationalism project. The reaction to this increased sense of national importance can be observed in the warnings from many commentators that China seeks a new regional and world order, though others point to the realities of military and technological abilities which would restrict such ambitions.

Liqing Li demonstrates how the student population has long been instrumental with regard to internal political change in China, and how this continues to be the case up to the present day. Students in the state-run university system are required to attend classes in political education, and it is argued that the student body can be manipulated to take part in demonstrations, including those which have a nationalist message. Thus, to ask individuals from the student body to be the subjects in her study relating to the attitude objects of feelings and beliefs about nationalism, seems a legitimate strategy.

Interestingly, as we have seen, she uses the concept of 'national habitus', borrowing from Bourdieu and others, to show that we can observe how the 'expected answers' from respondents can be garnered when a particular method is employed, but how deeper insights might emerge when another (different) method is used. The 'national habitus' is determined by the jurisdiction in which the citizen grows up, being a result of the myriad societal and family inputs as she matures in that particular society, and might include an amalgamation of attitudes, pre-conceptions, perceptions, responses and beliefs which the citizen might have regarding questions of nationalism; it is this 'national habitus' which might lead to automatic or less considered responses to the researcher, replicating the expressions of nationalist discourses. In this light, we can see how the attitudes of Li's respondents regarding nationalism are conventionally pro-China.

When questioned more deeply, the citizen respondent might deliver rather more nuanced responses. In Li's words, from Chapter 2:

By examining the contradictory responses and reactions students gave to different questions included in the same questionnaire and through the researcher's further probing in interview, in what follows, I show that behind the take-for-granted-ness of the usual nationalist discourses of the nation, there are also complex stories about how university students view and articulate nation and nationalism.

For example, the respondents' responses towards the Taiwan issue mostly resonated with the orthodox stance advocated by the regime. When asked for their views on Taiwan, a majority of students expressed the attitudinal belief that Taiwan should always be a part of the Chinese nation, and that the interference of foreign nations into the sovereignty of Chinese territory was not acceptable. However, there was more reserve, and a greater distance from what is perceived as the government line, when the respondents were asked about the street demonstrations which are widely reported in the context of state-promoted nationalism. This is where attitudes (pro-China) in some instances differed from beliefs. There was a widely held belief, or suspicion, that such demonstrations were orchestrated by government agents, that the targets of such demonstrations were carefully selected, and that misguided demonstrators were likely to be involved in random acts of violence.

In Chapter 4, Chen Nie takes us into another context of another very contemporary area, and at the same time, an area of great change, as he presents his data relating to attitudes in the housing sector. Change, in this chapter, can be seen at many levels. Not only does he discuss housing in a context of national economic transition, a macro level change in itself, but he informs us that theorists and researchers have observed a change of mentality among people who now appear to value a home of their own as a worthwhile goal, offering financial security and an accumulation of wealth, improvements in mental health, life satisfaction and self-esteem. This psychological change seems to be associated with political strategies and national economic shifts; indeed, there is an argument that the growth of the preference for owner-occupation is the result of encouragement by government and of corporation, rather than being only the choice of the individual.

The young people who are interviewed have been subject to a number of important recent changes in housing policy. They live in the present era when housing has ceased to be a welfare entitlement, a heavily subsidised commodity, as it was for their grandparents and for some of their parents. Chen Nie reminds us of the 'zigzag' nature of the history of housing policy over the last five decades, which has switched from private provision, to state provision, and now back to the largely private provision of the current policy. For the Western reader, some of the context of Chen Nie's chapter may sound rather familiar. We can detect a certain globalisation of ideas, in the sense that discourses on the private ownership of the home, on rising prices for residential properties, on the need for intergenerational loans, and on global hot spots of property prices, are familiar to many of us in many parts of the world. This globalisation in housing issues is of course a direct result of the adoption by many governments, including China's, of the neoliberal policies which were outlined in Chapter 1.

But as well as the global dimension, this chapter also demonstrates a dimension of something which is very local, very Chinese. Chen Nie points towards the persistence of old traditions, resonating with those literatures which attempts to explain the roots of Chinese culture. He looks deep into the past, where he finds a continuity of traditional attitudes in the deep love of the home, and a traditional belief in the importance of home and rootedness to one's psychological health. And in the scale of the financial assistance from parents to their offspring when purchasing very expensive flats in Beijing, there are echoes of the traditional Confucian strength of the family bond. That the young are prepared to pay exorbitant sums for Beijing property shows an acceptance of the market economy, while at the same time, the intergenerational loans which allow such purchases are a manifestation of the traditionally strong links between one generation and the next.

Chen Nie restates the challenge to both to the established order in housing research and the points to the limits of quantitative methods in this area. Most housing studies within a Chinese context follows the same route: the emphasis of much research in housing on the legislative and institutional structure of the housing sector and government policy is seen an important determinant of housing outcomes. Government or media-determined definitions are often unreflexively accepted as fact-like. Meanwhile, in Chapter 4, the focus is on the process of choice, and Chen takes seriously the role of human subjects in housing processes rather than concentrating on structures and those more impersonal forces.

In summary then, Chen Nie's research in Chapter 4 amongst young people in Beijing reveals feelings which include positive attitudes towards owner occupation, negative attitudes towards the private rental sector and rather ambivalent attitudes towards social welfare housing. He unpacks positive attitudes to home ownership and argues that there is a hidden complexity. He makes a careful analysis of historical perspectives regarding housing and identifies a cultural common ground, which is a desire to settle down, a rootedness in a particular location, and a reluctance to move. The positive attitudes to home ownership are a result, on the part of the individual, of financial motives and the above common cultural ground, but also a result of the discourse around housing policy.

In Chapter 5, Yu Chen touches on a very topical issue, much discussed in the West, relating to the feelings, beliefs and behaviours surrounding education, and specifically surrounding the attitudes of high school students as they progress to university. Traditionally, education is the route to officialdom in China, and so it can be seen as instrumental to power, esteem and comfort, if not riches. Perhaps we can argue that this belief in education in China is somehow qualitatively different from Western views, in that the collective memory of the imperial examination system has imbued education with an apparently unassailable status. Perhaps as a result of these deep roots, we see little internal contradiction in the responses from all the interviewees about the value they attach to schooling and progression onto university, and the esteem bestowed upon the individual and her family.

There may be an expression of tradition in this piece, but Yu Chen's chapter is not free of the context of change. Indeed, her investigation is set against the revolution of higher education expansion, and the move from an elite system to a mass system, a move which holds out the promise of a consequent revolution in opportunity for those who are currently excluded from those possibilities. Of course, the expansion of HE is itself set against the transformation of China's economic fortunes, and concurrent with that transformation is the marketisation of many sectors, including that of HE.

In these circumstances it is not surprising that HE in China has attracted wide attention from the media and from academics. At the heart of Yu Chen's investigation is the discourse around social equity and mobility. It is here that she sees a contradiction between societal attitudes and current social activity. In her own words:

> Chinese values demand that individuals work as hard as possible in their daily social life because Chinese people believe social mobility is universally possible in terms of the degree of hard work in the education system.

This can be seen as another utopian view, in this instance, of social mobility; we saw a different utopian view expressed by Wei Fang in the context of the democratisation of new digital technologies. Yu Chen concludes that current studies seem to be inadequate when it comes to the discussion about the impact of social and economic factors upon social mobility in general, and in this instance, enrolment to HE in particular, and the attitudes which underlie these impacts; it is from this point that she attempts to provide empirical evidence relating to these social and economic factors.

Yu Chen dwells on issues of class, and reminds us of the much trumpeted feature of Chinese Confucian society regarding the willingness of most families, and in particular middle class families, to invest privately in their children's future; pressure from parents is a popular discourse with Western media and literature. Of course, this behaviour is not singular to China, though perhaps, as I have indicated, there are qualitative differences between Chinese families and others in this regard. Nevertheless, it appears to be the ability and the drive of the middle class which sets them apart from others in Chinese society, and where we see the tension between belief and behaviour. Though there might be in China a general belief in education – and Yu Chen's evidence, and others', suggests this – it is the supportive behaviours towards their children, which sets the middle class apart from other groups.

And so we can see another emergent structural issue arising from Yu Chen's data. For Wei Fang, the social fracture is the rural – urban divide. For Yu Chen, it is class, and the issue of class is translated into attendance at a particular category of school, either the senior high school, or the key senior high school, the latter boasting higher quality staff and facilities. Of course, there is no doubt an overlap between the two fractures of location and class. But the evidence is that attendance at particular schools within the state structure is key to the future of individuals. What also emerges are the traditional values around the family: close bonds, parental involvement, respect for parents. Further, the reproduction of the established, current order of privilege and entitlement appears to be taking place, and there is a stubborn resistance to change.

References

Bourdieu, P. 1993. *Sociology in Question.* Translated by R. Nice. London, Sage.

Bourdieu, P. 1998. 'L'essence du neo-liberalisme/The essence of Neo-Liberalism' from *Le Monde Diplomatique.*

Faure, G.O. 2002 *China: New Values in a Changing Society.* Accessed at www.ceibs.edu on 6 September 2014.

Index

1950s 30, 67, 111–12, 131
1960s 69, 112
1970s 1, 67, 113, 133
1980s 67, 97, 189; early 17, 98, 114, 160, 163; late 80, 161; post-1980s generation 109, 123; reforms 116
1990s 14, 85, 119; CCP government 117; creation of home-owning societies 97; early 80, 157; end of 142; late 160, 163; Mao fever 67, 92n3; mid 6, 70–1; new policy developments 156; post-1990s generation 123; strategic expansion of HE 182

academic results 18, 154, 169, 177
achievement 177; academic 40–2, 49, 182; educational 42; individual 16; occupational 159
Agnew, J. 104
air pollution 7
ambivalence 7, 50, 57, 189; amplification 9
ambivalent attitudes 9, 146, 192
American Life Project 26–7
anti-Americanism 3; among Chinese youth 6; rising anti-American sentiment 71
attitude construct 3, 8–9, 99; formation 8

balance 72, 92; perspective 104; state and market 15; yin and yang 4
Ball, S. 16
Bargh, J.A. 21, 23
Baym, N. 22, 24
BBSs (Bulletin Board Systems) 34
Beijing 68, 70, 138; fieldwork in 17; home ownership 112, 122–4, 129–30, 192; house prices 125–6, 132; hukou 4, 142, 144–5; Low Rental Housing (LRH) scheme 142; Ministry of Education 163–7; political circles 69; private rental 133–9; scholars 6; social welfare housing 143; Tiananmen incident 67, 88, 147n4; university 72, 157, 169, 172, 180–1; university students 73, 75; young migrants 147n7; *see also* Beijing University, Tsinghua University
Beijing Area Studies Survey of Beijing Residents (BAS) 4
Beijing University 157, 172, 180–1; Research Centre on Contemporary China (RCCC) 4
Berg, L. 72–3
Bergman, M.M. 3, 8
Bildner, E. 1, 7
Billig, M. 77
Blogs 34
Boase, J. 25
Bourdieu, P. 106–8, 158, 161, 189–90
boycott of French products 90
Boyd, D. 28, 46, 49
Bryman, A. 33, 72

capital 14–16; economic, social, and cultural 58n16; gains 126; human 157–8, 165; income, occupation and educational 5; lack of 179, 181; social 17, 56, 189; theory 107
capital city 4, 49, 122
capitalism 1, 14, 100, 112
Carlson, A. 67
Castells, M. 102
CCID Saidi-consultant 32
Cerny, G. 16
Chan, D.K.S. 27, 45
Chan, K.W. 31
Chang, M. 67–8, 70–1
change-makers, actual and potential 5
Chen, J.J. 116–17
Chen, W. 69, 123

196 Index

Chen, X. 3, 40
Chen, Z. 69, 123
Cheng, T.J. 31
Chesebro, J. 21, 23
China 7, 67–9, 78, 82, 91, 161; administration system 58n4; classes of society 160; development 83, 98; dissatisfaction with structures 86; economic growth 132, 153; economic reform 162, 193; economy 1–2, 155; Everbright Bank 123; future elites 72, 85; General Social Survey 4–5; higher education 165, 169, 171–2, 175–6; housing reform 115, 118, 135; human rights 79; improving status 80; macroeconomic transformation 119; modern history 29; national context 75; national greatness 89; national identity 92n7; national strength and dignity 88; neoliberal policies 192; position 77; relations with outside world 11, 15; rural population 30; sovereignty 66, 76, 90; strategy for home-owning society 120; transitional 146; university students 17, 65; Youth and Children Research Centre 70; Youth Daily poll 6; *see also* contemporary China
China Internet Network Information Center (CNNIC) 32–4, 38
Chinese 3–7, 42–3, 54, 71, 105, 109, 121, 125, 161, 164, 186–7, 193; Academy of Social Sciences 4, 160; cities 114; citizens 1–2, 8, 16; context 176; cultural origin 111, 192; culture 83, 147n8; education 153–6, 165; embassy bombed 65, 68, 90–1, 92n2; government 78, 86, 157; *guanxi* culture 57, 188; housing policy 113; housing system 97–8, 108, 129, 136; immigrants 40; intellectuals 30, 88; internet 32–3, 37; internet users 58n2; nation 70, 191; nationalism 66–9; parents 41–3, 166; people 67–9, 130; population 31, 112; rural–urban inequality 22, 29; society 47, 115, 158–9, 171, 174–5, 182; students 64; young people 21, 124, 179; youth 38, 49; yuan 147n3; *see also* contemporary Chinese
Chinese Communist Government (CCG) 30
Chinese Communist Party (CCP) 30, 66–8, 70–2, 75–6, 115, 179, 190; Central Committee 112; government 77, 117
Chinese Educational Bureau 70
Clapham, D. 101, 105
Clark, W. 101, 121

Cohen, M.L. 30
colleges 11, 36, 49, 72; independent 163
competition 15, 43; educational 159, 161; rental 135–6; states 16
competitive advantages 16; economy 161; education 154–5; rents 116
competitiveness: international 157; national 16
Confucian philosophy 111
consensus 11, 16, 65; worldwide 68
consumer 5, 187; groups 132; of HE 163; items 115, 159; individual preferences 101; single culture 15; youth-oriented culture 46; welfare 155
consumerism 43; consumerist attitudes 32
contemporary China 1, 3, 186; anti-foreign nationalism 71; anti-Western nationalism 67; attitudinal study 8; economic transformation 17; nationalism 64–5, 73, 85–6, 91; Research Centre on (RCCC) 4; society 18, 110; students 70, 76; urban society 122–3
contemporary Chinese 1; attitudes and behaviour 4–5, 187; culture 4; housing system 129, 146; nationalism 69; society 18, 110
convergence 186–8; of human activities 15; network 27
core middle class *see* middle class
corruption 7, 43, 88
Creswell, J.W. 10, 82
crisis: Asian Economic 165–7; CCP legitimacy 68; of faith 67; fiscal 16
cross-gender 54; peers 41–4, 47, 58n13; relationships 41–5, 54, 58n12; youth 45, 49
cultural 5, 18, 47, 130, 146, 160; aspects 31; assets 161; background 167, 172, 179; barriers 85; boundaries 10; capital 58n16, 158, 181; category 30; common ground 147, 192; construction of cities 50; context 13, 65, 74, 129; defensiveness 93; elements 4; entity 66; factors 40, 45; identity 190; issues 15; landscape 103; levels 14; nationalists 82; norm 88–9; origins of attitude to housing 109, 111; resources 182; status 162, 168; tradition 187
Cultural Revolution 111, 113, 115–16
culture 10, 12, 74, 102; Chinese 4, 43, 66, 83, 111, 147n8, 192; Chinese housing 109; consumer 15, 46; dynamic 29; *guanxi* 54, 57, 188; Han people 71; middle-class 162; national political 158

Damm, J. 32, 34
De Menthe, B. 4, 187
Deng Xiaoping 1, 67, 115
Denscombe, M. 122
digital 186, 188; divide 189; lives 11; preferences and behaviours 187; revolution 153; technologies 17, 193
distribution: consumer items 159; opportunity 188; social capital 56
distribution of resources 18, 161, 182; differentiated 31; unequal 21, 25, 43
Duncan, N. 100, 104

Ebo, B.L. 21, 24–5
economic development 2, 118, 123, 164–7, 189
economic growth 16, 32, 98, 119, 123, 132, 142, 153, 160–1, 163, 165, 182
Edensor, T. 74–5
Engels, F. 102, 115
environment 1, 3; better quality 100; built 101; changing 121; internet 24–5; less intimidating 132; for raising children 143, 147n8
environmental 22; concerns about air pollution 7
European 12; dominated 14; nations 1; transitional countries 98, 108
exchange rates 147n5; flexible 15

face-to-face 24; communication 22–3, 28, 38; interviews 3–4, 7, 28, 34, 39, 55, 73; meetings 48; setting 46
Fannie Mae National Housing Survey 100
Faure, G.O. 3–4
Fazio, R.H. 8–9
female 36, 39–40, 46, 48, 51, 54, 56; figure in Chinese culture 147n8; friends 41, 45; students 72, 79, 84–7, 89–90; young people 33–4
feminist perspective 8
Fenton, S. 81, 92
Forrest, R. 101–2, 108–9, 121
Fox, J. 80–1
Franklin, B. 107–8
free market economy 1–2; methods 15; profit-making 135
Friedman, E. 1, 15, 69
Fukuyama, F. 15–16

GDP per capita 77–8
Giddens, A. 106–8, 154
Gilderbloom, J. 103
globalisation 13–17, 21, 68, 191

globalists 14–15; hyperglobalists 14
grandparents 127, 191
Grinter, R.E. 26
guanxi 54; culture 57, 188
Guo, W. 157
Guo, Y. 70, 76–7
Gurney, C. 102, 104, 141, 143

half-core middle class *see* middle class
Hammersley, M. 12–13
Harvey, D. 15–16, 102
Hatch, M.J. 11
Hayek, F. 1, 15
He, B. 76–7
Held, D. 13–14
Hert, P. 21, 24
higher education (HE) 11, 14, 175, 186, 189; access 17–18, 84, 159, 172, 182; Chinese 153, 156; competition 161; development 155; expansion of 179, 193; limited opportunities 40; National Entrance Examination (NHEEE) 154, 162; social class 162, 177; social inequality 160, 181; systems 157, 168
higher education (HE) platform 179–80; for the political arena 158; for social success 154
Ho, D.Y. 42
Ho, K.-C. 34
Holliday, A. 13
Holstein, J.A. 12–13
Hong Kong 7, 27, 108, 126; management system 147n5
hong qi (Red Flag) 115
Horizon Consultancy Group 7
house prices 128, 134; in Beijing 126; current 132; soaring 101, 120, 124–7, 135; upward trend 108
householders 165
households 101, 106, 109, 115, 121, 128; below the national standard 120; dependency on wage labour 102; expenditure 114, 116; higher-income 142; owner occupation 132, 141; registration system 144; saving rates 117; status of the household head 112, 120; working class homeowner 104
housing: affordable 147n6; conditions 112, 115, 120; Economic Comfort (ECH) scheme 118–19, 142–6, 147n8, 147n9; Two-Limitation Housing (TLH) programme 142–3
housing allocation 121; dissatisfaction 115; public system 118; welfare 119

housing market 17, 97–9, 112, 125–6, 131, 146; booming 108, 122, 124, 128, 147; buying 144–5; commercial 142; fully-fledged 120; mature 109; new 119, 121; private 113, 135; private rental 123, 136

housing system 98–9, 108–9, 120–1, 123, 136, 146; Chinese 97, 129; development 107; dualist 102, 132, 143; new 118; pre-reform 130; privatised 131; public 111, 124; quasi-clan 114; socialist 122; social welfare 119, 142

housing tenure 11, 15, 99; choices 121, 123, 146; major 112; preferences 102; social attitudes towards 98, 107–10, 122, 146

Huang, Y. 68, 71, 109–16, 119, 121–3, 130–1

hukou 30; Beijing 145, 188; local 142–4; non-agricultural 31; rural 58n4, 58n7; system 4, 30–1, 113, 188; urban 5, 31, 58n4

human rights 14, 79; abuses 77

income 144, 159, 161; average 5; disposable 134; family 158, 163; high 57; higher 142; household 114; individual 16; limitations 144; low 102, 119–20, 142–3; raising 155, 158; rural family 42; source of additional 165; stable 110–11; urban middle class 160

inequality 7; of HE opportunities 161, 177; housing 112–13; rural–urban 17, 22, 29, 30, 32; social 21, 25, 160, 189; university choice 181

information and communication technologies (ICTs) 31–2

Instant Messaging (IM) 26, 33–5, 40

integration 15; international 14; with the outside world 68, 156; political 157–8

integrationist scholars 189

intergenerational communication 42; loans 17, 191–2; transfer of wealth 124, 127, 146

internet 21–2, 25–7, 32–3, 37–8; cafes 40, 43; communication 39, 45, 188; development 29, 31; diffusion 17; era 23–4; friendships 48, 50; mobile 44; relationships 58n13; social networking platform 34; spaces 2; users 58n2

Interpretivist theory 11

intervention 44; adult 57; Chinese central government 164; foreign 190; parental 42–3, 58n12; state 2

interview semi-standard 12; semi-structured 10, 34

Israel 38

Jacobs, K. 105–6
Jacques, M. 82, 85
Jessop, B. 16

Kang, J. 21, 23–4, 38, 123
Kant, I. 14
Kaplan, K.J. 9
Katz J.E. 26
Kemeny, J. 98–100, 102, 105–6, 132, 136
key schools 154, 168–72, 176; parents 173; participants 175; students 179–82; university applicants 177; *see also* non-key schools
King, P. 105–6, 108
King Jr., Martin Luther 24
Kirkby, R. 113–15
Kuipers, G. 74–5

landlord 131, 135–7, 139, 141; selectivity 132
landlord-owned housing properties 113
landlordism 113
LaPiere, R.T. 2, 64, 89, 92
Lea, M. 21–2, 24
Lee, J. 67, 108, 112, 117–20, 132, 135, 147n5
legitimacy 15, 70; CCP 67–8; institutional 31
Lenhart, A. 26–7, 29
Li Lanqing 164
Li, Q. 118, 120, 162
Liang, S.M. 29, 100, 110
Likert, R. 9; Likert scale 7, 9
Lin, N. 159
Liqing Li 186, 189–90
Liu, F.S. 43–4
Liu Xiaobo 79, 84, 93n8
living standards 7, 118
Livingstone, S. 26, 38, 44–5
loser 170–1, 175–6; losing face 41
Lu, H. 29–30
Lu, L. 5, 16
Lutz, J. 69–70

Macao 7
McKenna, K.Y. 21, 23–4, 26, 38
Mandarin 7, 186
manipulated 18, 71, 190
Mao Zedong 16, 115; Mao era 17; Mao fever 67, 92n3; Marxism-Maoism 68; social and economic experiments 69

marginal middle class *see* middle class
marginalised 84, 120–1, 142–3, 145–6, 147n9
market 2, 14, 116, 124, 135, 144, 161; analysis 99; anti-market revolution 112; based economy 98; current value 132; economy 157, 192; forces 15, 109, 168; housing rent 118; job 102; labour 145; open 103, 123; oriented 108, 120, 146; overheated 121; private rental 138–9; regulation 115; stock 125–6
marketisation 17, 21, 193; housing 116
marriage 113, 119, 124, 127, 144
Marsh, D. 11
Mattelart, A. 14–15
Mesch, G. 28, 38, 45–6
middle class 5–6, 118, 182, 193; culture 162; new 161–2; students 163; upper 162, 176; urban 160
migrants 4; Chinese immigrants 40; rural 51, 161; unauthorised 31; urban 132; workers 51, 53, 132, 145; young 147
Miles, M.B. 10, 12
Ministry of Education 163
mobility 158, 160–1; social 42, 155, 164–7, 171, 176, 182, 193; upward and downward 30
Mok, K.H. 14, 160

National Higher Education Entrance Examination (NHEEE) 154, 162–3, 167–8, 173–4
nationalism 64, 72, 81, 83, 88–92; attitudes to 186; Chinese 66–7, 80; fervent 74; perceived importance 190; post-Mao 69; questions of 189; rising 17, 65, 68, 70–1, 73, 85–6; state-promoted 191
neoliberal 98, 142; agenda 16; policies 15, 192; urbanisation 135
neoliberalism 13–15
Ngok, K. 157
Nobel Peace prize winner 79, 84, 93n8
non-key schools 154, 174, 178; participants 180; students 169–70, 172–3, 176, 179, 181–2; university applicants 177; working-class students 168, 171
nuance 1, 10, 182, 186; nuanced data 187; nuanced responses 190

O'Connel Davidson, J. 12
one-child policy 8, 42–3, 58n12, 84
online games 34–5, 37, 58n8
Ozga and Gewirtz 13

parental educational background 163; financial resources 127; generation 109; involvement 194; pressure 170–1
parents 7, 17, 123; college experience 29; devotion 42; educational attainments 158; emphasis on education 40–1, 160, 166, 171–2, 175–6, 178, 180–2, 191–3; expectations 43–4, 49; financial assistance 125, 127–8; intervention 42, 58n12; occupation 52; political status 179–80; respect for 42, 194; restrictions 43, 50, 89; structured behaviours 173; *see also* grandparents, teachers
peers 17, 45–7; cross-gender 41–4, 47, 58n13; intellectual and social 181; local 47–8; online 49, 189; pressure 49; relationships 42–4
Peilin, L. 4–5
People's Republic of China (PRC) 6, 67; attitudes 2–3; citizens 72; dominant group 71; government 31; higher education system 157; official press agency 78
Perry, E. 66, 155
Peter, J. 26, 38
Pew Global Attitudes Survey 2–3, 6–7
Pew Research Centre 3, 7; Internet project 26–7
place of origin 34, 46–7, 49–50, 53, 57
platforms 35, 37, 48, 58n8; making friends 36; online communication 26–7, 34; online relationships 43; social media 15
political education 3; classes 190
political-economic 15; agenda 16
population 30–2, 71, 112, 144; Chinese 160; general 51; growing 113; home ownership 123; student 190; urban 5, 7
Princeton Survey Research Associates International 7
private housing 109, 112, 119, 123, 131, 135; best 114; cheap rented 138; confiscated by the state 113; consumption 104; ownership 147n4; provision ended 142, 149; stigmatised 117; urban 116
private rental 17, 132–3, 139–41; housing 111–12, 123; makeshift 142; market 126; poor quality accommodation 123; sector 112, 131, 134–8, 146, 192
property 101–2, 124; Beijing 192; current market value 132; global hot spots 191; housing 119; owners 110; owning 109, 125–7, 142, 145; private 16, 100, 112, 117; rights 114, 120

Index

public housing 109, 115–16, 119, 130; advantages to renting 131; sale of 118; subsidised of 123; system 120, 124; tenants 111, 114; transferred into 113
public housing allocation 112; system 118; by work units 113–14

QQ 33–4, 35–7, 39–40, 58n8, 58n9; account 58n16; buddy list 46, 58n6; spaces 52; *see also* Qzone
qualitative approach 10, 64, 122, 146; data 6, 179; differences 193; interviews 11, 92n5; methodology 3, 92; research 33–4, 98–9, 121
quantitative content analysis 5; data 6, 179; examination 98; investigation 122; marginalisation 146; methods 99, 105, 121, 192; perspective 142; research methods 45, 92n5; study 33–4
Qzone 34–5, 58n9

Reay, D. 172, 176
reflexive 13, 90; approach 65, 73
reflexivity 13, 92
Renren 34–7, 58n8
rental: dualist system 136; socialist system 108
Report on Urban Private Housing Property and Suggestions for Socialist Transformation 112; *see also* property
respect 25; for Chinese culture 83; not deserving 85; for the old 47; from others 177; for parents 42, 194
Rheingold, H. 22, 25
Rice, R. 21, 23–4, 26
Rosen, S. 69–70
rural 30–2, 34, 50–7, 58n16, 161–2; areas 17, 113, 187, 189; background 85; *hukou* 58n4, 58n7; migrants 132; peasants 29, 66, 110; status 33; students 36, 39–42, 46–8; young people 21–2, 40, 188
rural–urban differences 53, 56; divide 187–8; gap 29–31, 50; inequality 17, 22, 29–30, 32; migrants 51, 113; relations 30–1; students 162

Said, E.W. 12
satisfaction 1; life 101, 191; ratings 2; spiritual 115
Schmidt, V.A. 15
self-examination 13, 155
self-presentation 21, 44
Sewell, W. 83, 159

Shaanxi province 18
Shanghai 72–3, 112, 122; Housing Provident Fund 147n5; Housing Reform Plan 118
Shen, S. 67–8
Siegel, J. 21, 23–4
Singapore 2; Central Provident Fund 147n5
Smith, Adam 175
social attitudes 2, 4–5; different 108; towards different housing tenures 107
social constructivist 11; perspective 106
social equity 18, 165–6, 182, 187, 193; increasing 161; radically transformed 17, 21
social inequalities 147n4, 160, 164
Social Networking Sites (SNSs) 26–8, 34; student habits 29
social structures 31, 86, 103–4; effects of 108; existing 18, 147n4; of the student body 162; transformed 160; village 110
social welfare housing 121–3, 135–6, 142; accessing 143–4; ambivalent attitudes to 192; geographical distributions 147n9; marginalised 145–6
socialist transformation 111–12, 116, 131
socio-economic background 18, 160–1; circumstances 158; entitlements 31; factors 28; problems 154; status 52, 159; transformation 16
Sproull, L. 21–2, 24
standards 57, 86, 172; international 157; living 7, 118; national 120; tenure 129; youth 54
State Council (SC) 116, 118–19, 147n6
state planning 2, 164
Steinfield, C. 26
Stiglitz, J. 16
Sullivan, M. 82, 88
Sun, L. 4
superpower 6
Swidler, A. 89

Taiwan 73; autonomy 69; issue 76–7, 80, 82, 84, 191
teachers 40–4, 162, 168, 170, 175–6, 179; highly qualified 154; pressure from 49, 173
Thogersen, S. 162–3
Tiananmen Gate 67
Tiananmen Square 88; demonstration 67–8, 190; incident 70, 147n4; student protest 88
Tibet 7, 77

transformation 17, 21, 32; economic 193; HE 165, 167; of housing policy 98, 122; incremental 120; macroeconomic 119; market policy 146; social 4, 103; socialist 111–12, 116, 131; socio-economic 16
transformationists 14–15
trends 14; in living arrangements 17; shaping America 7
tripartite model 8, 181
Troyna, B. 13
Tsinghua University, Beijing 157, 169, 172, 181

Unger, J. 160, 163
United Nations 158
United States (US/USA) 1, 6, 79; attitudes to housing tenure 108; bombing of the Chinese embassy 65, 68, 90; home ownership 102; real estate 97; social networking 26–8; suspicion of 69; teens 29, 38
university/universities 50, 55–6, 134, 154, 160, 163, 166, 169, 175–9; applicants 153, 165, 167, 177, 179; chosen 72–3; degrees 161–2, 174–5; elite 17–18, 28, 77, 88, 91; entering 125; good 172–3, 176; graduating from 144–5; Harvard 97; high status 155, 157, 168, 170–1, 180–2; not going to 56; progression to 192–3; selected 92n4; students 35, 49; system 187, 190; US 32; Western 156
University of Michigan's Detroit Area Study 4
university students 178, 187; anti-foreign 67, 71; attitudes and perceptions 64–5, 91; China's 17, 65, 69; elite 72; moral and political attitudes 80; national attitude 73, 81; nationalism 69–70, 83, 191; social and economic backgrounds 159
unreflexively accepted 105, 192
urban 7, 17, 23, 29–30, 33, 50–3, 56–7, 115, 132, 142, 161, 188–9; areas 34, 41, 43, 58n7, 70, 112–13, 119; background 85; dwellers 121; educated elite 69; families 162; *hukou* holders 5, 31, 58n4; living standards 118; managerialism 102; middle class 160; students 36–7, 39, 42, 45, 47, 49, 54–5; young people 21–2, 32, 40; *see also* rural–urban
urban China 6, 17, 108, 111–13, 118, 124, 126; contemporary Chinese society 122–3; pre-reform 114; social welfare housing 143, 145, 147n9; transitional 99, 121, 132, 135, 141
urban housing 112; former suburban farmhouses 114; private 116; public reform 115; public rental provision 131; reform 118; social welfare 143, 145, 147n9
urban youth 17, 56; internet cafes 43; online 32, 54; online communication 57; perceptions 50–1, 53; prejudged as arrogant 51, 54; social networks 55, 58n7
urbanisation 17, 21, 113, 132; neoliberal 135
urbanites 50–1, 56

Vaira, M. 64
values 4, 10, 89, 101, 155; Australian 100; changing 187; Chinese 161, 193; cultural 158, 160; group 109; home-ownership 102, 104, 107; housing 121–2; moral 181; set of 3, 66; society 175, 188; traditional 194; Western 190
villages 7, 50, 52, 58n4, 58n7, 58n16, 155; friends 55–6; global 25; migrant workers leave 51; social structure 110; students from 53; urban 132
von Mises, L. 1, 15

Walther, J.B. 27–8
Wan, Y. 158, 164
Wang, F.L. 31
Wang, H. 17, 70, 98
Warren, C. 10–11
Washington Consensus 16
Wasserstrom, J. 70–1
Waters, M. 15
Watson, M. 16, 159
welfare housing 116, 118, 146; access to 145; allocation 119; marginalised public 121; purchasing existing 120; *see also* social welfare housing
Western scholarly viewpoint 8; scholars 3; scholarship 2
Whyte, M.K. 30, 113
winners and losers, stratified global order 14–15; *see also* loser
women's rights 8
World Bank 16, 155
World Trade Organization (WTO) 16
Wu, X.G. 31, 66–7, 156

Xi, J. 70
Xian province 18

Xinhua 78
Xinjiang 7
Xu, Y. 17, 79

Yang 113, 130, 170, 175, 180
Yang, R. 13–15
young people 21–2, 32–3, 37, 54–5, 88, 179, 188; access to institutional resources 189; attitudes 17, 29; in China 34–5, 91, 121, 123; Chinese 124; choices of SNSs 28; drop out of school 58n15; entering housing market 125; from the EU 26; going to university 165–7, 175–7, 182; higher status 56; homeowners 108–9, 120–1, 123–4, 126–7, 129; housing policy 191; housing rental 132–41; housing tenures 122, 146; marriage 119; migration to Beijing 147n7; owner occupation 192; parental help with home ownership 128; preferences 45, 48, 58n13; respect for parents 42, 194; structuring social worlds 49; social welfare housing 143–5; urban 40, 50, 57
young people online 29; communication 33–4, 48, 57, 188–9; digital technologies 186; friendships 37–40; Instant Messaging (IM) 26; internet 21, 32; practices 26; relationships 27, 35–6, 44, 50, 54, 58n9
young people's relationships 43–5; cross-gender 41–2, 54, 58n12; friendships 37–40; offline 57, 189; online 27, 35–6, 50, 54, 58n9; peer 46; with older people 47
youth 34, 47–8, 50–1, 57; action 87, 90; Chinese 6, 71, 187; cross-gender 41–5, 49; internet use 38, 43; online communication 27, 40; online friendships 51, 54; Research Centre 70; rural 53, 55–6, 58n16; rural migrant workers 161; rural and urban 17, 32, 57; student 69; village 58n7; youth-oriented consumer culture 46
Yu, Z. 65, 72
Yuan, J. 68

zero or neutral point 9
Zhang, M. 112, 114–15, 131
Zhang, X.Q. 112, 114–15, 118, 131
Zhang, Y. 42–3
Zhao, D. 67, 72
Zhao, S. 88–9
Zheng, Y. 68, 109